Marina Carr Plays One

Born in 1964, brought up in County Offaly, Marina Carr graduated from University College Dublin in 1987 with a degree in English and Philosophy. She was Writer-in-Residence at the Abbey and Trinity College Dublin. Her plays include *On Raftery's Hill* (Royal Court) and *Portia Coughlan* (Royal Court and the Abbey, Dublin); *By the Bog of Cats . . .* (Abbey, Dublin), *The Mai* (Peacock, Dublin/Abbey, Dublin/Tricycle/McCarter, Princeton); *Low in the Dark* (Project Arts Centre, Dublin); *Ullaloo* (Abbey, Dublin Theatre Festival); *Ariel* (Abbey, Dublin, 2002). Awards include *Irish Times* Playwright Award 1998, The Susan Smith Blackburn Award for *Portia Coughlan*, Best New Irish Play at Dublin Theatre Festival 1994, The E. M. Forster Prize from the American Academy of Arts and Letters, and The American Ireland Fund Award. She is a member of Aosdána.

by the same author

ON RAFTERY'S HILL
BY THE BOG OF CATS . . .
PLAYS ONE
(Low in the Dark, The Mai, Portia
Coughlan, By the Bog of Cats . . .)

MARINA CARR

Plays One

Low in the Dark

The Mai

Portia Coughlan

By the Bog of Cats . . .

**Introduced by
the author**

faber and faber

First published in this collection in 1999
by Faber and Faber Limited
3 Queen Square, London WC1N 3AU

Typeset by Country Setting, Kingsdown, Kent CT14 8ES
Printed and bound by Mackays of Chatham plc, Chatham, Kent

A CIP record for this book is available from the British Library

ISBN-13: 978-0-571-20011-5
ISBN-10: 0-571-20011-7

4 6 8 10 9 7 5 3

First published in this collection in 1999
by Faber and Faber Limited
3 Queen Square London WC1N 3AU

Typeset by Faber and Faber Limited
Printed in England by Clays Ltd, St Ives plc

All rights reserved
© The Estate of [illegible] 1999

For Dermot and William

The right of [illegible] to be identified as author of this work
has been asserted in accordance with Section 77 of the
Copyright, Designs and Patents Act 1988

A CIP record for this book is available from the British Library

ISBN 0-571-20011-X

Contents

Introduction

When I was a scut we built a theatre in our shed; we lay
boards across the stacked turf, hung an old blue sheet
for a curtain and tied a bicycle lamp to a rafter at the
side of the shed so its light would fall at an angle on the
stage. For costumes we wore brown nylons over our
faces. There were always robbers in our plays. Even
when you weren't playing a robber, you dressed like one,
for any second you could be caught or hung or shot.
Even the Good Guy dressed like a robber, so if the worst
came to the worst he could arrest himself. Everyone was
interchangeable. One minute you were the heroine on
the swing and the next you were in the stocks pleading
guilty to every crime invented. Our dramas were bloody
and brutal. Everyone suffered: the least you could hope
to get away with was a torturing. And still we all lived
happily ever after. Good and bad got down from their
ropes or off the rack or out of the barrel of boiling oil,
apologized to the Goodie – who was usually more
perverse than all the Baddies put together – and made
long soliloquies about 'never doing it again'. Everyone
was capable of redemption except Witches. We had no
mercy for Witches, but since the Witch had all the power
and all the magic, we could never finally throttle her
with all the righteous savagery of our scuttish hearts.
Just when we had her choked down to her last cheekful
of air or had her chest bared for the stake, she'd cast one
of her spells and escape on the handle of an old spade.

Scuts know instinctively that morality is a human
invention, fallible and variable as the wind, and so our
dramas were strange and free and cruel. But scuts also

have a sense of justice – bar the Witch, I don't know what she was about – and hence our desire for the thing to end well. We loved the havoc, the badness, the blood spillage, but loved equally restoring some sort of botched order and harmony. Ignorantly we had hit upon the first and last principles of dramatic art. And the Witch? Maybe she was Time. Time we didn't understand or fully inhabit, and yet we respected and feared her. And fell away humbly under her spells and charms and curses. If I'm after anything when I'm writing plays, it's the scuts' view of things as they are or were or should be, and perhaps once in a blue moon be given a sideways glance of it all as the first dramatist might see it and how it should be done.

Marina Carr
February 1999

LOW IN THE DARK

Low in the Dark was first performed by Crooked
Sixpence Theatre Company at the Project Arts Centre,
Dublin, on 24 October 1989, with the following cast:

Curtains Brid Mhic Fhearai
Bender Joan Brosnan Walsh
Binder Sarah Jane Scaife
Baxter Peter Holmes
Bone Dermod Moore

Director Philip Hardy
Designer Liz Cullinane
Costumes Leonor McDonagh
Lighting Brian O'Rourke
Music Bunnan Beo Ensemble
Stage Manager Lorraine Whyte

Characters

Bender, in her fifties, attractive but ageing
Binder, Bender's daughter, in her mid-twenties,
a spoilt brat, whimsical
Baxter, in his mid-thirties, Curtains' lover
Bone, in his late-twenties, Binder's lover
Curtains can be any age, as she is covered from
head to toe in heavy, brocaded curtains and rail.
Not an inch of her face or body is seen
throughout the play

The Set

Stage left Bizarre bathroom: bath, toilet and shower.
A brush with hat and tails on it

Stage right The men's space: tyres, rims, unfinished
walls and blocks strewn about

The floor is chequered in cream and black

Act One

SCENE ONE

Soundtrack on, lights on middle stage space.
  Curtains walks down the middle space, looks right, looks left then looks straight ahead.

Curtains Before they ever met the man and woman had a dream. It was the same dream. The woman dreamt she came up from the south to meet the man from the north. It was the same dream. The man dreamt he came down from the north to meet the woman from the south. It was the same dream with this difference . . .

Binder (*gets up from the toilet where she has been sitting as if on a throne*) Open those bloody curtains!

  Curtains, caught mid-story, gives herself a vigorous dusting with a carpet beater and walks off.

Why does she never open her curtains? Even an inch!

Bender (*from the bath*) Even half a one!

Binder (*yelling after her*) Open those bloody curtains!

Bender I'd love to rip them off her! There is a life to be lived, I'd say as I'd rip them off, or didn't you hear? And then I'd tell her, it's not every woman can say that she's been loved!

Binder Go on! Give us a go in the bath.

Bender (*pushes her away*) Go away!

Binder You look old today!

Bender (*nonplussed*) I'll be older tomorrow.

Binder There's grey in your hair!

Bender Yours is falling out.

Binder You've put on weight!

Bender That's the baby.

Binder Another one?

Bender And why not?

Binder It's not fair.

Bender To who?

Binder To anyone . . . to you, to him!

Bender It might be a her.

Binder Never, babies are always boys.

Bender Even when they're girls.

Binder And it's not fair to me! I'll have to sit here and wait and listen to you screaming!

Bender A good scream would do you the power of good!

Binder I've nothing to scream about.

Bender That's your tragedy.

Binder (*looking at herself in the mirror*) Do you like my hair?

Bender I love your hair.

Binder And . . .

Bender And your lips.

Binder Yeah, I love them too, will I put on more lipstick?

Bender Sure why not, give me some too.

Both put on lipstick.

Here! Put him in the shower. (*She's just had a baby, baby crying sounds.*)

Binder Why didn't you tell me? (*Holds up the baby.*)

Bender You accuse me of screaming too much, so I had a silent birth this time.

Binder Did it hurt?

Bender After the first million you get used to it.

Binder Can I feed him?

Bender Go ahead!

Binder (*breast-feeding and examining the baby*) It's a she!

Bender What'll we call him?

Binder Alexander.

Bender We have an Alexander!

Binder There's no harm in another one.

Bender Please yourself.

Binder She sucks like a man.

Bender She'll have luck so! (*Finishes her drink, lights another cigarette.*) I wish her luck . . . I wish her all the luck in the world, give me another drink!

Binder You drink too much!

Bender I don't drink half enough! I deserve one after that ordeal . . . remember, not even a scream.

Binder That was very underhand of you.

Bender A drink for her sake and put him in the shower and give him a doll!

Binder They're for the girl-babies.

9

Bender Well then give him a train and give his mother a drink!

Binder I'm her mother!

Bender Whose mother?

Binder It's my baby, so leave off!

Bender Yours? I just had him!

Binder It's a her!

Bender Silently!

Binder You're hallucinating again. I had him.

Bender Binder, don't start or I'll send you back.

Binder You can't! Remember you tried, I'm too big.

Bender I'll try again.

Binder He's my baby, and what's more I won't call him Alexander, horrible name!

Bender It was your idea.

Binder (*to the baby*) I'll call you Jonathon, won't I?

Bender We already have four Jonathons, anyway it's a girl, look I'll give you the next one.

Binder You always say that . . . anyway there won't be a next one!

Bender There's plenty where she came from . . . as soon as I get my figure back I'll have another and then another, because I am fertile!

Binder I had a dream last night your uterus fell out.

Bender I dreamt your ovaries exploded!

Binder At least I have ovaries and eggs, lots of eggs, much more than you because I'm young. I'm in my prime.

Bender I've had my fair share of eggs. Now give her to me.

Binder Take her then! (*Throws the baby.*) But don't expect me to hit her when she starts screaming!

Bender (*to the baby*) We don't expect anything from her do we?

Binder He's a very ugly baby!

Bender There's no such thing as an ugly baby. (*to the baby*) Is there? You're the image of your father, aren't you?

Binder Who's his father?

Bender None of your business! Isn't it enough that he has a father . . . somewhere . . . here now put him away gently. (*Kisses the baby and gives it to Binder.*)

Binder (*examining the baby*) I still think it's a she. (*Throws it in the shower.*)

Bender I'd better write to him. Get out the pen and paper!

Curtains enters, goes straight for the Venetian blinds and examines them.

Binder Hello, how are you?

Bender Oh, there you are!

Curtains I love your blinds, they really keep the light out.

Binder And the shower curtain?

Curtains (*examines the shower curtain*) Yes, it's magnificent! Truly magnificent!

Bender I bought it in a sale. Eh, where did you get your curtains?

Curtains (*outraged*) Don't be so impudent!

Binder We told you all about our blinds and our curtains!

Curtains (*smugly*) Did I ask you about them! No I didn't!

Bender Yeah, well you're always in here touching them up, looking for information about them. I even lent you one of the blinds and it came back filthy!

Binder I had to scrub it!

Curtains What about the stories I tell you about the man and the woman?

Binder I don't need your stories! I have my own man.

Bender So have I.

Binder You have not! You've no one, only me!

Curtains So you don't want my stories any more? (*Goes to walk off.*)

Bender No wait! We didn't say that.

Curtains I can always talk to myself you know. I don't need this abuse.

Bender Calm down will you . . . Was the man very handsome?

Curtains (*sitting in state on the toilet*) Yes.

Binder And strong?

Curtains Yes.

Bender And the woman?

Binder She was lovely.

Curtains Yes she was. And the woman said to the man, 'I believe you're born to haunt me.'

Bender The woman was right.

Binder The woman was wrong.

Curtains The woman was right.

Bender And what did the man reply?

Curtains He said nothing.

Binder Ah, why didn't he say something?

Bender I bet he said something, you're just too mean to tell us!

Curtains (*up and away*) Goodbye.

Bender No, wait!

Curtains has gone.

She always leaves us like this.

Binder Can I get in the bath?

Bender (*pushing her out of it*) No! We've to write that letter, are you ready?

Binder (*bored*) Ready.

Bender My dearest . . . My dearest? My dearest man, I am writing to tell you that you have another son . . .

Binder Daughter!

Bender That you have another child. It was a difficult birth but . . .

Binder It wasn't!

Bender It was a terrible birth, but I survived it. I think I would survive anything. It looks like you. Do you remember the night I conceived?

Binder (*stops transcribing*) Do you?

Bender Of course.

Binder Really?

Bender Yes.

Binder How did you know?

Bender I cried. Women always cry when they conceive.

Binder No they don't!

Bender Well they should . . . where was I?

Binder (*reads*) Do you remember . . .

Bender Grand. How is your music going?

Binder Are you sure he's a musician?

Bender Of course I'm sure.

Binder Supposing he's not?

Bender OK, OK cross that out . . . how is your . . .

Binder Work?

Bender That's too vague.

Binder But they usually work.

Bender OK, how is your work going? I wish you would come home . . . all my love.

Binder And the address?

Bender Just leave it there. He'll know it's for him when he comes.

Binder (*throwing the letter on the floor*) He'll never come, they never do.

Bender They always come in the end.

Binder Yeah when you're past wanting them.

Bender Do I detect a note of bitterness?

Binder Yes, I'm very bitter today.

Bender Why?

Binder Because I'm afraid I'll end up like you!

Bender Now I'm bitter!

Binder You've every right to be. Look at you!

Bender I'm always open to suggestion, but, aaaaah! Oh! Help me! Help! Aaah! Someone help me! It's coming! It's coming!

> *Binder rushes to put on a hat and tails and grabs a bunch of flowers. Dramatic music comes on. Binder runs to the bath. Bender is in the throes of childbirth.*

I thought you were never coming!

Binder My love, look! (*Shows the flowers.*) For you. (*Throws them on her.*)

Bender (*throws them back at her*) Get away from me! Aaah! Aaaah!

Binder Is dinner ready darling?

Bender GAAAS!

Binder Where are my slippers?

Bender Epiduuraaal!

Binder You've been very thoughtless these last few days.

Bender EPIDUURRRAL!

Binder Are you in pain?

Bender EPIDURAL! AAAH! AAAAH!

Binder It'll be over soon.

Bender It'll never be over! I'm going to die!

Binder (*pats Bender's head nervously*) You're not going to die! It's coming out.

Bender Is it? AAAH!

Binder Push! Push! Nearly there! It's a . . . push! It's a son! (*Holds it up.*) We have a son! (*Walks off with the baby.*)

Bender (*struggling out of the bath*) I have another son. (*Exits.*)

SCENE TWO

Baxter and Bone come on stage right. Bone has his arm around Baxter as if they are a married couple. Baxter wears high heels, a woman's hat, a dress, and a necklace around his neck. He looks pregnant.

Baxter (*woman's voice*) You're marvellous, darling, you really are.

Bone (*pointing to the wall*) So you like it?

Baxter (*examining the wall*) It's exactly what we needed . . . exactly.

Bone (*thrilled*) Do you think?

Baxter How high will you build it?

Bone Well how high would you like it?

Baxter I don't mind as long as it's higher than everyone else's.

Bone has begun building.

Can I help?

Bone I think you should do your knitting.

Baxter I want to help with the wall!

Bone Knit darling, knit!

Baxter sits in a chair reluctantly and begins knitting.
Pause. Brief tableau of the knitting and building.

How is the knitting?

Baxter (*still playing the role of a woman*) Grand, grand.

Bone And the baby?

Baxter (*puts a hand on his stomach*) Quiet today.

Bone (*still building*) And how are you?

Baxter A bit tired but otherwise . . .

Bone Are you happy?

No reply from Baxter except to knit faster.

With me?

The real Baxter erupts out of the role-play.

Baxter (*in a deep, man's voice*) I heard you!

Bone Well are you?

Baxter (*back to a feminine voice*) Yes.

Bone Are you sure?

Baxter Yes.

Bone Really?

Baxter (*deadpan*) I am very happy with you. I cooked you your favourite.

Bone (*delighted*) Did you? A whole tray of them?

Baxter Two trays! Twenty-four buns all for you.

Bone Ah, you'll have one.

Baxter (*in his real voice*) I will not!

Bone I'm sorry, I shouldn't have said that.

Baxter You know I hate those things! (*back to the woman's voice*) I only cook them for you.

Bone You're spending too much money.

Baxter (*knitting*) You're not earning enough!

Bone (*innocently*) Am I not?

Baxter I think you should get another job.

Bone Two jobs?

Baxter If you did you could have buns every day, and I could knit you a decent scarf. (*The scarf is about twenty feet long.*)

Bone But I'd never see you!

Baxter (*real voice*) Exactly.

Bone Watch it!

Baxter (*niggling female again*) Do you think is there any point in us going on?

Bone Of course there is.

Baxter Just asking.

Bone I hate it when you say things like that! You're trying to upset me.

Baxter I'm not!

Bone You are! (*Points to the wall.*) I do everything to please you!

Baxter (*real Baxter, throws down the knitting*) I'm fed up of this! It's pointless!

Bone (*determined to finish the scenario, as before, points to the wall*) I do everything to please you!

He waits for the response from Baxter. None is forthcoming. He forces the knitting into Baxter's hand, annoyed.

Yes you do, darling!

Baxter Yes you do, darling.

Bone And I love you for it!

Baxter And I love you for it.

Bone Now would you like some tea?

Baxter Now would you like some tea?

Bone knocks off Baxter's hat.

You always end it like this!

Bone You always force me to! If you'd just say what you're supposed to say.

Baxter (*taking off women's clothes and shoes*) Women don't talk like that!

Bone That one did! (*unsure*) How do women talk?

Baxter (*putting on his own shoes*) I don't know! They just talk, they never stop and there's no sense in anything they say, ever! Anyway I'm off!

Bone You're always leaving me here.

Baxter You could go somewhere yourself you know.

Bone Where?

Baxter Anywhere . . . just move around, I suppose.

Bone Here?

Baxter Here's as good as anywhere, it's just matter in motion, place is unimportant.

Bone Well, will we have some tea and buns before you head off?

Baxter Alright . . . but just tea for me.

Bone A little apple tart and cream?

Baxter (*delighted*) Apple tart and cream! What would I do without you? Hah?

Bone I don't know . . . I suppose . . . eh . . . I've eh, met another woman.

Baxter Another woman?

Bone (*apologetic*) Yes . . . it'll . . . it'll eh, probably be over soon . . . yeah.

Baxter Has it started yet?

Bone No.

Baxter Then how can it be over?

Bone Well, eh . . . after you start, eh . . . it usually finishes after a while.

Baxter That's no excuse.

Bone I know, I know . . . but when she talks . . .

Baxter (*cynical*) I know when she talks.

Bone And the lipstick on . . .

Baxter The soft hair . . .

Bone The smell on the pillow . . .

Baxter The shoes . . .

Bone The earring left behind . . .

Baxter Did she leave an earring?

Bone Yes. (*Produces one from his pocket.*) And a sock. (*Takes a pink sock from the other pocket.*)

Baxter Can I?

Bone gives him the sock.

Lovely colour.

Bone I washed it for her.

Baxter Did you?

Bone And hung it out to dry, and took it in, and ironed it.

Baxter You don't iron socks . . .

Bone (*taking back the sock*) This one you do.

Baxter Or shoes or underwear and what about me?

Bone (*examining the sock*) What about you?

Baxter You've upset everything, you know that!

Bone Yes.

Baxter And who's going to pick up the pieces when she's gone?

Bone Maybe this time she won't go.

Baxter She'll go! You'll pick a fight with her and she'll go! And then we'll run up and down mountains till the anger is gone. And when the anger is gone we'll drink until you have forgotten her. And when you've forgotten her, we'll play a few games and then you'll start all over. Can I see the sock again?

Bone Will you give it back?

Baxter Yeah.

Bone Sure?

Baxter Yeah!

Bone gives Baxter the sock and watches him examine it.

Bone Can I have it back now?

Baxter (*still examining*) Take it easy will you?

Bone Next thing you'll want her earring and then you'll disappear!

Baxter Can I, eh, can I try it on?

Bone It won't fit, I tried it already.

Baxter Small foot?

Bone Tiny.

Baxter (*trying on the sock*) Describe her?

Bone Ah, Baxter, don't! You'll stretch it!

Baxter I let you try on the blue slip!

Bone But it fitted!

Baxter With a stretch. (*examining the sock on his foot*) What's she like?

Bone She's long blond hair on her arms and long dark hair on her head and she's a handbag full of things.

Baxter What things?

Bone Women's things, I suppose.

Baxter Did you not look?

Bone I didn't get a chance.

Baxter Does she knit?

Bone I didn't ask her yet.

Baxter Suppose she doesn't.

Bone We'll cross that bridge when we come to it. (*He points at the sock.*) Look you're ruining it! (*He takes it off Baxter's foot.*) I'll have to wash it again now, your big ugly foot mark all over it!

Baxter There was a time you were very glad to have this big ugly foot for company!

Bone I'm sorry.

Baxter You're always sorry!

Bone gives him the sock.

How does she walk?

Bone I haven't quite mastered it yet, but it's something like this.

Does a female walk. Baxter copies him.

She takes short little steps and her feet turn in a little.

Baxter Cute. Do her eyes turn in?

Bone No, she has level eyes.

Baxter I love a slight squint. Remember the Blue Slip?

Both turn in their eyes.

One of her eyes turned ever so slightly.

Bone Gave her a dotty look.

Baxter Very attractive, that dotty look. Does she use her wrists?

Bone Yeah, she goes like this a lot.

Twiddles his right wrist. Baxter does likewise.

Baxter Like this?

Bone Something like that, and when she walks –

He starts walking again. Baxter follows him.

– she tosses her head.

He tosses his head. Baxter mimics.

And when she takes off her shoes, she takes them off from behind, like she puts her leg some way behind her and puts her head to the side and her hand down.

He demonstrates. Baxter copies.

Baxter The Necklace used to take hers off like that. And when she was putting on her bra she used to fasten it in the front first and then turn it around and put in her arms. (*He demonstrates.*)

Bone A lot of women do that.

Baxter They do not! Most of them fasten it from behind. (*He stretches his arms behind to indicate.*)

Bone (*trying to do it*) God I don't know how they manage it. Does the curtain woman wear a bra?

Baxter I think so.

Bone What do you mean you think so?

Baxter Sometimes I almost feel it but I've never seen it.

Bone Surely you know what a bra feels like?

Baxter Of course I know what a bra feels like! But there are many different types of bras. There's the platex, the cross-your-heart, the Saint Bernard, there's the two-in-one, the three-in-one . . .

Bone The all-in-one, there's the light-support, the medium-support, the extra-support . . .

Baxter And there's them tops like tee-shirts only they're bras, and yet they couldn't be classified as The Bra. Do you know the kind I'm talking about?

Bone I wasn't born yesterday. Is that the kind the curtain woman wears?

Baxter More or less.

Bone Which?

Baxter Less.

Bone So what you're saying is you don't know. You mustn't care about her very much or else you'd know what type of bra she wore!

Baxter She's a 38B, OK!

Bone Pink Sock's a 32A.

Baxter We all have our limitations.

Bone Well at least she has a handbag and her knickers are silk!

Baxter Curtains doesn't wear any.

Bone You're not serious?

Baxter She says they're a sign of weakness.

    Curtains enters, followed by Bender and Binder.

Bender And then what did the man say to the woman?

Binder He said shut up and lie down for a while.

Bender He did not! Curtains, what did he say?

Curtains He said, 'You're the crack in my pane of glass.' Hello, Baxter.

Baxter Hello, Curtains.

Bone Hello, Binder.

Binder Hello, Bone.

Bender Hello, Bender. Hello, Bender.

The pace accelerates.

Bone Binder, this is Baxter.

No one looks at anyone.

Binder Baxter, this is Bone.

Baxter Binder, this is Bone.

Bone Baxter, this is Binder.

Binder Bone, this is Baxter.

Baxter Bone, this is Binder.

Bender Bender, this is Bender.

Curtains Then the man got up one morning and looked out of his window. 'It's time', he said to himself, 'that I started riding.' So he got up on his bicycle . . .

Bone Can I?

Curtains Certainly you can.

Bone So he got up on his bicycle and he rode all over the Earth, he cycled over the sea . . . he cycled over the sea . . . (*Forgets.*)

Bender For it was a sturdy bicycle. One evening as he was flying over the highways, he saw the woman in his path.

Bone 'Get out of my road,' he yelled!

Binder But she would not, he said it again, louder this time . . .

Curtains Everybody.

All 'Get out of my road,' he yelled!

Binder Still the woman would not move.

Baxter 'I've two choices,' the man said to himself, 'I can knock her down or I can stop.' In fact he did both.

Curtains Which proves?

Bone Which proves that the bicycle is streets ahead of the human mind.

Curtains 'You!' she said. 'If you have courage get off your bicycle and come with me! I've . . .'

Bender 'I've nothing to give,' the man said. 'Don't worry,' the woman replied, 'I've learned how to steal.'

Curtains So the man and woman walked. They walked a million miles. Then the woman turned to the man and said . . .

Baxter 'Hello.'

Curtains And the man answered . . .

Binder 'Hello yourself.'

Curtains The woman said, 'How are you?' And the man replied . . .

Binder 'I'm fine, how are you?'

Curtains The woman did not reply.

Bone So the man said again, 'How are you?'

Baxter Still the woman did not reply.

Bender She did so!

Baxter She did not!

Bone Curtains, did she?

Curtains I suppose.

Bender She said to the man . . .

Pause, all look at Curtains.

Curtains (*starts to go off-stage*) 'I need change, I need to make strange, I need to kill an albatross, I need to lie with the golden ass.'

At this point she is off-stage. Baxter follows her.

Bender (*heading towards the bath*) And then the man said to the woman . . . (*She drifts into the bath, her voice trails off, she talks to herself.*)

Binder Bone.

Bone Binder.

Binder Will we?

Bone No! I've to build. (*He throws the sock at her.*) You know I hate women who leave their things after them!

Binder (*picks up the sock*) You washed it!

Bone I did not! When can I see you again?

Binder I'm here now.

Bone Now is no use.

Binder I made you some buns.

Bone How many trays?

Binder Three.

Bone I wanted two! There's your bloody earring as well! (*He throws it at her.*)

Binder How is the wall?

Bone Grand.

Binder Will I see you tomorrow?

Bone You might. Can I have the sock back?

Binder gives him the sock. Bone kisses her and goes off. Binder heads back to the bathroom.

Bender (*from the bath*) What did he say to you?

Binder He told me my lipstick was lovely.

Bender Give me some.

Binder gives it to her. She puts it on.

Did he kiss you?

Binder Yes he did.

Bender The cheek of him! Where?

Binder Everywhere!

Bender And you let him?

Binder Yes.

Bender I don't believe what I'm hearing.

Binder There's no harm in it.

Bender There's plenty of harm! You're disgusting! He's only using you.

Binder I love being used.

Bender I think you should finish with him for your own sake.

Binder Just because you've no one . . .

Bender Hah! I've had every man I've ever wanted! All I have to do is this! (*She clicks her fingers.*) And they run.

Binder In which direction?

Bender You need a good trouncing!

Binder I'll trounce you back!

Bender It's no joke having a child the likes of you!

Binder I never asked to be born!

Bender Oh yes you did! Screaming out of the womb you came, ripping everything in your path asunder and you haven't stopped since!

Binder You should have aborted me.

Bender Too late now.

Binder Yes.

Bender No use crying over spilt milk.

Binder Hmm.

Sound of babies crying comes over.

Bender I suppose we'd better feed them.

Binder I fed them already.

Bender All of them?

Binder Yeah.

Bender The Pope too?

No answer from Binder.

I don't know what I'd do without you.

Binder Don't start! I can't stand it when you get all emotional.

Curtains enters, goes straight to the Venetian blinds and starts opening and closing them.

Look, will you leave those alone.

Bender Come into the bath beside me . . . you seem very excited.

Curtains I've something to tell you both.

Pause. Binder and Bender look at her.

Binder Well?

Curtains I bought a new slip.

The following is accelerated.

Bender What colour?

Binder What size?

Bender Silk?

Binder Cotton?

Bender How much?

Binder Where?

Bender When?

Binder How?

Bender Why?

Curtains Stop!

She rummages around under her curtains and produces strings of beaded wood, Indian-style curtains. Four or five strands. All three examine it.

Binder It's amazing.

Bender (*jealous*) Ah, I had one of those.

Binder You never had.

Bender Sure they wear out in no time.

Curtains So you like it?

Bender I'd like to see all of it. Open the curtains and do a twirl.

Curtains You want jam on it.

Bender So you bought it. I got mine as a present. A present from an Indian called Chipachi.

Curtains Well, where is it now?

Binder He took it with him when he left her.

Bender He did not! I threw it at him. I said get out and take your slip with you. (*to Curtains*) Come on into the bath beside me, here, there's room.

Binder (*as Curtains gets into the bath*) You never let me in the bath.

Bender I loved your story today.

Binder It was beautiful.

Curtains I hope you're learning from it.

Bender Oh, we are.

Curtains Then the man looked at the woman . . .

Bender How did he look at her?

Curtains A long, slow look he gave her. 'Woman,' he said, 'I threw my bicycle in the ditch for you, and this is how you repay me!'

Bender The cheek of her! If I was that man I'd have left her there and then! Some bubble bath?

Offers bubble bath. No reaction from Curtains.

We all need a good scrub. He gave it to me for . . .

Binder I gave it to you.

Bender He gave it to me for the smell. 'I love the smell of you,' he said, 'after a bath.'

32

Curtains 'Big deal,' the woman said, 'I got out of the sewer for you.'

Binder Bet that shut him up!

Curtains Not at all! He started to look at the woman again . . .

Bender Razor? (*Offers razor.*)

Curtains The woman let him look and let him look and said nothing.

Bender (*still holding the razor*) Me neither.

Binder The hairier the better.

Bender But not on the face.

Curtains Finally, the man said, 'Your silence is driving me crazy.'

Binder For some reason they don't like them on the face.

Bender Well, pull it out when he's not looking.

Curtains Then the woman turned to the man and said, 'How many lovers have you had?' 'One,' the man answered.

Bender And if he sets the pupil on the shaven patch, give him the gentle eye.

Binder You know that flutter that kills them! (*Does one.*)

Curtains 'One,' the man answered.

Bender The danger has passed.

Binder Really? Only one?

Curtains 'One,' the man answered, 'one and all the rest.'

Bender Let him torture himself a little for having

doubted you, then just when he's beginning to doubt himself, say, you're such a beautiful man darling . . .

Binder What did he mean by 'one and all the rest'?

Curtains 'Ah yes, one,' the woman replied.

Bender Beautiful man always throws them! Think it's the juxtaposition. Let him come to terms with it, there's time.

Binder There's plenty of time.

Bender Then say it again, you're such a beautiful man darling.

Binder and Bender. So hairy!

Bender throws down razor.

Curtains (*getting out of the bath*) 'Ah yes, one,' the woman said, 'one is all one ever has, the rest come too early or too late.' (*She exits.*)

Bender What's she talking about? (*She drinks pensively, then sings.*) Dandelion wine will make you remember. (*Pause.*) Do you remember?

Binder (*reading*) Yes, I remember.

Bender Put on the hat and tails.

Binder Ah, Bender!

Bender Do you remember?

Binder (*puts on the hat and tails, bad humour*) Yes, I remember!

Bender Let me finish! . . . The first time we heard that song?

Binder (*impatient*) Yes, I remember!

Bender Tell me about it.

Binder (*with arms folded, she rattles it off*) You wore a pink dress, very low cleavage, there were too many lights and too few drinks.

Bender And then?

Binder We drank.

Bender And . . .

Binder We left.

Bender Go on.

Binder (*singsong*) I ripped the clothes off you, the few you wore.

Bender I was always decent!

Binder begins taking off the hat and tails.

Put those back on!

Binder I've done it a hundred times!

Bender Please, Binder . . . just once more, for me.

Binder (*puts them back on*) Well, make it quick!

Bender And put some feeling into it this time!

Binder (*with feeling*) We walked through the trees and the moon . . . the moon was there . . . (*ordinary voice*) Well, come on!

Bender struggles out of the bath.

Bender Slow down, will you! The moon?

Binder (*annoyed*) What about the moon?

Bender Where was it?

Binder Below us.

Bender (*coy*) Never!

Binder Yes, it was. We were looking at it through the lake.

Music on at this stage.

Bender Now I remember.

Both look down.

Isn't it? . . . isn't it? . . . isn't it just?

Binder Yes, it is.

Bender And the stars?

Binder The stars are there too, they'll be there long after this planet has turned to dust.

Bender (*breaking their arm link*) He never said that!

Binder Well, I'm saying it.

Bender Keep to the rules! Go on.

Binder puts an arm around Bender, they walk.

Binder Did you know that Fionn MacCumhail hunted on these very mountains?

Bender No, I didn't.

Binder That this lake is called Pallas Lake, named for Pallas Athene who swam here once.

Bender No, I never knew.

Binder Do you know anything? Do you?

Bender (*breaks the embrace*) No! That comes later, much later and his tone was never that harsh!

Binder What comes next then?

Bender St Brigid's Well.

Binder (*arm around Bender again*) And over here is St Brigid's frog-spawned well. And up here is the fairy fort, we used to play around it as children.

Bender You live in a beautiful place.

Binder That's true . . . it's beautiful . . . yes, it is.

Bender Will we talk about us?

Binder What about us? We're alive, we're together, we're rotting.

Bender You make it all seem so pointless.

Binder Well, is it not?

Bender No, we're young.

Binder That's true.

Bender We've our whole lives ahead of us.

Binder Can't argue with that.

Bender We're happy.

Binder Are we?

Bender Do you still love me?

Binder Of course.

Bender Say it!

Binder I love you.

Bender Have you said it to others?

Binder Hundreds, and I'll go on saying it. I'll say it a million times. I'll say it even when I don't mean it. I'll yell it to the space between the branches, I'll whisper it as they nail the lid on.

Bender That's exactly how he said it.

Binder (*taking off hat*) Must've been a rare tulip.

Bender None rarer, none rarer.

They exit.

SCENE THREE

Bone enters, lays a brick, sits in a deck-chair and starts knitting. Baxter arrives with a necklace around his neck and nail polish in his hand.

Baxter How is the knitting?

Bone Grand, grand.

Baxter (*offers nail polish*) Will you?

Bone (*offers knitting*) If you will.

Baxter It's my turn.

Bone I did the necklace yesterday.

Baxter I did the knitting last night.

Bone You did not. I was with the Pink Sock last night.

Baxter I sat in that chair for hours, must've knitted a yard at least.

Bone It's my turn.

Baxter It's not!

Bone How is Curtains?

Baxter Closed, and the Pink Sock?

Bone Puce . . . she never opens the curtains?

Baxter Never.

Bone You're lying.

38

Baxter She never opens them.

Bone Does she make apple tart?

Baxter Yes.

Bone And cream?

Baxter Sometimes cream.

Bone When she feels like it.

Baxter It's worth waiting for.

Bone Has she said anything you'll remember after she's gone?

Baxter Well has the Pink Sock?

Bone She's too busy baking.

Baxter Curtains says nothin'.

Bone Not even a phrase?

Baxter (*offering the nail polish again*) Look, will you do this or won't you?

Bone Always the necklace!

Baxter Always the knitting!

Bone (*pointing to the nail polish*) She's gone!

Baxter (*pointing to the knitting*) She'll never arrive! (*Begins to open the nail polish.*) I'll do her myself.

Bone OK! OK! Give it to me.

> *Baxter gives him the nail polish. Bone sits down, takes off a shoe and begins painting his toenails in a female pose. Baxter takes off the red necklace and puts it in his pocket.*

Baxter OK, are you ready?

39

Bone Ready.

Baxter (*does a little walk, then turns*) Well.

Bone (*woman's voice*) Hello, darling.

   They kiss.

How was your day?

Baxter Fine, and yours?

Bone Very busy.

Baxter You're painting your nails again.

Bone Yes, it's wearing off. Are you hungry?

Baxter No, I can wait.

Bone Well, I should cook you something soon because I'm going out at eight o'clock.

Baxter I thought you were staying in this evening.

Bone Well, I've changed my mind.

Baxter That's not what she said! She said I'm sorry, but I made this arrangement that slipped my mind until a few minutes ago.

Bone (*real Bone*) She was very forgetful.

Baxter Can you not cancel it?

Bone (*back in the role*) Do you really want me to?

Baxter Yes.

Bone OK, I'll stay in. Happy?

Baxter Yes, are you?

Bone Yes. (*Hands him nail polish, ordinary voice.*) Here!

Baxter No, wait! It's not finished yet!

Bone Hurry up.

Baxter You're spoiling it all! Can we start again?

Bone No!

Baxter I love your dress.

Bone (*back in female role*) Do you?

Baxter (*exploding*) It's not 'Do you'! It's 'I wear it for you'! I love your dress!

Bone I wear it for you.

Baxter (*pleased*) Do you?

Bone Yes.

Baxter Red's your colour.

Bone Red's my colour.

Baxter And sometimes rust.

Bone And sometimes rust.

Baxter I bought you a present.

Bone Oh.

Baxter puts the necklace around Bone's neck.

It's lovely.

A long look ensues.

Baxter OK, it's my turn now.

Bone takes off the necklace and gives it to him.

Baxter Wait! (*He takes the necklace, puts the lid on the polish and puts the necklace around his neck.*)

Bone Do you want me to do Curtains?

Baxter No.

Bone OK, the Pink Sock! (*Hands Baxter the pink sock.*)

Baxter (*puts the sock on his hand like a glove*) I don't know what she says.

Bone Make it up. Come on.

Baxter (*woman's voice*) Do you like my lipstick?

Bone Yes, I do.

Baxter And my sock?

Bone Yes.

Baxter I want a baby.

Bone So do I.

Baxter Will you buy me a present?

Bone Of course I will.

Baxter I want a bath.

Bone You want to trap me.

Baxter I do not.

Bone Yes, you do, you women are all the same.

Baxter I'm different.

Bone I want to be free. I think we should finish.

Baxter (*gets up from the chair*) OK, goodbye.

Bone Come back here! Where do you think you're going?

Baxter (*sitting again*) You said you want to finish with me.

Bone And I do.

Baxter (*gets up again*) All the best so.

Bone No, that's not what she'd say! She'd say, 'Don't leave me.' She'd say, 'I need you Bone.'

Baxter I need you Bone.

Bone You don't.

Baxter Alright, I don't.

Bone No! You do.

Baxter I do.

Bone You don't

Baxter I don't.

Bone You do!

Baxter I don't!

Bone You do!

Baxter No, you need me!

Bone Me? I don't need anybody.

Baxter Neither do I.

Bone I wish you'd stop talking about your mother.

Baxter I wish you'd stop talking about yourself.

Bone You're very aggressive.

Baxter I am not.

Bone You are.

Baxter (*moves towards him, shouts*) I am not!

Bone OK, you're not.

Baxter Will you marry me?

Bone Why?

Baxter Because, that's the why.

Bone That's no reason to marry.

Baxter Then because we can hate one another legally.

Bone I love the Pink Sock!

Baxter (*normal voice*) Really? (*Takes off the sock.*)

Bone Yes.

Baxter Then you're lucky. (*Gives him back the sock.*)

Bone Am I?

Baxter Will we build for a while?

Bone OK.

   They build.
    Curtains comes on followed by Bender and Binder.

Bender I'd love to meet that man.

Curtains (*angrily*) You'll never meet him. He belonged to the woman!

Binder Go on. Continue the story.

Curtains I don't feel like it now.

Bender Was it something I said?

Binder Please, Curtains . . . and the man said to the woman . . .

Curtains He didn't say anything!

Bender Yes, he did! He said . . .

Curtains Who's telling this story?

Binder She's sorry.

Bone (*stops building*) Is it time for the story?

44

Curtains (*looking at Baxter who remains building*) As soon as Baxter is ready!

Baxter I heard it last night. (*He walks off.*)

Curtains So the man and woman walked, not speaking unless spoken to, which was never as neither spoke. Going along the path in this amiable fashion they came upon a woman singing in a ditch. 'Sing us your song,' the man said. The woman sang.

In Salamanca I mislaid my daughter,
In Carthage they killed my son,
In Derry I lost my lover,
In this ditch I've lost my mind.

'You've ruined our day,' the man said. 'Don't be so cruel,' the woman said and turning to the woman in the ditch, she asked, 'Is there anything we can do except help you?' The woman did not reply. So the man and woman hit her and moved on.

Curtains goes off, followed by Bender.

SCENE FOUR

Bone and Binder remain on stage. Bone has the twenty-foot scarf around his neck. Binder is knitting the scarf which Bone is wearing. They begin walking around the space, Binder following Bone.

Bone Can I carry your handbag?

Binder Another bun?

Bone Three please. (*Turns to receive buns out of her handbag.*) How is the knitting?

Binder Grand, grand.

Bone And the baby?

Binder What baby?

Bone And how are you?

Binder Pissed off.

Bone Are you happy?

Binder Can I have a bun?

Bone With me?

Binder Well can I have a bite?

Bone Of course.

Gives her a bite of the bun. Gives her a kiss. Both still walk, Bone ahead.

Binder I want a baby!

Bone Do you like the wall?

Binder Will I put on more lipstick?

Bone I built it for you.

Binder Women always cry when they conceive.

Bone I do everything to please you.

Binder (*stops walking, knits furiously*) I'd love to get a man pregnant!

Bone Slow down will you, you're knitting too fast.

Binder He'd arrive home shaking. 'Well, what's up?' says I . . .

Bone begins walking around Binder in a wide circle, wrapping the scarf around her.

Bone Darling, you know when you make buns? . . .

Binder 'I'm pregnant,' he says . . .

Bone The temperature has to be just right . . .

Binder 'Are you?' says I, giving him a level look . . .

Bone Has to be 150 degrees . . .

Binder 'Yes,' he whispers, 'must've got caught' . . .

Bone And you have to pre-heat the oven . . .

Binder 'And who's the mother,' I'd say, kind of harsh . . .

Bone For fifteen minutes exactly . . .

Binder 'Need you ask,' he'd say and the tears would start . . .

Bone Otherwise they don't taste the way they should.

Binder 'OK! OK,' I'd say, 'I'll stand by you for what it's worth, but I'm not promising anything, now dry your eyes.' Another bun?

Bone I haven't finished these yet.

Binder How is the wall?

Bone It's coming on great.

Binder And the lawn?

Bone Mowed it yesterday, mowed it today and I'll mow it tomorrow.

Binder You're marvellous, darling.

Bone No, you are.

Binder I'm very fertile.

Bone How is the knitting?

Binder Millions of eggs going to waste!

47

Bone And how is the baby?

Binder Quiet today, how is the Black and Decker?

Bone Drilling away, and how are you?

Binder A bit tired but otherwise . . .

Bone Will you come and live with me?

Binder I want to marry you!

Bone Same thing.

Binder It's not. I want a house with a bath and a man in it and a baby, all together, all for ever, all for me.

Bone I want a permanent relationship for a month or two, and sure who's to say the third month would be the death of us? Are you happy?

Binder No, I'm not!

Bone I want a woman who knows how to love. I want laser beams coming out of her eyes when I enter the room. I want her to knit like one possessed. I want her to cook softly.

Binder I want a man who'll wash my underwear, one who'll brush my hair, one who'll talk before, during and after. I want a man who'll make other men look mean.

Bone Can I carry your handbag?

Binder Another bun?

They exit.

SCENE FIVE

Curtains runs on followed by Bender who is beating her with a carpet-beater. She gives her three or four good belts. Suppressed howls from Curtains for the first three, a howl for the fourth. Bender is enjoying it. Perhaps Curtains is too.

Curtains Thanks very much.

Bender Wait, I'm not finished yet.

Curtains Ah, I think I'm clean enough.

Bender No, there's a bit of dust here!

She gives her a sudden belt on the spot. Curtains howls.

Curtains That's fine, thank you.

She puts out a hand for the carpet-beater. Bender belts her hand, the hand disappears behind her curtains.

Bender (*still belting her*) If you'd just take them off! I could belt you till tomorrow and there'd still be dirt flying!

This speech is punctuated by belts at regular intervals.

Curtains No harm in a bit of dirt. (*Winces with each belt.*)

Bender stands back to admire her efforts. She flicks bits of dust off Curtains here and there.

Bender Just one more on this section!

She takes a run at Curtains, belts her with all her might. Curtains falls, Bender is panting.

Clean as a new pin! Wait!

She gives Curtains one more belt while she's down.

Curtains (*on the floor*) I feel great now.

Bender Oh, we nearly forgot about the face, Curtains.

Curtains You're right.

She turns her head towards Bender and receives a swipe.

Great, just great. (*She gets up, takes the carpet-beater, puts it under her curtains, then sits on the toilet.*) So the man and woman walked some more . . .

Bender (*now in the bath*) Did they?

Binder enters. Bender motions her to ssh. Binder sits.

Curtains And they came to a hill where three men were nailing three women to three crosses. 'What have we here,' the man said. 'I want vinegar,' the one on the middle cross yelled. 'Get me vinegar!' 'Would wine do?' the woman asked. 'Has to be vinegar!' the one on the cross screamed. The one on the right roared, 'WE'LL BE BACK! WE'LL BE BACK!' And the one on the left said, 'Put silk on a man and he's still a goat, put silk on a goat and she's still a woman!'

Bender Oh my God, immaculately receive me.

Binder Conceive me spectacular.

All In the name of the mother, the daughter and the holy spirit. (*Pause.*) Ah! (*Pause.*) MEN!

Bender That was, eh, really moving.

Curtains I put everything into those stories.

Bender Well, it was lovely to see you.

Curtains It was. (*She doesn't budge.*)

*Binder goes to the shower, throws three babies on
Bender and sits with two, both breast-feeding.*
   *Curtains gets up and goes over to the shower.
She grabs an armful of babies, and orchestrates the
feeding of the babies. Soundtrack of babies gurgling
and crying comes over.*

One day the woman turned to the man and said, 'It's
time you had a baby.'

Binder (*to Bender*) It's time you stopped having them!

Bender (*looking at the three babies on her*) And who
have we here?

Binder The three Jonathons.

Bender My darlings, all my little darlings, and what ages
are these three?

Binder You had them!

Bender Jealous?

   *Curtains distributes babies by the armful to Bender
and Binder, and also grabs babies back at random
from them.*

Curtains 'Have one yourself,' the man said to the
woman.

Binder I think you should go on the pill.

Bender After this one I'll go on it.

Binder That's what you said the last time. Think you're
a fucking artist or something?

Bender I am an artist, a bloody genius in fact! Show me
the art that is life! You can travel the whole world and
nowhere, nowhere will you find it except in the big

stretch-marked belly of a woman. Now, Jonathon, you'll have to wait while Jonathon and Jonathon drink first.

Curtains 'Babies are for women,' the man said to the woman. 'I think we have a crisis on our hands,' the woman said . . .

Bender (*throws baby at Curtains*) He's all done!

Curtains throws a yellow baby at Bender, and throws a pink one at Binder.

(*to Binder*) You're cold towards me today. I gave you everything!

Binder You gave me life, that's all.

Bender I've received less and been grateful for it. Give me the pink one!

Binder What's wrong with the yellow one?

Curtains Today she prefers pink.

The yellow baby is swapped for the pink baby. All three of them are involved in the throwing and the catching.

Binder The yellow one's whinging!

Bender It wasn't from the wind he got it, just like the father, a right auld whiner!

Curtains He'll grow up disturbed, kill you when he's twenty-one.

Binder Wish I had.

Bender I never prevented you from learning calculus, did I? Give me the yellow one!

Another swap.

Curtains 'Sit down there on that stone till I tell you

something,' the woman said to the man. The man did as he was told.

Bender (*to the yellow baby*) My baby, my poor little unloved, unwanted helpless thing. I wish to God your fathers would come home.

Binder I knit, he builds, he builds, he knocks it down and he builds again.

Curtains The woman is born full and dies empty. The man is born empty and dies full. He dies full unless he miscarries.

Bender God, I'm stuck, just like that black hobo on East 51st one evening. 'Lady,' he said, 'lady I'm stuck here a long time!' 'So am I,' I answered, 'so am I.'

Binder Caught him rooting in my handbag twice. I said, 'Why are you ransacking my handbag?'

Curtains He dies full unless he miscarries.

Bender But I gave him a dollar and he gave me a light, then he invited me to stay with him on the cardboard . . .

Binder And the lawn, the lawn is beautiful . . .

Curtains The man began to panic, 'Where's my bicycle?' he said. 'I want my bicycle!'

Bender The pair of us could still be there, a trash can for a pillow . . .

Binder And his Black and Decker! He'd drill the eyes out of my head if I'd let him.

Curtains 'Your bicycle can't help you now,' the woman said, 'you have to come with me.'

Bender His lice-ridden head on my breast, maybe I would have been happy there, maybe.

Curtains 'Come with me,' the woman said to the man!

She dumps the remaining babies on top of Bender who is in the bath.

'Come with me and I will change you beyond recognition!' (*Exit.*)

Bender Where's the Pope?

Binder On your mountain!

Bender That's the Doctor!

Binder Show?

Bender holds up a baby.

That's him.

Bender I know my children! This is the Doctor! Here on my right breast is the Black Sheep! (*Points to the yellow one.*) On my left, the President! Now, where's the Pope? (*accusingly*) You have him!

Binder I haven't!

Bender (*panics*) Well, where is he? (*She throws babies out of the bath.*)

Binder Calm down, he's probably in the shower.

Bender I want the Pope! Get me the Pope!

Binder (*flings the Pope at her*) He's not Pope yet!

Bender Woe betide you when he is! Neglecting him like that! (*She gives reverential and preferential treatment to the Pope.*)

Binder You fed him already! (*Exits.*)

Bender I'll feed him again. I want him fat and shiny. Holy Father, (*bows to the baby*) you'll pull your auld mother up by the hair of her chinny chin chin, won't you? We'll have tea in the palace and I'll learn Italian and the pair of us side by side, launching crusades, banning divorce, denying evolution, destroying the pill, canonizing witches. Oh, a great time we'll have, you singing the Latin with a tower of a hat on you, the big stick in your rubied fist and them all craw-thumping around the hem of your frock and whispering for miracles. And me sitting there as proud as punch in the middle of the incense and the choir. Oh, a great time we'll have, the pair of us, we will surely. (*She's in the shower among the babies. She closes the shower curtains.*)

SCENE SIX

Curtains comes on with Baxter underneath her curtains. She begins moving, slowly at first, swaying back and forward. Her breathing becomes audible, the swaying increases in tempo, the breathing increases. The swaying becomes jerky. She is now gasping, and the swaying reaches its height. All the curtains are shaking. Climax. Breathing subsides. The swaying subsides to silence. Hold for a few seconds.

Baxter appears from behind the curtains, naked from the belly up. (He mustn't be seen until this point.) He puts on his necklace and waits expectantly. She hands him out a slice of apple tart. Baxter looks at it then looks at her.

Baxter Any, eh . . . any cream?

Curtains (*shakes, a squirt of cream*) Do you think I'm sexy?

Baxter Of course.

Curtains Sexier than the Necklace?

Baxter I'm not in the business of comparing.

Curtains Well, I am. There's a landscape that lovers inhabit or so I'm told.

Baxter Yes, you only realize you've been there when you've left. The fever is too high. You're not on this earth and you've no desire to be, and you've . . .

Curtains Rubbish! You know nothing about love.

Baxter I know one thing about love. If it's there you don't have to talk about it.

Curtains You're with a talker.

Baxter Then talk to yourself.

Curtains So the man and woman came upon a man with a good leg and a bad leg and a halter around his neck. 'Why do you wear that halter around your neck?' the woman asked.

Baxter remains impassive. Bone and Binder drift on stage.

Curtains Binder, you know this story.

Binder 'I'm looking for the horse who wore it,' the cripple replied. 'Then you're sick,' the man said . . .

Bone 'So sick I'd be for finishing you off right now.' The woman said, 'I think that's an excellent idea.'

Curtains 'No wait!' the cripple said. 'I have to find her, I need to see her, I want to explain, for the horse is gone, the horse is gone and the halter remains.' 'Very well,' the woman said, maiming his good leg. He thanked her and hobbled on. As they were walking along the man and woman fell in love . . .

Bender (*from behind the shower curtain, a roar*) What?

56

Curtains (*shouts*) They fell in love!

Bender (*running from the shower*) Go back! Go back! This is the part I've been waiting for.

Curtains I've just started on this story.

Bender (*disbelieving*) Has she, Binder?

Binder Yes.

Bender Wait! Wait! I want to settle myself for this. Lipstick, Binder!

> *Binder produces lipstick, puts some on and hands it to Bender who puts some on. Curtains' hand emerges from curtains. She puts some on.*

Bone (*taking out aftershave*) Some aftershave, Baxter?

> *He puts some on. Baxter puts some on.*

Curtains Is everybody comfortable?

Bender (*bursting with excitement*) Hurry up! Hurry up!

Curtains So the man and woman fell in love . . .

Bender Did they?

Curtains They fell deeply even. The man put it down to the accident of birth, the boredom of the path and the finality of death.

> *The men nod.*

The woman put it down to the perfume, the lipstick and the finality of the tit.

> *The women nod.*

'My love,' the man said to the woman, 'let's make hay before we're snowed in altogether.' 'Certainly we'll make hay *a stor mo chroi* [love of my heart]', the woman replied. For the woman loved the man and the man loved the woman.

Bender Wonderful.

Bone Go on! Go on!

Baxter Sssh.

Binder Listen, will ye.

Curtains So . . .

All So?

Curtains So they made hay and they made hay and they made hay, and one morning they woke and the harvest was done.

Bender It was not! They made hay and more hay! Didn't they, Binder?

Binder Yes, they did! They made hay and more hay!

Curtains They didn't! The harvest was done!

Bone I don't believe you!

Baxter You're making it up!

Curtains (*with finality*) The harvest was done! 'Let's walk some more,' the man said with a hint of contempt in his voice. The woman began to cry.

Bender That's not fair! Why did he have to make her cry?

Baxter He didn't make her! Her bladder was too near her eyes, that's all!

Binder He did so make her! She was fine the night before, wasn't she, Curtains?

Curtains She was ecstatic.

Bone And what about the man? Maybe he couldn't help the contempt!

Baxter He only asked her to walk!

Bender I know that note of contempt. I know it so well. It lurks in the saying, not in what's being said.

Bone I think you're over-reacting.

Bender (*points the finger*) That's it! The very note I'm talking about! The note that says, 'There's no magic here.'

Curtains So the man and woman walked some more. They walked the world seeking a topic of conversation.

Bender What did I tell you?

Curtains At the end of his tether, the man spoke of the hills of the north . . .

Binder The woman spoke of the hills of the south . . .

Baxter He hinted at desperation sung in ditches.

Bender She hinted at desperation not sung at all.

Baxter He mentioned mysteries that might claw at your bones.

Curtains They agreed to be silent. They were ashamed, for the man and woman had become like two people anywhere, walking low in the dark through a dead universe. There seemed no reason to go on. There seemed no reason to stop.

Lights down.

Act Two

SCENE ONE

Lights up. Curtains is standing centre stage, impassive. Bone and Binder walk on, both pregnant. Bone is following Binder, who now wears the scarf. Bone knits. Both nod at Curtains. Curtains nods back.

Binder How is the knitting?

Bone Grand, grand. How is the baby?

Binder Acting up. Another bun?

Bone Men always cry when they conceive.

Binder And the wall?

Bone I suppose it's an emotional time for them.

Binder And how are you?

  They exit.

Baxter (*from behind the curtains*) Any apple tart?

  There is a lot of movement underneath the curtains.

Curtains So the man and woman continued walking . . .

Baxter Cream? (*Pause.*) Thank you.

Curtains And the man said to himself, 'I've two choices . . .'

Baxter Did they never get tired?

Curtains 'I've two choices, I can run or I can hide,' the man said . . .

Baxter I hate your stories.

Curtains Curtain up your mouth!

Baxter Uncurtain yours!

Curtains If you think you're getting in the window tonight, forget it!

Baxter There are other windows.

Curtains Then go and find one.

Baxter The Necklace never spoke like you.

Curtains Well, she should have.

> *Bone and Binder enter still knitting, still pregnant, Bone still following Binder.*

Bone Please, Binder, can I carry your handbag?

Binder First the knitting, now the handbag!

Bone Just for a few minutes.

Binder OK. (*Gives him the bag.*) Don't root in it this time, you mess everything.

Bone I promise I won't. (*He's already rooting in it. He produces tampons and goes to put two in his pocket.*)

Baxter (*from behind the curtains*) Lovely day.

Binder I hope this weather keeps up.

Baxter How are you doing, Bone?

Bone Grand and yourself?

Binder (*catching Bone with tampons*) Bone!

Baxter Could be worse.

Binder Bone, they're women's things!

Bone Are they? (*He puts a pill in his mouth.*)

Binder And so is the pill! Anyway it's pointless taking it now, you're already pregnant!

Bone I took every precaution.

Baxter I want a baby!

Binder Did you?

Bone It was your carelessness and now you take it out on me.

Binder (*touches her stomach*) And what about your carelessness?

Bone You begged me for a baby!

Binder I begged you for one baby, not two!

Baxter Bone, how did you manage it?

Binder Can I have my handbag back?

Curtains The woman said to the man, 'Let's go away somewhere.' 'We're already away somewhere,' the man replied . . .

Bone I made some buns for you.

Binder I made some for you.

Bone Will we eat our own then?

Binder Will we swap?

   They swap.

Bone How is the baby?

Binder Fine, how is the baby?

Bone Quiet today, and the knitting? (*He's knitting.*)

Binder Grand, grand and how are you?

Curtains So the man and the woman fought . . .

Bone Did they?

Bender (*comes on and gets into the bath*) They did not!

Curtains They did so! They fought in the morning before they got up. They fought all day as they walked and they fought in the evening before they slept!

Bender Liar! They made hay and were happy.

Binder Yes, that's what they did.

Curtains One evening the man turned to the woman after they had fought and before they slept. 'I suppose a good ride is out of the question,' the man said.

Baxter (*from behind the curtains*) Men don't talk like that! (*Gets out of the curtains.*)

Bender Oh yes they do!

Curtains 'You mean you want to make love,' the woman replied . . .

Bone Make love! I call a ride a spade!

Binder Then you'll be digging for ever!

Curtains The man paused. 'If we can still call it love, then yes I want to make love . . .'

Bender 'I don't feel like it,' the woman said.

Curtains 'Soon we'll be sleeping in separate ditches,' the man said. The woman said nothing.

Binder She didn't have to. She let her body talk.

Curtains 'You're starting on this power between your legs stuff again,' the man said.

Bender 'It's the only power you've left me with, I might as well use it. Goodnight.'

Baxter 'I could always force you,' the man said.

Curtains 'Yes, you could always force me,' the woman replied.

Bone 'But I never would,' the man said.

Curtains 'Oh, you're so good to me,' the woman said and slept.

Curtains walks off. Binder drifts into the bathroom and goes up to the window.

Bone I feel like an animal.

Baxter Don't mind her.

Exit Bone and Baxter.

SCENE TWO

Bender is in the bath, smoking. Binder has her head stuck out of the window.

Binder (*out of the window*) Hey you!

Bender gets out of the bath immediately.

Variation on the fall? With me? . . . Not up to it? You're not up to much, are you?

Bender (*pushing Binder aside*) Don't be so rough with him! (*She leans out of the window, feminine, gentle, baby voice.*) Hello . . . fine, and you? Tired? Me too . . . would you like a bath? A hot one? With loads of bubbles and we could have a little chat and maybe some wine? . . . Do you like red or white?

Binder Or blood?

Bender (*pushes Binder onto the floor*) You shut up! (*soft voice again*) Red? Me too.

Binder She prefers white, anyway there's no wine up here, not a drop!

Bender Sorry . . . what's your name anyway? Salvatore . . . foreign . . . yes I know it means saviour, and your last name? Di Bella . . . The beautiful Saviour . . . that's lovely, that's really lovely . . . Mine? (*to Binder*) He wants to know my name.

Binder Wait till he hears it.

Bender My name? Well now, when you translate it . . . it means . . .

Binder (*pushing Bender aside*) Her name is Bender and when you translate it, it still means Bender!

Bender Stop it!

Binder Because she is a bender! All her life she's done nothing but bend! She bends over, she bends back, she bends up, down, under and beside. She is Bender! And me? I'm . . .

Bender (*knocks Binder down with a clout*) Don't mind her! I don't know what she's saying!

Binder Now you go away and leave us alone! We have no room for your misery. (*She gets into the bath.*)

Bender I'm sorry . . . he's gone . . . I wonder where he'll go.

Binder Isn't it enough that he's going somewhere!

Bender The sooner you have that baby the better!

Binder The sooner you stop having them! I'm fed up looking after them!

Bender I'll go on the pill!

Binder You said that before!

Bender This time I will . . . (*Puts the hat on Binder's head.*) And you, great impregnator, scattering your seed all over the Earth, of late; making tremendous efforts to screw the moon, would you not gestate with me a while?

Binder It's out of the question!

Bender That's not what he said! You love to say horrible things to me when you've the hat on!

Binder (*throws the hat at her*) Do it yourself so.

Bender (*picks up the hat, slams it on her head and takes on a male pose*) Listen, I have my work. (*Takes off the hat.*) What about me? (*hat back on*) Don't I spend all the time I can with you? (*hat off*) It's not enough, I miss you. (*hat on*) I miss you too. (*hat off*) That's a lie. (*hat on*) It's not. (*hat off*) It is. (*hat on*) It's not. (*hat off*) It is. (*hat on*) It's not. (*hat on and off at accelerated speed*) 'Tis, not, 'tis, not, 'tisnot, 'tisnot, etc. (*Eventually she throws the hat off.*) Ah, go to hell!

> *Binder is out of the bath by this stage. She has put some music on, some romantic love song, and is dancing away with the hat.*

Binder Come on, Bender, dance with me.

Bender I don't feel like dancing.

> *Binder continues dancing. Bender goes to the window.*

I wish Salvatore Di Bella would come back, we'd be happy together, I know it.

Binder (*puts on the hat, Italian accent*) Eh Bellissimo, com estai? Sono Salvatore Di Bella, I am the greatest lover in the world, come with me and we will do many things together, we will swim in the Caspian Sea (*Bender begins to laugh*) and drink the vino, blood or white?

Bender Blood.

Binder Ah, me too, the blood I love, and after we drink and swim and eat, then *mi amore* –

Puts arms around Bender, they dance a slow dance.

– then we will talk of many things, but light, and we will not stop to think, never, because *mi amore*, when you stop to think, then is *triste, molto triste*, because the universe, she is an incurable wound, blistering on the belly of the void, she is one vast unbearable grief.

The dance and music stop. They exit.

SCENE THREE

Bone enters, hugely pregnant, wearing one high-heel shoe and one man's shoe. He looks at the wall, looks at the knitting then makes a decision.

Bone A brick! (*He lays a brick.*) A stitch! (*He knits a stitch.*) A brick! (*He lays another brick.*) A stitch! (*another stitch*) A brick! A stitch! (*He sits in a chair in admiration, hand on belly. He looks at the knitting then looks at the wall.*) That's how it's done.

Baxter has arrived.

Baxter How is the baby?

Bone Splashing around.

Baxter Can I listen? (*He kneels and puts his ear to Bone's belly.*)

Bone Still alive?

Baxter Of course.

Bone I have dreadful nightmares about it.

Baxter That's normal. (*Still on the floor, he looks up at Bone.*) Bone, I asked you not to wear high heels when you're pregnant.

Bone I'm only wearing one.

Baxter Even so, you'll get varicose veins, then you'll say I neglected you.

Bone Well, you are. We used to have great times together, way back before the necklace.

Baxter Yes, way back before the knitting . . . you used to sew, beautiful needlework. I could sit and watch you all night.

Bone And you ate only meringue . . . you had taste then.

Baxter And you wouldn't so much as look at a bun. God! We had such dignity.

Bone Blue was your colour.

Baxter Ah yes, the Blue Slip, she was light, she was happy.

Bone (*hand on his stomach*) It was all easier then, I was younger, freer and cheesecake was the thing.

Baxter If I'd only stopped for a little think, never dreamt a necklace or apple tart could bring a man so low.

Bone (*patting his stomach*) Soon there'll be hope, new life.

Baxter I hope it's a girl-baby.

Bone So do I.

Baxter I'll buy her a necklace to haunt some fool or other.

Bone And we'll teach her to sing and dance.

Baxter How to put lipstick on.

Bone How to flutter the eyelids.

Baxter How to say no, when she means yes.

Bone And yes, when she means no.

Baxter And we'll tell her fairy tales of happy ever after.

Bone So she won't strangle herself in the cradle . . . suppose it's a boy-baby.

Baxter Never, babies are always girls.

Bone Not always.

Baxter Bone, I don't think we'd survive another man-child.

Bone I'll do my best.

Baxter I want a girl-baby and that's final!

Bone You don't know what I go through!

Baxter And what about me? No one's forcing you to have it!

Bone It should be the most natural thing in the world to have a baby!

Baxter A girl-baby, yes.

Bone Your snide remarks won't get us anywhere.

Baxter You think it's easy for me watching you? Swelling day by day, while I canter round barren as a mule!

Bone You could cross the great water yourself you know.

Baxter I crossed it once . . . nearly killed me. (*Pause. He takes two buns out of his pocket, shyly.*) I made you some buns.

Bone (*moved*) You think that much of me?

Baxter (*still holding the buns*) I suppose.

Bone Not shop bought?

Baxter No.

Bone Am I getting through to you at last?

Baxter I wouldn't go that far . . . look, take them will you?

Bone (*taking the buns*) I . . . I . . . I don't know what to say.

Baxter Silence might be better.

Bone But surely this is an occasion which calls for a phrase.

Baxter (*pleased*) Maybe.

Bone Or a word even . . . can you think of one?

Baxter No. (*Watches Bone eating a bun with pleasure.*) Can you?

Bone No.

Baxter (*impatiently*) Take your time.

Bone (*still thinking*) Still no.

Baxter Bear in mind my weakness for the spoken word.

Bone (*still thinking*) I'm really sorry, Baxter, it just won't come.

Baxter (*disappointed*) It's OK. OK.

> *Pause.*
> *Bone eats a bun still searching for a word. Baxter is deflated.*

Bone Would a meaningful look maybe compensate?

Baxter Depends on the look.

Bone OK, walk a bit and then turn, you'll find I might surprise you.

Bone assumes a tragic look. Baxter walks and then turns with a big smile. He sees Bone's look, his smile decreases to a sad expression. He shuffles around, head down, hands in pockets.

What's wrong, Baxter?

Baxter (*hurt*) You look like I've poisoned you.

Bone Well, have you?

Baxter If that's what you think! (*Goes to walk off.*)

Bone Baxter, I'm sorry, that was really cheap of me after all the trouble you went to. Give me one more try?

Baxter Alright then.

Baxter turns and walks. Bone assumes a grin from ear to ear, Baxter turns, his face impassive, he looks at Bone, a long look, gradually a smirk, which eventually broadens into a dazzling smile.

Bone (*grin frozen on his face*) Well?

Baxter (*still smiling*) You see you can do it if you want to.

Bone There's hope for me yet.

Baxter I'll stand by you through thick and thin for that look.

Bone Will I look at you again?

Baxter Let's not overdo it, the heart's not up to such powerful feeling.

Bone Oh, the baby, she just kicked.

Baxter Are you alright?

Bone It's normal isn't it?

Baxter It is not? C'mon I'm taking you to the Doctor!

Both exit.

SCENE FOUR

Bender and Binder come on reading True Romance *magazine.*

Bender (*reading*) 'Doug moved closer to Sofia, his hot breath on the nape of her tiny neck. He held her tightly in his tanned, hairy, muscular arms. Sofia shrieked! "Doug," she said, "I can't." "Of course you can," he murmured, his tongue in her ear. "No! Doug! Please, I have leukaemia," Sofia gasped. "Well I haven't!" Doug answered, his fingers travelling down her spine and . . .'

Curtains (*coming on*) So the man and woman walked some more and . . .

Bender Shut up!

Curtains So the man and woman . . .

Bender and **Binder** Shut up!

Curtains Will I show you my new slip?

Bender Saw it already, anyway it's not new any more. It'll soon be in flitters.

Curtains It will not! Eh, can I look at your blinds?

Bender If you tell me where you got those curtains, you can have the blinds.

Binder And the shower curtain.

Curtains I bought them in a sale. (*Whips down the shower curtain and begins attaching it to her curtains.*)

Bender You did not!

Curtains I did.

Bender I've never seen curtains like those in a sale.

Curtains Then I made them.

Binder You told me you couldn't sew.

Curtains I lied.

Bender You're lying now! (*Whips the shower curtain off her.*) And don't dare look at it again.

Curtains (*sits on the toilet*) So the man and woman walked . . .

Bender Excuse me! (*She pulls Curtains off the toilet, lifts the lid, spits in the toilet, closes the lid and gets into the bath.*)

Curtains (*sitting on the toilet again*) So the man and . . .

Binder Excuse me! (*Pulls Curtains off the toilet, spits, closes lid.*)

Curtains (*on the toilet again*) So the man and woman . . .

Bender gets up like a shot. Curtains leaps up. Bender spits in the toilet. Curtains watches her then races to the bath and spits in the bath. Bender spits in the toilet. Curtains spits in the bath, four spits each, tit for tat style.

Curtains is back on the toilet. Bender is back in the bath. Both mouths are working furiously to collect spit. They look at one another. Both get up slowly, Bender standing in the bath. They stalk one another,

*sumo-wrestler style, face to face, then a synchronized
spit. Curtains runs off. Bender remains in the bath,
standing, looking after her.*
   *Binder has been reading a newspaper throughout,
the deaths column.*

Binder Didn't you know Adams?

  No reply.

He's dead . . . says here he died peacefully, in brackets.

Bender He would.

Binder Another fella here died peacefully too.

Bender Who can die peacefully?

Binder And this one. (*Reads.*) 'Mary Rose Lee, 97,
beloved of Jimmy,' suddenly, in brackets.

Bender No one dies suddenly at 97! She's probably been
dead for years only Jimmy didn't notice. Sure how would
he? He's probably 99, blind, deaf, toothless, crawling
around, waiting himself to be struck suddenly or
peacefully. Or maybe he's dead too, only they don't
notice because of the upset over Mary Rose. And a
couple of months from now they'll put another notice
in the paper, 'Jimmy Lee, died,' suddenly, in brackets.
And poor Jimmy has been dead a long time, even longer
than Mary Rose and God knows how long she was dead
before they copped on. Sure they might never even have
been alive.

Binder I want to live for ever.

Bender You've a lot to learn.

Binder Or if I die, I want to die for someone or
something.

74

Bender No one dies for anyone any more, they're all just dropping off peacefully or suddenly, or slashing their wrists in private or shooting one another in the back. Where's the noble death gone to? That great noble death, that great noble life.

Binder Like Cuchulainn and Ferdia?

Bender Yes. (*Puts on hat.*) Tonight my friend, my beloved brother, I anoint your wounds, I cook for you the wild pheasant of the forest, I make your bed soft to lie on, sleep well my friend, sleep well and may your dreams prepare you.

Binder You make him sound like a woman.

Bender Great men always sound like women. They feel as sharply as we do, they contradict themselves left, right and centre and they cry a lot too.

Binder I've never seen a man crying.

Bender Then you're mixing with the wrong sort.

Binder How do you make them cry?

Bender There's no set rules. Some of them'll cry for a reason and some of them'll just cry anyway.

Binder Very strange. (*Puts hat on Bender's head.*) C'mon, it's my turn.

Bender I don't feel up to it.

Binder I always do it for you.

Bender (*resigned*) Which one?

Binder (*hands her a red scarf*) The black musician.

Bender (*ties the scarf around the hat*) Can I do it in the bath?

Binder looks at her.

OK, OK.

She gets out of the bath. Binder puts on lipstick, and checks herself in the mirror. She walks into middle space and stands there demurely. Music starts playing, reggae. Bender walks over, a jaunty black walk.

(*into Binder's ear*) Hi, baby cake, you wanna jive with me a while?

Binder Sorry?

Bender You wanna dance?

She doesn't wait for a reply, she takes Binder's hand and they move a few steps. Dance. Bender the confident rhythm of most blacks when they dance, Binder self-consciously.

Well, you ain't no New Yorker, honey.

Binder Irish.

Bender Say what?

Binder From Ireland.

Bender I'd never have guessed. My grandmother's Irish.

Binder (*suspiciously*) Is she?

The phone rings in the bathroom. Both stop dancing then, a mad rush to the phone.

Bender It's my turn to answer it!

Binder It's mine. (*She makes a dive for it, seductive voice.*) Hello.

Bender is struggling to get it off her, both roll around on the floor, struggling with the receiver. Bender eventually gets it off Binder, holds her by the hair and lies on her at the same time.

76

Bender (*seductively*) Hello. (*to Binder*) It's a man!

Binder (*gives her a punch*) I know it's a man!

Bender Yes . . . yes . . .

Binder Let me listen!

Bender I know, I know, overdue? Yes, yes . . .

Binder What's he saying?

Bender (*fighting her off and seductive at the same time*) Did we not pay it?

Binder (*a roar*) I can't hear him!

Bender (*moves to let Binder hear*) Don't worry about it. We'll pay it . . . when?

Binder Keep him talking!

Bender Well, when would you like us to pay it? . . . Soon . . . what do you mean by soon? . . . Today? . . . (*to Binder*) He's going!

Binder (*grabs the phone off Bender*) What time today? . . . Before 5.30, eh, sorry we can't make it before 5.30 . . . Tomorrow . . . OK . . . (*to Bender*) He's going!

Bender takes the phone from Binder.

Bender What time tomorrow? . . . Any time . . . that's very considerate of you . . . Are you sure? . . . Sorry, excuse me, sorry, I can't hear you all of a sudden. (*Winks at Binder.*) Yes, could you repeat what you just said, yes, yes, yes, OK. (*Shouts.*) Wait! . . . well . . . how are you anyway? (*Pause.*) He's gone!

Binder I told you not to get personal, they hate it when you get personal!

Bender I couldn't help it!

77

Binder We could have kept him there half an hour at least!

Bender (*still on top of Binder*) I didn't mean it, alright!

Binder You meant it! You knew he preferred me so you had to move in! Hadn't you?

Bender Preferred you! The croaky little voice of you with your ostrich eyes and your pancake diddies!

Binder (*whispers*) Menopause, men o pause, men . . . o . . . pause!

Bender Stop it! (*Starts hitting her.*)

Binder Menopause, hot flush, empty womb.

Bender (*chasing her*) Stop it! Stop it!

Binder The womb will be empty and the tomb will be full!

Bender Stop it!

They are off by this stage.

SCENE FIVE

Baxter and Bone run on. Bone is hugely pregnant, Baxter is exercising him.

Baxter (*running on the spot*) Right! Down on the floor!

Bone Ah, Baxter! (*Gets down on the floor.*)

Baxter Come on, Bone, just a few more.

Bone I'm tired.

Baxter Come on, you don't want to get all flabby. Just three more.

Baxter flexes Bone's legs four times.

That's grand.

Bone (*still on the floor, from behind his hump*) I'm seriously contemplating an abortion.

Baxter Are you crazy?

Bone I have a right to choose.

Baxter You have not! There's a life there inside you! A destiny, all its own.

Bone Stop it! You're just trying to make me feel guilty. It's painless, an overnight job. I could be back building tomorrow.

Baxter Bone, please don't do it, for your own sake, you'll never recover.

Bone Rubbish! It's only a few cells, a mistake on Binder's part, that's all.

Baxter There are no mistakes, no accidents in this world.

Bone Here I am, a man with a girl-baby about to come out and I'm terrified!

Baxter I'll help you.

Bone What am I going to do when the waters break? Hah?

Baxter I'll be here.

Bone Supposing you're not, and the big waterfall comes, louder than Niagara! And, and a girl-baby bulldozing her way through me! Sure I'll probably die, you'll be sorry then!

Baxter Hang on! I'd nothing to do with this baby.

Bone Well, you don't want me to get rid of it and you do damn-all else except make me exercise till I drop!

Baxter Bone, think. Think for a minute! You might never have another one.

Bone One is enough, believe me. If it's a boy-baby I'll shoot it!

Baxter It'll be a girl.

Bone How do you know?

Baxter You're all over the place. With boys you're neat. I think you should have a Caesarean.

Bone Why so?

Baxter Well, my mother had a Caesarean, my grandmother had a Caesarean, my great-grandmother had a Caesarean. If I ever have a baby I'll have a Caesarean.

Bone You were a Caesarean baby?

Baxter Of course.

Bone No wonder you're so balanced. I was a natural birth. From paradise I came, through the chink, to this galaxy of grief. I'll never forget it and I'll never forgive her for it. Purged from the womb, jostled down the long passage, the umbilical around me neck, the grunting, the groaning, the blood, the shit, the piss, and the first scream, there was the point of no return. A rough start to a rough journey I tell you. I wouldn't wish life on my worst enemy, I'll have an abortion.

Baxter We're all abortions, some later than others, that's all. But look on the good side Bone. Life is short, soon we'll be dead.

Bone Not soon enough.

Baxter What are you going to call her?

Bone I'm not having her.

Baxter Either way she'll need a name. Call her after her mother.

Bone No. Green maybe, that's a nice name.

Baxter Or Red.

Bone Red's not too bad, how about October?

Baxter Or December or Sunday?

Bone Or Thursday or Midnight?

Baxter Three o'clock? Four o'clock? Five o'clock?

Bone Five o'clock? Let me think about it.

Baxter Six? No, six is too common, half past five maybe or quarter to six, but not six.

Bone I know what we'll call her.

Baxter What?

Bone Wall.

Baxter Well, if you're getting personal, why not Necklace?

Bone It's my baby.

Baxter OK, OK ... how about Wall-Necklace?

Bone Wall-Necklace, that's lovely, that's what we'll call her. (*Gets up.*) Well, I'd better go for my check up.

Baxter Do you want me to come with you?

Bone No, Pink Sock's taking me, thanks anyway. (*Exits.*)

Baxter No problem.

He looks around for something to do. He lays a block then puts a hand on his stomach, feeling for a baby. Disappointment. He puts a hand on the necklace.

We parted . . . amicably. I said take whatever you want. 'Are you sure?' 'Yes.' You took everything. Everything except the two easy chairs, the carving knife and the bed. You weren't about to take that to your new abode. Not the evening you left, nor the next evening, but an evening long after, I walked through the streets, empty but calm, fell sideways over a stone. Not a thing between me and eternity but a sliver of moon and your memory.

SCENE SIX

Curtains enters and goes towards Baxter.

Curtains One time . . .

Baxter puts his hands up.

One time the man and the woman . . .

Baxter Don't talk to me about the man and the woman. (*Exits.*)

Curtains (*to herself*) One time the man and the woman . . .

She stops. The carpet-beater is in action. Music begins. She performs a little carpet, bead and curtain dance. Bender comes on.

Bender Here, let me help you with that!

The carpet-beater disappears. Curtains turns away from Bender.

Bender I'm sorry for spitting at you.

Curtains It was I who spat at you.

Bender I'm really sorry.

Curtains No, I am.

Bender (*getting angry*) Listen! I'm really sorry for spitting at you the way I did.

Curtains It's I who is sorry. I spat first!

Bender No way! I spat first!

Curtains Well, I spat harder and my aim was perfect! And I'm really sorry and it won't happen again.

Bender (*smug*) I got you right between the two eyes. That was a dreadful thing to do.

Curtains Yes, it was.

Bender I remember a time when I would never have treated anyone like that.

Curtains So do I. Now I'd spit on anyone.

Bender Me too.

Curtains If I tell you something, will you keep it a secret?

Bender Yes.

Curtains One night the woman spat on the man.

Bender What did he do?

Curtains He was asleep. And another time the woman carved her name on the man.

Bender Did he not wake?

Curtains Of course he woke, but it was too late.

Bender What was her name?

Curtains Christ! I'm telling you that a woman carved herself into the back of a man and all you're worried about is her name! 'I'll leave my mark on you, I'll leave my mark, even if it kills you,' the woman said!

Bender And did it?

Curtains It killed them both.

Bender Terribly sad.

Curtains No it's not. There are worse things than dying.

Bender Like?

Curtains There's living when you know you've never been alive.

Bender It seems to me you've only ever spoken out of loss.

Curtains What's to be gained?

Bender You might as well get in the coffin.

Curtains You're already in it.

Bender Your mass is over.

Curtains You're on their shoulders.

Bender They're hammering your lid on!

Curtains You're going down!

Bender After you!

Curtains Your tombstone's up!

Bender Yours is inscribed!

Curtains Yes it is! Yes it is! Yes it is! And there's moss where my eyes used to be, and I can't say if I'm clay or dust or dust or clay.

    Exit Curtains.

SCENE SEVEN

Bender shrugs and wanders around the space. She picks up the brush with the hat and tails on it. She dances with it.

Bender (*while dancing*) You and I could have done it all. Yes, you and I . . . all is flux you said, had to look it up in the dictionary. (*Pause.*) Yes, all is flux, and your catch phrase, 'The only law we are certain of is the law of uncertainty, and the cold cold kiss.'

She bends to kiss the brush. Baxter has arrived with the necklace around his neck as usual. He watches her kissing the brush.

Baxter (*after a pause*) Are you my mother?

Bender (*puts hat and tails aside*) If you're my son.

They embrace, a mechanical embrace. He kisses her, she kisses him.

Baxter I've grown.

Bender Have you a woman?

Baxter I had.

Bender None of my sons have women.

Baxter I think I had if I'm not mistaken.

Bender (*getting into the bath*) Did you love her?

Baxter Yes.

Bender Not my son, my sons love only their mother!

Baxter (*dead, almost*) I love my mother.

Bender (*dead, too*) I love my son.

85

Baxter Can I come in the bath?

Bender Certainly you can.

Baxter gets into the bath, not facing her.

What's your name, son?

Baxter Mother . . .

Bender Yes, my son.

Baxter Mother, it's Baxter.

Bender Baxter . . . (*trying to remember*) Baxter . . . were you the one who beat me?

Baxter Used you to wear red?

Bender Never wore red.

Baxter The one I hit wore red.

Bender Bet she deserved it.

Baxter No.

Bender Stealing a son off his mother like that. I'd hit her as well. A good clout puts manners on them when they're young . . . what's your name again?

Baxter Baxter.

Bender Baxter . . . were you the one that was crazy on train sets?

Baxter Hate trains!

Bender The one who brought me flowers?

Baxter I used to draw pictures for you.

Bender Pictures.

Baxter You loved them?

Bender Did I?

Baxter Hundreds of them, one after the other, for you.

Bender Can't remember . . . sorry . . . I miss you.

Baxter Do you?

Bender Yes.

Pause.

Baxter I miss you.

Bender Do you?

Baxter Yes.

Bender (*offering breast*) Are you hungry?

Baxter Not any more. (*Gets out of the bath and kisses her.*) Lovely to see you.

Bender (*going off*) Call again soon, do you hear me now, call again, next time I'll remember you. (*Exits.*)

SCENE EIGHT

Bone and Binder storm on. Baxter, who has been on his way off, stops.

Baxter Binder, how do you get a man pregnant?

Binder Ask Bone, it was his fault.

Curtains (*coming on*) So the man and woman came to a fork in the road . . .

Bone If Binder wasn't so careless! Never thinks of anyone but herself.

Binder Your nerves are at you again, I see. I think you should go for a lie down.

Bone Another bun, please?

Baxter hands him a bun. Binder goes to hand him one.

Baxter Any apple tart?

Curtains goes to give him some. Bone gets there first.

Curtains (*a bit put out*) Cream?

Baxter No thanks.

Binder (*to Bone*) Darling, I know it's not easy for you.

Curtains (*to Baxter*) We could try again.

Baxter This is my safe period! I told you a hundred times.

Bone (*to Binder*) You've just no conception of what it's like carrying a girl-baby.

Binder It's no joke carrying a boy-baby either!

Bone Girls are harder.

Baxter I'm not asking for much!

Curtains At the fork in the road, millions of other men and women were gathered.

Baxter It's your attitude I hate!

Curtains Maybe you just can't conceive you know.

Baxter More likely there's something wrong with you.

Curtains Look, it happens sometimes, you're just not fertile.

Baxter I think you should have some tests. I want a girl-baby! It's them Curtains! I know it is.

88

Binder I bought you a handbag.

Bone Baxter already bought me one.

Binder (*peeved*) Did he?

Baxter At least he appreciates a present when he gets one. Where's the bracelet I gave you?

Curtains Binder broke it.

Binder I did not!

Curtains She was jealous!

Binder It fell.

Baxter Bone, Binder broke the bracelet.

Bone Did you?

Binder I suppose.

Baxter You suppose!

Binder (*to Bone*) Well, she said you were an eejit.

Bone Well, I am an eejit.

Baxter Yeah, he is an eejit.

Curtains That's what I said.

Binder I'm an awful eejit. I'm sorry, Baxter.

Curtains Forget it!

Bone No we won't forget it! How dare you call me an eejit?

Binder Yes, how dare you call him an eejit?

Baxter Don't speak to her in that tone of voice.

Curtains Eejit!

Baxter Don't you dare call him an eejit!

Curtains I was talking to you.

Bone He's no eejit!

Baxter Of course I'm an eejit!

Binder I could have told you he was.

Bone No, you're an eejit!

Baxter Yeah, you're some eejit!

Binder I am not an eejit!

Bone She's not an eejit!

Binder Maybe I am an eejit!

Bone She is an eejit!

Baxter No she's not!

Binder I must be an eejit!

Bone She's no eejit!

Baxter She's a big eejit!

Curtains Eejit!

Binder No, you're the eejit!

Curtains Yes, I am an eejit!

Baxter You are not!

Curtains I am!

Bone She is!

Baxter Well, I'm not!

Binder Neither am I!

Curtains Eejit!

Bone That's me!

Baxter No, it's me!

Binder It's me!

Curtains We're all eejits!

Others We are not!

Curtains We're no eejits!

Others We are so!

All EEJIT!

*They scatter to the four corners of the stage and exit,
except Binder who storms into the bath.*

SCENE NINE

Bender enters, sees Binder in the bath.

Bender Come on! It's my turn for the bath!

Binder I just got in.

Bender You've been there for years!

Binder (*pointing to her belly*) How does my son look
today?

Bender You're going to have a girl-baby!

Binder I am not!

Bender Please yourself. (*trying to get into the bath*) Go
on, push over!

Binder (*feeling her belly*) Oh! He just kicked.

Bender Well, kick him back! (*Boxes Binder's belly.*)
There! Think they can take over the whole joint!

Binder That wasn't me baby, that was the old hag!

Bender (*sits on the toilet and boxes her own belly*) And don't you start! (*to Binder*) Bet he doesn't budge for the rest of the day!

Binder He's crying, you've bruised him!

Bender He's just swimming around, anyway it's a girl-baby. Girl-babies aren't so bad. I was a girl-baby, so were you.

Binder (*fussing over her stomach*) And look what happened to me.

Bender Will you stop that! You'd swear it was the Messiah you had in there.

Binder Maybe it is.

Bender You're soft because it's your first . . . what does he say to you?

Binder Not much.

Bender Did he ask you to stay with him?

Binder Yes he did.

Bender Well, go on!

   No answer from Binder.

(*puts on a hat*) Did he say will you stay with me? Or (*changes the position of the hat, different intonation in her voice*) will you stay with me?

Binder Can't remember.

Bender Yes you can! You just don't want to share it with me.

Binder He said, will you stay with me.

Bender (*mimics him*) Will you stay with me? The cheek of him! And what did you say?

Binder I forget.

Bender (*hitting her with the hat*) What did you say? Go on! (*Hits her again.*)

Binder I said I can't.

Bender Why?

Binder Because of her.

Bender Because of me?

Binder stares forward. Bender taps her with the hat.

And what did he say then?

Binder He didn't say anything then.

Bender He did so! You told me before he did.

Binder I said, 'She needs me!'

Bender (*hits her with the hat*) I don't! Go on! And he said . . .

Binder I said she can't survive on her own! (*Gives Bender a vicious look.*)

Bender Liar! And what did he say?

Binder He said, 'I need you too.'

Bender And you said . . . 'She's the most important person in my life . . . more important than you even . . .' Isn't that what you said?

Binder It is not! We never mentioned you.

Bender You told me the pair of you spoke at length about me!

Binder I made it up!

Bender You did not! There were candles and wine and music, and he said, (*puts on the hat*) 'She must be an amazing woman . . .'

Binder He never said that!

Bender Beautiful even! Isn't that what he said? Yes! That's how it happened. (*Puts the hat on, mimics him again.*) Will you stay with me? (*hat off*) Who does he think he is! I suppose he told you he loves you.

Binder As a matter of fact he did.

Bender Once they tell you they love you it's downhill all the way! Might as well get out before it turns sour.

Binder You talk as if my life is over.

Bender Well, look at you, lying in my bath with a mountain on you like Kilimanjaro, your legs all knotted up, your skin gone to hell.

Binder Well, at least the father isn't invisible!

Bender Give him time! Give him time.

Binder I'll get my figure back.

Bender Heard that one before. Did he buy you a present?

Binder He asked me what I'd like.

Bender And what did you say?

Binder I said I didn't really want anything.

Bender You never say that! You say, I want that dress, I want those shoes, I want this perfume . . .

Binder I don't want any of those things.

Bender That's not the point! Keep him thinking of you! Never stop wanting! And when he has given you everything you could possibly want, you say, 'Thank you, darling, but I really didn't want any of those things.'

Binder I'm going! (*Gets out of the bath.*)

Bender (*stands in her way*) No, listen to me you, because I know something that you don't.

Binder Because you've done it all!

Bender Yes! I've done it all.

Binder See you.

Bender Come back here!

She goes to grab her. Binder looks at her. Bender stops. Binder begins to move off.

No, we'll make a phone call.

Binder I'm tired of your phone calls.

Bender I'll let you do all the talking.

Binder has gone. Bender wanders around the space, with the hat and tails, etc.

When we spoke, and it wasn't often, we spoke mostly of the landscape or of food. One night I thought the silence would never end. You were listening to each wave, the different sounds, you said. You wondered when the tide was high in Ireland was it low in England. I said I didn't know, said I would find out, never did. In bed we spoke least of all. He no longer had words to describe that landscape and I had not the courage. So we lay there, side by side like two corpses, horrified at our immobility. And if we merged, must've been by some accident. No passion there for a long time now. My eyes sought the ceiling above him, while his moved towards the back door.

Blackout, exit Bender.

SCENE TEN

Darkness.

Baxter Bone! Bone, where are you?

Lights come up. Baxter has a huge swelling or hump or pregnancy on his left shoulder. He is doubled over, necklace around his neck as usual. Bone arrives, puts his ear to Baxter's back and listens.

Well?

Bone (*listening*) Ssh!

Baxter (*panics*) Is she alright?

Bone Ssh will *you!* (*Silence.*) Not a bother on her.

Baxter Give her a kiss will you, I can't reach.

Bone kisses Baxter's hump then he kisses his own belly.

Well, go on, talk to her!

Bone (*to Baxter's back, softly*) Hello, baby.

Baxter Louder!

Bone (*a little louder*) Hello, baby.

Baxter (*impatiently*) She can't hear you!

Bone (*shouts*) Hello, baby!

Baxter That's better, that's better. (*Tries to straighten up, can't.*) It's not easy I tell you.

Bone No one ever said it was . . . (*Points to his own baby.*) Will you check her?

Baxter Right . . . come nearer.

Bone puts his belly to Baxter's ear, he listens.

She's grand, grand.

Bone Will you rub in some olive oil?

Baxter That's the Pink Sock's job.

Bone Pink Sock's gone.

Baxter Where?

Bone It began, it ended, you know.

Baxter Yes . . . terribly sorry, Bone.

Bone Yes.

> *Baxter struggles with the pain of his hump. Both their movements are slow and painful now.*

Baxter OK, get out the olive oil.

Bone How am I going to manage on my own with a girl-baby?

Baxter I'll stand by you. (*dreadful pain, groan*)

Bone Look, sit down will you.

Baxter Ah, you know I can't sit down!

Bone Well, lie down.

Baxter I'm not a dog!

Bone No one said you were!

Baxter Then stop telling me to lie down!

Bone You lay down yesterday.

Baxter Did I?

Bone And the day before.

Baxter My glorious past. Well, today I'll kneel. (*Kneels with great difficulty.*) It'll soon be over, Bone!

Bone Easy for you to talk, you've Curtains to look after you.

Baxter I told you I'd stand by you.

Bone Stand by me! You can't even sit.

Baxter Or lie down.

Bone Can you not?

Baxter Unless someone knocks me. Check if she's still breathing will you?

Bone (*checks*) She's grand. Are you taking your iron?

Baxter No, are you?

Bone No.

Baxter Great times ahead. (*Looks over his shoulder, pats his hump.*) Isn't that right?

Bone (*hand on stomach*) I'll have to be a mother and father to her now.

Baxter And you will too, and I'll help you any way I can. (*groan*) And sure she'll have her nibs here to play with.

Bone Hope they won't grow up masculine.

Baxter Not at all. Sure how would they, with me baking and you knitting.

Bone Will you finish with Curtains?

Baxter Never really started.

Bone (*suddenly terrified*) Baxter! I think they're out to kill us.

Baxter I think they have.

Enter Bender and Binder with the scarf around their necks. Binder is knitting, Bender is leading.

Bender (*monotone*) How is the knitting?

Binder (*robotic*) Grand, grand, and how are you?

Bender (*getting into the bath, no feeling*) A bit tired, and the baby?

Binder (*sitting on the toilet*) Fine, and the baby?

Light change, all in silhouette, a spot on Curtains who has just entered.

Curtains So the man and woman joined the millions of men and women at the fork in the road. The millions of men turned to the millions of women and said, 'I'll not forget you.' The millions of women turned and answered, 'I'll not forget you either.' And so they parted. The men heading north and the women heading south. Before they ever met the man and woman had a dream. It was the same dream, with this difference. The man dreamt he met the woman north by north east. The woman dreamt she met the man south by south west. Long after it was over, the man and woman realized that not only had they never met north by north east or south by south west, much worse, they had never met. And worse still, they never would, they never could, they never can and they never will.

Theme music comes on, she turns and begins walking off.

One day the man looked out of his window. 'It's time,' he said. So he got up on his bicycle and he rode all over the earth and he cycled all over the sea. One evening as he was flying over the highways he saw the woman in his path. 'Get out of my road,' he yelled, but she would not. 'I've two choices', the man said, 'I can knock her down or I can stop.' He did both. 'You,' she said, 'if you have courage get off your bicycle and come with me.'

End.

THE MAI

The Mai was first produced in the Peacock Theatre, Dublin, on 5 October 1994, with the following cast:

The Mai Olwen Fouere
Millie Derbhle Crotty
Robert Owen Roe
Connie Michele Forbes
Grandma Fraochlán Joan O'Hara
Beck Bríd Ní Neachtain
Agnes Máire Hastings
Julie Stella McCusker
Cellist John O'Kane

Director Brian Brady
Designer Kathy Strachan
Lighting Aedín Cosgrove
Design Co-ordinator Karen Weavers
Music Mícheál O Súilleabháin
Stage Director Collette Morris

Characters

The Mai, forty
Millie, her daughter, sixteen and thirty
Grandma Fraochlán, her grandmother, one hundred
Robert, The Mai's husband, forty-two
Beck, her sister, thirty-seven
Connie, her sister, thirty-eight
Julie, her aunt, seventy-five
Agnes, her aunt, sixty-one

Time

Act One Summer 1979
Act Two One year later

Act One

A room with a huge bay window. Sounds of swans and geese, off. Millie is standing at the window. (Note: Millie remains onstage throughout the play.) Enter Robert. In one arm he has a travel bag, in the other a cello case. He looks around, examines the room in amazement, opens the double doors upstage, sees a music stand, turns aside thinking, and brings the bag and cello case into the room. He closes the door.

The Mai passes the window, turns to look out on Owl Lake, hears a cello note – decides she is dreaming. She enters the room, wearing a summer dress and carrying an armful of books. She places the books on the bookshelf, a few here, a few there. Drawn to the window, she looks out at the lake, waiting, watching. She places a few more books, then moves again to the window.

A low cello note floats across the room. The Mai – startled – freezes, listens; the cello plays, melodic, romantic, beautiful. The Mai moves to the double doors. She slides them across to reveal Robert engrossed in his playing. She listens, wanting to interrupt, yet also not. Now the piece finishes. Silence. For the first time Robert looks at her, cello bow in his hand.

Robert Well – well – well.

He taps her shoulder, hip bone, ankle, on each of the 'Wells'.

The Mai Just look at you.

Robert You're as beautiful as ever.

The Mai Am I?

Now he plays the cello bow across her breasts. The Mai laughs.

Softer.

Robert Like this? Hmm?

The Mai Yeah.

Robert (*waves the bow around the room*) What's all this?

The Mai I built it.

Robert All by yourself? How?

The Mai Just did.

Robert And Owl Lake, my God, it's incredible.

The Mai You'll see it better in the morning.

Robert In the morning. Will I? How did you know I'd come back?

The Mai Don't know – just knew.

Robert lifts The Mai and carries her to a chair by the bay window, taking a bag from his belongings en route. He takes a scarf from the bag and ties it around her neck.

It's lovely.

Robert (*produces perfume, tears the wrapper, and sprays it all over her*) It's the one you wear, isn't it, or have you changed?

The Mai It's the one I wear.

Robert And these (*flowers*) are for you.

He produces a bottle of whiskey and a cigar.

And this is for you (*whiskey*) and I'll have a shot as well.

The Mai goes to the drinks cabinet, pours the whiskeys. Millie moves forward, looks at Robert, looks at The Mai.

Now let me see, is it Orla or Millie?

The Mai Millie.

Robert Millie.

The Mai She's sixteen now.

Robert I bought sweets for the children – but I suppose you're too big for sweets.

The Mai She's not too big for sweets yet.

Robert places a box of sweets in Millie's hands.

Millie Where were you?

Robert Here – there –

Millie Everywhere. We were here all the time and in the old house.

Robert I know you were.

Millie Mom, will I get the others?

The Mai Not yet, in a little while.

Millie Your jumper's lovely.

The Mai You'd better hide it or she'll have it on her.

Robert (*takes off the jumper*) Here, put it on. (*He puts it on her.*)

The Mai It's lovely on you – have a spray of perfume. And don't tell the others yet. I want it to be a surprise for them.

Robert and The Mai exit hand in hand to the bedroom.
Millie looks after them, moves around cleaning up,
goes to the study, sounds a note on the cello, listens,
looks out on Owl Lake.

Millie When I was eleven The Mai sent me into the
butcher's to buy a needle and thread. It was the day
Robert left us. No explanations, no goodbyes, he just got
into his car with his cello and drove away. So The Mai
and I went into town and sat in the Bluebell Hotel where
The Mai downed six Paddys and red and I had six
lemon-and-limes. Then The Mai turned to me with her
sunglasses on, though it was the middle of winter, she
turned to me and said, 'Millie, would you ever run up to
the butcher's and get me a needle and thread.' Now at
eleven I knew enough to know that needles and thread
were bought in the drapery, but I thought maybe it was
a special kind of thread The Mai wanted and because
of the day that was in it I decided not to argue with her.
So up I went to the butcher's and asked for a needle and
a spool of thread and of course they didn't have any.
Back I went to the Bluebell, sat beside The Mai and
said rather gruffly, 'Mom, they don't sell needles and
thread in the butcher's.' 'Do they not, sweetheart?' The
Mai whispered and started to cry. 'Are you all right,
Mom?' I said. 'I'm grand,' she said. 'Go up there and
order me a Paddy and red.' When I came back with the
drinks The Mai said, 'Don't you worry about a thing,
Millie, your Dad'll come back and we will have the best
of lives.'

Lights change. It's later that evening. Enter The Mai
in a slip, wildly happy. She collects a bottle of whiskey
off the cabinet and moves across to the window.

The Mai Look at the swans taking flight, Millie, aren't
they beautiful? (*And she drifts off.*)

Millie The Mai set about looking for that magic thread that would stitch us together again and she found it at Owl Lake, the most coveted site in the county. It was Sam Brady who sold the site to The Mai. For years he'd refused all offers, offers from hoteliers, publicans, restaurateurs, rich industrialists, Yanks, and then he turned round and gave it to The Mai for a song. When asked by irate locals why he'd sold it to The Mai, a blow-in, Sam merely answered, '*Highest bidder!*'

And so the new house was built and, once she had it the way she wanted, The Mai sat in front of this big window here, her chin moonward, a frown on her forehead, as if she were pulsing messages to some remote star which would ricochet and lance Robert wherever he was, her eyes closed tightly, her lips forming two words noiselessly. Come home – come home.

Light change. Daytime. The cello bursts into song, wild, buoyant, practising. A huge currach oar moves across the window with a red flag on it. Connie appears, stares in the window, nosey. She bangs the oar in her nosiness.

Grandma Fraochlán (*off*) Would ya watch where you're goin'!

Connie (*shouts back*) Would you ever stop givin' orders from the car!

Grandma Fraochlán (*grumbling*) Shoulda carried it meself!

Connie Ara dry up! Millie, how are you? Give us a hand with this, will you? Would it go through the window?

Millie opens the window.

The Mai Ah you've arrived.

Connie Hello, Mai.

The Mai Easy, easy, mind the window.

Grandma Fraochlán (*off*) Mind me oar!

Connie God give me patience with that one! Nearly got us killed, her and her bloody oar.

The Mai Leave it outside, we'll sort it out later.

Connie She'll nag us till it's in the bed beside her.

The Mai Ara for God's sake, she's not sleepin' with it now!

Connie Don't even ask! How are ya, *a stóir*?

The Mai Toppin', and yourself?

Connie The house is amazing, Mai, beautiful. (*She hears the cello.*) So he's here?

The Mai Yeah, isn't it wonderful?

Connie Here, try it up this way.

Grandma Fraochlán enters, leaning on Millie.

Grandma Fraochlán Show! Did ya do any damage to it?

Connie It's fine! Would you move out of the way or you'll be knocked down!

Grandma Fraochlán Ah Mai, great ta see ya, *a chroí*.

The Mai You've poor Connie moidered. (*She kisses Grandma Fraochlán.*) Could we not put it in the garage?

Grandma Fraochlán Well then ya can put me in the garage along with it.

Connie That's the place for ya!

Grandma Fraochlán (*nods towards the study*) And when did he arrive?

Connie There! I have it! Millie, run round and catch it!

Grandma Fraochlán Aisy, aisy, go aisy on it!

Connie Would you ever! Honest ta God, you'd put years on me!

Grandma Fraochlán Sorry, *a stóir,* but it's all I've left of him now. Why didn't ya build a bigger winda, Mai?

Connie I've never seen one bigger! Ya needn't be turnin' on The Mai now! We had to saw through the banister to get it into our house.

Grandma Fraochlán Every time I move, ye have a hullabaloo about me oar!

Connie Go in! Go in! Before I throw ya in the lake. We have it! We have it.

The oar is finally in.

Grandma Fraochlán Me bags, where are they?

Connie I've only two hands, Jesus!

The Mai How's Derek?

Connie Askin' for you, the kids too.

Grandma Fraochlán I feel a bit weak, need a piece a chocolate. Connie, where's me chocolate?

Connie Comin'! Comin'!

She goes off. The Mai leads Grandma Fraochlán in.

Grandma Fraochlán Ya couldn't've chose a nicer place, Mai, only –

The Mai Only what?

Grandma Fraochlán Well it's not the sea, is it? Why didn't ya move back ta Connemara like ya said ya would?

The Mai Ah I wouldn't get Principalship of another school so easy.

Grandma Fraochlán You'd be employed anywhere. Ya built this house for him, didn't ya?

The Mai And for myself and for the children.

Grandma Fraochlán Ya survived this long without him, why are ya bringin' all this on yourself again?

Connie enters with bags.

Connie There you go.

Grandma Fraochlán Where's th'other bag?

Connie Millie must've brought it in.

Grandma Fraochlán And me pension wallet, where's that?

Connie How'd I know! Where'd you put it?

Grandma Fraochlán Gev it to you.

Connie Did you? When – (*She looks in handbag.*) – Oh, right, there you go.

Grandma Fraochlán Chocolate.

Connie Which bag is it in?

Grandma Fraochlán Can't remember, look in all of them.

Connie glares at her.

The Mai Here. I have chocolate bought in for you.

Grandma Fraochlán (*taking the chocolate*) And where's the hundred pound the President gev me for me birthday?

Connie raises her hands in exasperation.

Well, where is it?

Connie (*growls*) You spent it!

Grandma Fraochlán Did I? When?

Connie Last week.

Grandma Fraochlán On what?

Connie On tobacco and pipes and chocolate and snuff and cigarettes and the Lord knows what!

Grandma Fraochlán Thah's alright so. Did I buy anythin' for you?

Connie No, you didn't.

Grandma Fraochlán Very thoughtless of me, it's th'auld memory. Sorry, Connie.

Connie (*lighting a cigarette, relieved the transfer is nearly over*) Ara I don't want anything.

The Mai and Connie exit. Connie beckons The Mai, wants to see around the house.

Grandma Fraochlán Millie, a glass of mulberry wine there to put manners an the ghosts.

Millie (*gives her a glass*) Grandma Fraochlán?

Grandma Fraochlán (*dreamily, eating chocolate and drinking wine*) Hah, lovey?

Millie The name alone evokes a thousand memories in me. She was known as the Spanish beauty though she was born and bred on Inis Fraochlán, north of Bofin. She was the result of a brief tryst between an ageing island spinster and a Spanish or Moroccan sailor – no one is quite sure – who was never heard of or seen since the night of her conception. There were many stories about him as there are about those who appear briefly in our lives and change them for ever. Whoever he was, he left Grandma Fraochlán his dark skin and a yearning for all that was exotic and unattainable.

The Mai enters.

Grandma Fraochlán (*looking around*) I don't know about all this, Mai.

The Mai You're just like the rest of that Connemara click, always hoping that things will turn out for the worst! Well they won't! Because Robert is back and he's here for good and that's all I care about.

Grandma Fraochlán I won't open me mouth again!

The Mai Ah now don't be like that. You know I'm delighted to have you here. Grandma Fraochlán, you don't realize how awful it's been these last few years, and now I have the chance of being happy again and I can't bear anyone to say anything that'll take that away.

Grandma Fraochlán Ya shouldn't think like that, Mai. You're strong, ya must be, look at all ya done this last few years. Anaway, how is he?

The Mai Never seen him more alive. You'd never think we were married seventeen years. I feel like a bride all over again.

Grandma Fraochlán An' ya look like one too. You're th'image of Ellen, God rest her.

The Mai Am I?

Connie enters.

Grandma Fraochlán More and more every day. Ellen got all the brains and all the beauty of my lot, just like you did out of Ellen's lot.

Connie And I suppose Beck and myself are scarecrows.

Grandma Fraochlán (*ignoring her*) In me darkest hour
I often wished that God had taken one of the others and
left me Ellen. Isn't that an awful wish from the mouth of
a mother?

Connie You should be struck down.

Grandma Fraochlán And she was so proud of her three
little girls – Mai, Connie and Beck. Didn't she pick lovely
names for ye at a time in Connemara when everyone was
called Máire or Bridgín or Cáit. Oh she was way ahead
of her time –

Connie Ah don't start.

Grandma Fraochlán Won scholarships and prizes into
the best schools and colleges in the country –

Connie We know! We know! (*raconteur voice*) She was
the only woman in her class doing Medicine the year she
entered the Dublin university, and she did it all be
herself, I had nothin' in those days –

Grandma Fraochlán Shame on ya mockin' your own
mother! And then that summer in Dublin, halfway
through her college degree, on a wild night of drink and
divilment, me darlin' girl got pregnant be a brickie.

Connie Ara give over!

Grandma Fraochlán (*lost in memory*) Oh Lord, nineteen
years of age, she had to marry him, what else could she
do, it was nineteen thirty-eight.

A few mock tears from Connie.

You'd want to show a bit more respect.

Connie I've run out of respect.

The Mai We know all this, Grandma Fraochlán.

Grandma Fraochlán Then heed it! You're too like her for my peace of mind!

Connie (*listening to cello, looking around*) Well I don't know how you did it, Mai, it's a mansion – I mean Derek and I are on very good incomes and we'd never attempt something like this. Has he written anything worth talking about these last few years?

The Mai He has. Loads.

Connie That's all very well but what're ye goin' to do for bread and butter.

The Mai He's going back teaching in the college in the autumn.

Connie I thought he walked out of there after Julie's Michael gettin' him the job an' all.

The Mai Well, he's sorted it out, they're delighted to have him.

Grandma Fraochlán (*who has been dreaming and muttering to herself during the above exchanges*) Would you say I'll go to heaven, Mai?

The Mai Why wouldn't you, if there's such a place.

Grandma Fraochlán If indeed, but seriously now do you think I'm paradise material or am I one of Lucifer's wicked old children?

The Mai (*laughs*) Paradise material definitely.

Grandma Fraochlán I've been havin' woeful drames lately. I keep dramin' I'm in hell and I'm the only one there apart from Satan himself –

Connie He'd be well matched.

Grandma Fraochlán And through a glass ceilin' I can see everyone I ever cared about, up beyond in heaven, and d'ya know the worst part of the dream is Satan and meself gets on like a house on fire. We're there laughin' and skitterin' like two schoolgirls. Isn't that a fright?

The Mai Ara it's only a dream. Any word from Beck?

Connie She rang last week. Have you heard from her?

The Mai Not in months.

Connie She's in great form, met a new man.

Grandma Fraochlán Another one.

Connie This time she said it's for real.

Grandma Fraochlán That's what she said the last time and the time before. What does he do?

Connie I told you I didn't ask her.

Grandma Fraochlán Well what does his father do or did ya not think of axin' that aither?

The Mai These things don't matter any more.

Grandma Fraochlán I remember the first time I met the nine-fingered fisherman. '*Is mise Tomás, scipéir, mac scipéara*,' he said. I knew where he was comin' from, one sentence, one glance of his blue eyes and me heart was in his fist.

The Mai Has she any plans to come home?

Connie You know Beck. Well I'd better be off.

The Mai Have something to eat first. I've dinner made for you.

Connie I can't, Mai, I've a hundred and one things to do and Derek's expecting me, but thanks anyway.

Grandma Fraochlán (*who has been muttering to herself*) But it doesn't matter – I'm proud of Beck, proud of

Connie and proud of The Mai. Three great women! (*A bit tipsy, gets up to embrace them.*)

The Mai Sit down, *a stóir*.

Grandma Fraochlán Mighty women the lot of ye!

Connie She's off!

Grandma Fraochlán If Ellen could see ye now! D'ya think she'd be happy with the way I reared ye? I'm so proud of ye! (*Swinging her glass, she spills the wine.*)

The Mai Mind the wine!

Connie Jesus, The Mai's new rug!

> *Grandma Fraochlán pays no heed, continues swinging the glass.*

Bye, *a stóir*.

> *She kisses Grandma Fraochlán.*

Grandma Fraochlán (*in full flight, ignores Connie's exit*) And I'm proud of Beck too, though she's flittin' from one country to the next with not a stitch on her back nor a shillin' in her purse. Doesn't matter. I'm proud. Mighty proud.

> *The Mai and Connie drift off during this. We see The Mai waving Connie off.*

Millie Grandma Fraochlán became a little sentimental after a few glasses of mulberry wine, and after a few more she began to call up the ghosts and would wrestle with them until sleep overtook her. These ghosts were as numerous as they were colourful. One of her favourite buddies from the ghost department was the Sultan of Spain.

Grandma Fraochlán (*incensed*) Now Sultan! You give

me one good reason why women can't own harems full
of men when it is quite obvious that men owns harems
full of women! G'wan! I'm listenin'! G'wan! Answer me
that! And cut out that desert swagger! (*She listens
earnestly, then with growing annoyance.*) Seafóid Sultan!
Nowhere in the holy books does it say that! (*Listens.*)
I'll get upset if I want to! G'wan! Off with yourself!
There's no gettin' through to you! Don't know why
I even waste me time with ya! Off! And God help the
harem that has to put up with ya!

Millie And she'd banish him back to his tent in the
desert or to his palace in Morocco or his villa in Spain or
to the exotic ghost section of her ancient and fantastical
memory.

Grandma Fraochlán (*putting on lipstick*) That you,
Tomás?

Millie A more intimate ghost was the nine-fingered
fisherman, Grandma Fraochlán's beloved husband, who
was drowned in a fishing accident some sixty years ago.

Grandma Fraochlán (*holds up lipstick*) Remember ya
bought it for me – 1918 at the Cleggan fair – still have it
– Why wouldn't I? Remember the Cleggan fair, me nine-
fingered fisherman, we went across from Fraochlán in
the currach, me thirty-eighth birthday, a glorious day –
(*Listens, laughs softly.*) I knew you'd remember, you'd
got me a bolt of red cloth and I'd made a dress and a
sash for me hair. Remember, Tomás, remember, and you
told me I was the Queen of the ocean and that nothing
mattered in the wide world, only me. And we danced at
the Cleggan fair and you whispered in me ear – sweet
nothins – sweet nothins.

> *Grandma Fraochlán dances with the air; cello pro-
> vides music, Irish with a flavour of Eastern. Let her*

*dance a while. The music stops. Grandma Fraochlán
stands there lost in memory. Robert enters.*

Robert You OK there, Grandma Fraochlán?

Grandma Fraochlán (*wiping off lipstick*) Grand, grand.

Robert Settling in all right?

Grandma Fraochlán (*sharply*) Are you?

Robert (*smiles*) Yes, it's lovely here.

Grandma Fraochlán (*looking at him, the Mirada Fuerte*)
I think you only come back because ya couldn't find
anythin' better elsewhere and you'll be gone as soon as
ya think you've found somethin' better –

Robert You don't know the whole story and I'd advise
you not to be –

Grandma Fraochlán I know enough! You didn't see her
strugglin' with them youngsters, all yours – in case you've
forgotten – scrimpin' and scrapin' to get this house built
and when everythin's laid on, you appear on the doorstep
with a bunch of flowers. Ah! (*gesture of dismissal*)

Robert People change.

Grandma Fraochlán I'm not on this planet one hundred
year without learnin' a thing or two. People don't
change, Robert, they don't change at all!

Robert Well maybe if you and the rest of The Mai's
family weren't livin' in our ear –

Grandma Fraochlán I'm here as an invited guest in The
Mai's new house and I'll leave when The Mai axes me to
leave and not before!

Robert Grandma Fraochlán, I don't want to fight with
you.

Grandma Fraochlán Why couldn't ya just leave her alone? Ya come back here and fill the girl's head with all sorts of foolish hope. Your own father left your mother, didn't he?

Robert He never left her! He went to America for a few years. It was after the war, he had to get work, but he came back, didn't he!

Grandma Fraochlán And thousands stayed, war or no war, or brung their wives and children with them. But not you, no, and not your father, and sure as I'm sittin' here, you'll not be stoppin' long, because we can't help repeatin', Robert, we repeat and we repeat, the orchestration may be different but the tune is always the same.

> *Robert exits. Grandma Fraochlán dozes. Light changes. Beck enters with a gift.*

Beck Now you're not to tell anyone.

Grandma Fraochlán I won't, I won't, what is it?

Beck The Mai'd kill me if she ever found out.

> *Grandma Fraochlán opens the gift.*

Happy birthday, Grandma Fraochlán.

Grandma Fraochlán An opium pipe. Glory be, Beck, ya didn't!

Beck Didn't I tell you I would.

Grandma Fraochlán I haven't seen one of these in – in –

Beck Is it the right kind?

Grandma Fraochlán Sure it is. (*She takes a puff to test it.*) There's great pullin' in that – Now did ya get anythin' to put in it?

Beck Course I did. We'll have a wee smoke later on down in your room.

Grandma Fraochlán (*still examining it*) With the windas open, aye. We couldn't have one now, could we?

Beck (*a look around*) What ya think?

A devilish smile from Grandma Fraochlán.

Come on.

Grandma Fraochlán You're the original angel, Beck, the original angel.

They exit. Evening. Lights up on The Mai and Robert. He plays a piece for her. She listens.

Robert (*finishing*) Well?

The Mai It's very dark.

Robert You're not crazy about it.

The Mai No, it's beautiful but –

Robert But what?

The Mai I thought you'd write something lighter – happier – that's all.

Robert Maybe next time I will.

The Mai Why'd you come back?

Robert Why'd I come back? Difficult one – it's not so great out there, Mai.

The Mai Is it not?

Robert No.

The Mai And I thought you came back for me.

Robert I think maybe I did – you really want to know what brought me back?

The Mai Yeah I do.

Robert I dreamt that you were dead and my cello case was your coffin and a carriage drawn by two black swans takes you away from me over a dark expanse of water and I ran after this strange hearse shouting, 'Mai, Mai,' and it seemed as if you could hear my voice on the moon, and I'm running, running, running over water, trees, mountains, though I've long lost sight of the carriage and of you – And I wake, pack my bags, take the next plane home.

The Mai So you've come back to bury me, that what you're sayin'?

Robert Why do you always have to look for the bleakest meaning in everything?

The Mai It's usually the right one.

Robert Not everything has to be final and tragic, Mai, not everything. And dreaming about death always means something else. Dreams aren't that vulgar, they're coy, elusive things. They have to be, the amount of times I've dreamt about you dying, and here you are healthy as a trout.

The Mai And just how many times have you dreamt of me dying?

Robert I don't remember.

The Mai That many?

Robert Don't tell me you haven't dreamt about me dying?

The Mai Once – only once – Was the night before we got married –

Robert Yeah –

The Mai Remember Grandma Fraochlán had put you sleeping in the kitchen in front of the range?

Robert Yeah –

The Mai And I was in the back room with Connie and Beck?

Robert Yeah – And you crept out to me when the whole house was asleep.

The Mai Yeah – And we drank all Grandma Fraochlán's mulberry wine.

Robert Yeah – And we had to whisper so we wouldn't wake the old crone.

The Mai Yeah –

Robert (*looking at her*) So, your dream.

The Mai I dreamt it was the end of the world and before my eyes an old woman puts a knife through your heart and you die on the grey pavement, and for some reason I find this hilarious. Then the scene changes and I'm a child walking up a golden river and everything is bright and startling. At the bend in the river I see you coming towards me whistling through two leaves of grass – you're a child too – and as you come nearer I smile and wave, so happy to see you, and you pass me saying, 'Not yet, not yet, not for thousands and thousands of years.' And I turn to look after you and you're gone and the river is gone and away in the distance I see a black cavern and I know it leads to nowhere and I start walking that way because I know I'll find you there.

Robert That's an awful fuckin' dream to tell anyone.

The Mai Well, you asked me to tell you.

Robert The night before we got married?

The Mai Yeah – remember it like it was yesterday.

A pause. They look at one another. Hold a while.

Robert Mai, I've finished nothing this past five years – nothing I'm proud of.

The Mai Have you not?

Robert I need you around me –

The Mai So you came back for your work?

Robert No. Not only – All those years I was away, not a day went by I didn't think of you, not a day someone or something didn't remind me of you. When I'd sit down to play, I'd play for you, imagining you were there in the room with me.

The Mai I used to talk to you all the time.

Robert I used to hear you.

The Mai Used you?

He looks at her, plays her toes with his cello bow.

Robert Don't you know you are and were and always will be the only one? Don't you know, no matter what the hurtling years may do to us? (*He hands her tickets.*)

The Mai Tickets – For Paris – Both of us?

Robert And why not?

The Mai I've never been to Paris.

Robert I know. C'mon, let's go into town for dinner.

Millie Can I go with ye?

Robert Ah? (*He defers to The Mai.*)

The Mai Some other evening.

Millie Tch!

Robert Poor Millie's bored.

Millie Well I am! There's nothin' to do round here except chase tractors or listen to Grandma Fraochlán blatherin' about the nine-fingered fisherman.

Robert I'll take you in tomorrow for a surprise.

Robert and The Mai go out.

Millie (*watching them depart*) Maybe we did go into town the following day, I don't remember. It is beyond me now to imagine how we would've spent that day, where we would've gone, what we would've talked about, because when we meet now, which isn't often and always by chance, we shout and roar till we're exhausted or in tears or both, and then crawl away to lick our wounds already gathering venom for the next bout. We usually start with the high language. He'll fling the Fourth Commandment at me, *HONOUR THY FATHER!* And I'll hiss back, a father has to be honourable before he can be honoured, or some facetious rubbish like that. And we'll pace ourselves like professionals, all the way to the last round, to the language of the gutter, where he'll call me a fuckin' cunt and I'll call him an ignorant bollix! We're well matched, neither ever gives an inch, we can't, it's life and death as we see it. And that's why I cannot remember that excursion into town if it ever occurred. What I do remember, however, is one morning a year and a half later when Robert and I drove into town to buy a blue nightgown and a blue bedjacket for The Mai's waking. Still reeling from the terrible events of that weekend, we walked through The Midland drapery, the floorboards creaking, the other shoppers falling silent and turning away, they knew why we were there and what we'd come for, afraid to look yet needing to see, not wanting

to move too closely lest they breathed in the damaged air
of Owl Lake that hung about us like a wayward halo.
No shroud for The Mai. It was her wish. In one of those
throwaway conversations which only become significant
with time, The Mai had said she wanted to be buried
in blue. So here we were in a daze fingering sky blues,
indigo blues, navy blues, lilac blues, night blues, finally
settling on a watery blue silk affair. Business done, we
moved down the aisle towards the door. A little boy,
escaping his mother, ran from the side, banged off
Robert and sent him backwards into a display stand.
About him on the floor, packets of needles and spools of
thread all the colours of the rainbow.

> *Daylight, sunshine, cello music, sound of children
> playing off. Beck enters in swimming togs and a
> bathrobe, screeching and yelping from the lake.*
> *Enter The Mai with a boy's trousers, sewing them.*

Beck Well that's the end of my swimming for another
summer. (*She pours a drink.*) Will you have one?

The Mai When I've finished this (*sewing*).

Beck (*goes to window, waves at the children*) You're so
lucky to have them all. I don't suppose I'll ever have a
child now.

The Mai You're still young enough.

Beck Mai, I'm thirty-seven.

The Mai Wasn't St Elizabeth ninety-two when she had
John the Baptist?

Beck You never take no for an answer, do you?

The Mai And didn't the Duchess have Grandma
Fraochlán when she was forty-five and didn't Aunt Julie
have Barclay when she was forty-three?

Beck And didn't she make a right job of him! No, I won't have any now. I suppose there has to be one spinster in every generation.

The Mai Honest to God, Beck, you'd swear you were on your last legs. Tell me more about this Wesley fella?

Beck Not much to tell.

The Mai Don't be so cagey, you know I'm dyin' to hear.

Beck He's fifty-three and he thought I was thirty. He was married once before and he has two teenage sons who I got on better with than Wesley. I like being around young people, Mai – anyway Wesley was jealous, he was like a big baby sulkin' in the background but I didn't care. Brian, the older one, used to take me surfing and on my thirty-seventh birthday, thirty-first to them, he drove down from his college, a whole hundred miles, just to give me a birthday present. Of course Wesley couldn't handle this at all.

The Mai Poor Wesley.

Beck Yeah – he wasn't really my sort, too educated for me, though I must say I've always been attracted to educated men, probably because of my own dismal academic record.

The Mai You could've gone on and studied if you'd wanted.

Beck Not at all, I'm thick. Always was.

The Mai You were never thick.

Beck Five *E*s in my Leaving Cert.

The Mai Will you see him when you go back?

Beck Mai, I'm married to him.

The Mai You're not!

Beck In a registry office five months ago, don't ask me why.

The Mai Ah, why didn't you tell us?

Beck Because I'm getting a divorce.

The Mai Ah you're not, Beck. Listen, congratulations anyway. (*Gets up to kiss her.*)

Beck Ara would you stop! Now don't say a word to anyone. The last thing I need is the Connemara click in on top of me.

The Mai I won't open me mouth. Was it a lovely ceremony?

Beck It was, it was wonderful.

The Mai I would've gone. Why didn't you invite me, Beck? Do you have any photos?

Beck I burnt them all.

The Mai Ah you didn't, what happened?

Beck The only reason he married me was because he was afraid of getting old and being left alone.

The Mai Is that what he said?

Beck No, of course that's not what he said. He made it seem like he was doing me a favour.

The Mai Well it's not exactly Tristan and Isolde –

Beck Don't get me wrong, he was kind, kind enough until one night I got a little drunk and believed myself to be a lot closer to him than I actually was and I told him I wasn't thirty-one and that I wasn't in fact a qualified teacher but a low-down waitress.

The Mai Ah, Beck, why did you have to tell him all those lies in the first place?

Beck Mai, you don't know what it's like out there when you're nothing and you have nothing, because you've always shone, always, you've always been somebody's favourite or somebody's star pupil or somebody's wife, or somebody's mother or somebody's teacher. Imagine a place where you are none of those things.

The Mai It hasn't always been easy for me, Beck.

Beck You don't know what you're talking about.

The Mai You didn't see me after Robert left me! What a struggle it was. You never wrote or phoned and Connie never came to see me, and yet the pair of ye kept in contact all the time, and now you sit in my new house and tell me I don't know what it's like.

Beck I never knew what to write, Mai. You know I'm useless in a crisis.

The Mai You don't have to be. That's the easy option. You've an awful lot to offer anyone, if you'd just believe in yourself.

Beck The truth is, Mai, I've damn all to offer anyone. I can barely stay alive myself without getting involved in your hopeless affairs with Robert.

The Mai He's my husband and he's back and I love him, so don't you freeway in here and tell me it's hopeless.

Beck Well it is, and Connie says so too.

The Mai Well why doesn't she say it to my face? I never see Connie any more. Anytime I suggest we meet she's busy. I'm fed up of it, Beck.

Beck Well that's between Connie and yourself, none of my business.

The Mai Ye're thick as thieves, always were.

Beck You had Grandma Fraochlán, we had one another.

The Mai That's no explanation. That's childhood. We had no choice then.

Beck And we've had none since! Wesley said I had the deportment of a serving girl – low voice, head down, don't interrupt anyone.

The Mai It's a very cruel thing to say to anyone.

Beck Well it's the truth, isn't it!

The Mai It's not how I would've described you or how anyone who cared for you would.

Beck Doesn't matter. It's over now anyway.

The Mai You won't go back to him?

Beck I never give second chances, Mai. Don't believe in them. Anyway I knew it wouldn't last.

The Mai Then why did you marry him?

Beck Ah I don't know.

The Mai You don't know?

Beck (*exploding*) I told you I was thick! I don't know! Maybe because everything I touch turns to shite! Now will you stop asking me all these questions!

The Mai I'm sorry, Beck – I didn't mean to –

Beck Don't apologize! I'm the one who's sorry. I've no right to take it out on you. I'm just a bit under the weather these days. I'm thirty-seven years of age, Mai, and what've I got to show for it? Nothing. Absolutely nothing!

The Mai You're still young, Beck. Why don't you do some kind of course here, get a job, settle down?

Beck I don't see the point, Mai. I can't think of any good reasons to do anything ever again. (*Drinks.*)

The Mai and Beck exit.

Millie Needless to say, within days the story of Beck's liaison had travelled through the family like wildfire. None of The Mai's doing. No, Beck herself felt the need to tell everyone that she had been married, however briefly. I think maybe to raise herself a little in everyone's estimation.

Julie and Agnes appear in fur coats, with similar handbags, outside the window, peering in, nosing around.

Agnes (*looking around furtively*) Well, what do you think?

Julie A lot of money's been spent here. I wonder where they got it from.

Agnes Everythin's on credit these days. Would you look at the size of that window?

Julie (*peering in the window*) An ordinary house wouldn't do them. No, The Mai'd have to do the bigshot thing. I'd say they haven't two pennies to rub together. Is it my eyesight or is that a Persian rug?

Agnes (*taking out glasses*) Show. It is. It is.

Julie (*taking glasses off Agnes, looking through them*) Not a mock one?

Agnes Show. (*taking glasses back*) The genuine article.

Julie They don't fall off the trees.

Agnes You can be sure of that, oh but isn't the view magnificent?

Julie They could've bought a picture of a view.

They pass across the window.

Millie Two of The Mai's aunts, bastions of the Connemara click, decided not to take the prospect of a divorcee in the family lying down. So they arrived one lovely autumn day armed with novenas, scapulars and leaflets on the horrors of premarital sex which they distributed amongst us children along with crisp twenty-pound notes. Births, marriages and deaths were their forte and by Christ, if they had anything to do with it, Beck would stay married even if it was to a tree.

Julie and Agnes enter, disarmed of their furs, but not their handbags which go everywhere with them.

The Mai (*off*) Make yourselves at home, I'll be in in a minute.

Agnes Well that was lovely.

Julie It was. I wonder how much the site cost.

Agnes What is it? Half an acre? You wouldn't get much change out of eight grand, not with a view like that.

Julie Eight grand! Where did The Mai get hold of money like that with all those young ones?

Agnes They're a fine healthy clatter.

Julie And she's manners on them. I'll say that for The Mai, she's a bit of *slacht* on that brood.

Agnes They've all plenty to say for themselves.

Julie Maybe a bit too much to say, and the posh accents of them. Must be the schools she's sendin' them to. They didn't learn to speak like that around here.

Agnes That's for sure.

Julie Still, they set to the washin' up and not a gig or a protest out a one of them.

Agnes And Robert there helpin' to serve up the dinner.

Julie Thanks be to the Lord Jesus, though it might be just for show.

Agnes No, I was watching him, he knew where everything was and what needed to be done.

Julie Thanks be to God he's back, one less to worry about. I wonder where he really was all that time.

Agnes Wasn't he in America?

Julie You can be sure that's only the tip of the iceberg; strange crowd, tell you nothin'.

Agnes What'll we say to Beck?

Julie We'll play it by ear. I wish to God she'd take that peroxide out of her hair.

Agnes She's a holy show in those tight black pants.

Julie I hope to God she's not pregnant.

Agnes Glory be, I never thought of that.

Julie (*proud she's thought of it*) Oh you have to think of everything.

Agnes She'd never have it.

Julie God forbid! A divorcee with a child, born after the divorce.

Agnes She'd never go for an (*whisper*) abortion, would she?

Julie We'll find out if she's pregnant first and, if she is, with the luck of God she'll miscarry.

Agnes Poor little Beck, she was always so nervous.

Julie A jittery little thing from the outset, all that opium Ellen took and Grandma Fraochlán feedin' it to her.

Agnes It's up to us, Julie, to see that she's all right.

Julie It is indeed. And isn't Grandma Fraochlán looking well?

Agnes She looks very stooped to me.

Julie Not at all, she'll have to be shot. Here they are now. Go easy for a while, we'll have a bit of a chit-chat first. (*cute wink to Agnes*)

Agnes (*cute wink back*) I'll wait for you to start.

Julie Grand. (*one more cute wink*)

Grandma Fraochlán enters on Beck's arm, followed by The Mai.

The Mai Ye'll have a glass of sherry.

Julie Not at all, we're grand.

The Mai offers one to Agnes. Agnes looks at Julie who is busy looking at Beck's belly. Agnes accepts.

Grandma Fraochlán (*filling her pipe*) Still teetotallin', Julie?

Julie When you give up the pipe I'll hit the bottle.

Grandma Fraochlán You'll never drink this side of paradise so. I'd hate to die and never have tasted sweet wine, wouldn't you, Beck?

Julie You're looking great, Beck.

Beck I'm pushin' on, Aunt Julie.

Agnes None of us are spring chickens any longer.

Julie (*to Grandma Fraochlán*) I see you're still on the mulberry wine.

Grandma Fraochlán And I'll be on it as long as I can swalla.

Julie You know it's against your doctor's orders. Mai, why're you letting her drink mulberry wine?

The Mai Ara it does her no harm and she enjoys it.

Julie She wouldn't be allowed it in my house.

Grandma Fraochlán Precisely why I never stay in your house, Julie, *a stóir*.

The Mai Now Grandma Fraochlán, don't start a row. Remember you promised.

Julie You were told no tobacco and no alcohol. I can't see why you can't obey two simple rules.

Grandma Fraochlán Tha Lord put grapes and tobacco plants on the earth so his people could get plastered at every available opportunity.

Julie Ah there's no talkin' to you.

Agnes You're very quiet there, Beck.

The Mai Have a whiskey, love, you're on your holidays.

Agnes Honestly, Mai, you get more and more like Ellen every day.

The Mai Grandma Fraochlán's always sayin' that.

Julie It's true and you've the same voice.

Agnes The very same. She'd be sixty now, a year younger than me.

Julie It was shameful what happened to Ellen.

Agnes It couldn't be helped.

Julie I'll never understand how a young woman in the whole of her health dies in childbirth in the best nursing home in Galway.

Grandma Fraochlán She was worn out from all them miscarriages and pregnancies.

Julie Twenty-seven years of age. You should've looked after her better, Grandma Fraochlán.

Grandma Fraochlán So it was all my fault, was it?

Julie I'm not saying it was.

Grandma Fraochlán Then what are ya sayin'?

Julie Nothin', only I remember a few nights before she got married, she appeared on my doorstep, three months pregnant with The Mai there, and she begged me to take her in until the child was born and she wanted me to go and talk to you and make you see that she didn't have to marry him.

Grandma Fraochlán And why didn't ya!

Julie If it was now I'd mow ya down!

Grandma Fraochlán We're all wonderful after the event, Julie, the maybe if we done this and the maybe if we done that! Why didn't ya come and make me see and why sit here and tell me a lifetime too late?

Julie Because I knew it would be pointless.

Grandma Fraochlán Well that's one knife you've buried in me and you're not here two hours. Where's the next one?

Agnes (*peacemaker*) What's Australia like, Beck?

Beck Oh it's beautiful.

Agnes Did you travel much around it?

Beck Yeah, I was all over.

Agnes And did you meet any aborigines?

Beck Several.

Agnes And what're they like?

Beck Well they're like ourselves, I suppose.

Julie Indeed'n they are not! They live in caves, don't they, and they're black, black as ravens with teeth of snow. Sure didn't I see them on the telly!

Beck Most of them live in houses now. Only a few still live in caves.

Agnes And did you see the ones in the caves?

Julie Wouldn't be my style at all!

Beck I did, I went on a camping holiday in the outback last summer.

Julie (*time for the jugular*) Was that where you met your husband?

Beck No, I met him in Sydney.

Agnes (*dreamy*) In Sydney, Australia.

Julie And when are we going to meet him?

Grandma Fraochlán You're not. The Mai told ya all about it on the telephone.

Agnes You're not really getting a (*whisper*) divorce, are you, sweetheart?

Beck I'm afraid I am.

Agnes Don't worry, don't worry.

Julie None of ours ever got a divorce!

Beck It just didn't work out, Aunt Julie. I tried. I really did.

Julie What's all this talk about working out. In my day you got married and whether it worked out or it didn't was by the way.

Grandma Fraochlán I didn't bring you up to think like that, Julie!

Julie You didn't bring me up at all. I brought myself up and all the others. You were at the window pinin' for the nine-fingered fisherman!

The Mai Ah there's no need to be shoutin' now, Julie.

Julie Sorry, I'm only tryin' to help Beck.

Agnes And what'll you do now, sweetheart?

Julie I don't like your carry on one bit, young lady! All this hoorin' around for years and finally someone marries you and you walk out on him. And I suppose you'll be back hoorin' around before we can bat an eyelid!

Grandma Fraochlán Ara, cop onto yourself, Julie! This is the age of freedom, isn't that right, Beck?

Julie I still call it hoorin' around!

Grandma Fraochlán Maybe a bit of hoorin' around would've done yourself no harm; might take that self-righteous *straois* off your puss!

Julie You watch your dirty Arab tongue!

The Mai Go easy, the pair of ye!

Grandma Fraochlán I'm half Spanish, half Moroccan for your infor –

Julie Oh it's half Moroccan this time, is it! Last time it was three-quarters Tunisian!

Grandma Fraochlán I told ya, ya eejit, my great grandfather was Tunisian! I'm only quarter Tunisian, half Moroccan and half Spanish!

Julie That makes five quarters! How many quarters in a whole?

Grandma Fraochlán A good kick up yours is what you need! Don't ya dare come the schoolteacher with me, ya little faggot ya!

The Mai Oh Jesus!

Julie No thanks to you I became a schoolteacher. If you had your way I'd still be out there on Fraochlán scrawbin' the seaweed off the rocks. Anyway it's all rubbish about the Tunisian and the Moroccan. You don't know where you came from!

Agnes This'll get us nowhere.

The Mai Wouldn't ya think ye could be civil to one another at this stage of ye'er lives (*Points finger to Grandma Fraochlán.*) And you promised you'd behave yourself.

Grandma Fraochlán Sorry, Mai, sorry. It's a swanky autumn day, isn't it, Julie?

Julie You haven't changed one bit, always fillin' our heads with stories and more stories –

Agnes Ah, Julie, leave it.

Julie Whose side are you on?

Agnes I'm not on any side. And sure who knows but you'll marry a decent man yet, Beck. (*a glare from Julie*)

After the (*whisper*) divorce, I mean.

Beck I think I'll end up like yourself, Aunt Agnes, without a man or a care in the world.

Grandma Fraochlán You'll pilla a fine man yet, Beck, don't mind any of them.

Julie Are you still talking about sex at your age?

Grandma Fraochlán Well I wasn't particularly, but now that ya mention it, what else is there to talk about at any age? You're born, ya have sex, and then ya die. And if you're one of them lucky few whom the gods has blessed, they will send to you a lover with whom you will partake of that most rare and sublime love there is to partake of in this wild and lonely planet. I have been one of them privileged few and I know of no higher love in this world or the next.

The Mai You make our men seem like nothing.

Grandma Fraochlán I only talk about me own.

Julie Well maybe you should talk about him less, seeing as he left ya penniless with seven offspring.

Grandma Fraochlán He didn't leave me. He was taken from me. He was given to me and he was taken from me, somethin' you would never understand, you who was seduced be ledgers and balance sheets, installed in a house with a slate roof and an automobile be a walkin' cheque book who counted his thingamagigs as he came –

Julie You're a vicious auld witch!

The Mai Grandma Fraochlán, that's enough! I mean it!

Grandma Fraochlán Sorry, Mai, sorry, Julie, sorry, *a stóir*, it's me filthy foreign tongue. Julie, I called you after the sunshine though you were a child of winter, me only winter birth, me first born, greatest love abounding in your making. Maybe parents as is lovers is not parents at all, not enough love left over. Did we fail you, *a stóir?*

Julie You're the same, still the same, a dagger in one hand, a flower in the other – Well it doesn't wash with me any more. (*getting upset*)

The Mai Ah come on now, Julie.

Beck (*to Grandma Fraochlán*) Come on, you and I'll go for a lie down.

Julie Sorry, she provokes me.

Grandma Fraochlán (*being led away by Beck and Agnes*) Me pipe! I'm not sittin' beyond in the room 'til that one's gone, without me pipe!

Agnes I have it, I have it.

Grandma Fraochlán And me mulberry wine.

Agnes Yes, yes.

Grandma Fraochlán You blame me for everthin'! You always have, and y'always will!

Julie Ara whisht, Mom, or you'll drive me mad!

The three of them exit.

She takes it out of me every time.

The Mai Ah she's not the worst.

Julie I'm sorry for fightin' in your new house, Mai –

The Mai Ara for God's sake.

Julie And don't hold it against me that I don't get on with her.

144

The Mai Of course I won't.

Julie A lot of things happened, Mai, long before you were born and I'm not just talkin' about Ellen.

The Mai Julie, none of us are perfect.

Julie I'm not talkin' about perfection. You didn't know her as a young woman. She was fiery, flighty. She had little or no time for her children except to tear strips off us when we got in her way. All her energy went into my father and he thought she was an angel. And then when she was left with all of us and pregnant with Ellen, she was a madwoman. Mai, I'm not makin' it up. She spent one half of the day in the back room pullin' on an opium pipe, a relic from her unknown father, and the other half rantin' and ravin' at us or starin' out the window at the sea.

The Mai Did she? She must've been heartbroken.

Julie I know, I know. Several nights I dragged her from the cliffs, goin' to throw herself in, howlin' she couldn't live without the nine-fingered fisherman, opiumed up to the eyeballs. She was so unhappy, Mai, and she made our lives hell.

The Mai It must have been terrible for you.

Julie And then Ellen, she was brilliant, that girl was going places but there was something in Grandma Fraochlán that must stop it, and she did. She made that child marry that innocent. He wasn't Ellen's steam at all and he only married her because Grandma Fraochlán saw he did. He married her and then he left her on Fraochlán to rot. Came home every summer, left her with another pregnancy. And she belittled your father all the time to Ellen, till Ellen grew to hate him and looked down on him. He couldn't write or spell very well and

Grandma Fraochlán would mock his letters until finally
Ellen stopped writing to him. And at the same time she
filled the girl's head with all sorts of impossible hope,
always talkin' about the time she was in college, and
how brilliant she was, and maybe in a few years she'd
go back and study. And it only filled Ellen with more
longing and made her feel that what she had lost was all
the greater. And do you know the worst, the worst of it
all, Ellen adored her and looked up to her and believed
everything she said, and that's what killed her, not
childbirth, no, her spirit was broken.

The Mai Are you serious?

Julie Well that's what I saw. Just be careful with Robert,
don't let her interfere, she doesn't realize the influence
she has over all of us. I'm seventy-five years of age, Mai,
and I'm still not over my childhood. It's not fair they
should teach us desperation so young or if they do they
should never mention hope. Now where's my coat? Oh,
I almost forgot, here's a little something. (*She produces
an envelope from her breast.*)

The Mai I wouldn't dream of taking it.

Julie (*puts the envelope into The Mai's dress, and
produces another from her other breast*) And that's for
Beck. Don't let on I gave it to her. I can't be seen to be
supportin' a divorcee.

The Mai There's no sense to this –

Julie He wasn't an aborigine, was he?

The Mai Who?

Julie Beck's husband?

The Mai (*controls a titter of amusement*) No – aah – he
wasn't.

Julie Not that I've anythin' against them. It's just these mixed marriages rarely work. There's plenty more (*indicating envelope*) where that came from, so don't ever be stuck. I know you've had it rough.

Julie and The Mai exit.

Millie Owl Lake comes from the Irish, *loch cailleach oíche*, Lake of the Night Hag or Pool of the Dark Witch. The legend goes that Coillte, daughter of the mountain god, Bloom, fell in love with Bláth, Lord of all the flowers. So away she bounded like a young deer, across her father's mountain, down through Croc's Valley of Stone, over the dark witch's boglands till she came to Bláth's domain. There he lay, under an oak tree, playing his pipes, a crown of forget-me-nots in his ebony hair. And so they lived freely through the spring and summer, sleeping on beds of leaves and grass, drinking soups of nettle and rosehip, dressing in acorn and poppy. One evening approaching autumn Bláth told Coillte that soon he must go and live with the dark witch of the bog, that he would return in the spring, and the next morning he was gone. Coillte followed him and found him ensconced in the dark witch's lair. He would not speak to her, look at her, touch her, and heartbroken Coillte lay down outside the dark witch's lair and cried a lake of tears that stretched for miles around. One night, seizing a long-awaited opportunity, the dark witch pushed Coillte into her lake of tears. When spring came round again Bláth was released from the dark witch's spell and he went in search of Coillte, only to be told that she had dissolved. Sam Brady told me that when the geese are restless or the swans suddenly take flight, it's because they hear Bláth's pipes among the reeds, still playing for Coillte.

Ghostly light on the window. Robert stands there with The Mai's body in his arms, utterly still. Millie watches them a minute. Ghostly effect.

A tremor runs through me when I recall the legend of Owl Lake. I knew that story as a child. So did The Mai and Robert. But we were unaffected by it and in our blindness moved along with it like sleepwalkers along a precipice and all around gods and mortals called out for us to change our course and, not listening, we walked on and on.

Lights down.

Act Two

The following summer.
Enter The Mai in a summer dress. She goes to the window, looks out, reaches into the pocket of her dress, takes the envelope with the card and ten-pound note out, looks at them hopelessly, and puts them back into her pocket.
Beck and Grandma Fraochlán call, offstage.

Beck Mai, how are you?

Grandma Fraochlán Happy birthday, Mai.

The Mai waves at them from the window; they cross the window.

The Mai Ye had a good journey?

Grandma Fraochlán I'm gettin' too auld for all this movin' about, Mai.

They pass into the house.

The Mai It's great to see you again, Grandma Fraochlán. (*Kisses her.*)

Grandma Fraochlán You'll be glad ta see the back of me before long.

The Mai How's Connie?

Beck Askin' for you. Where's your gang? The house is very quiet.

The Mai I sent them into the pictures. I wanted a bit of peace.

Beck And Robert?

The Mai Gone away for the weekend.

Grandma Fraochlán And why didn't you go with him?

The Mai Ah – the children – you know.

Beck I'd have stayed if you'd only asked.

The Mai Ah it doesn't matter.

Grandma Fraochlán It does. Why didn't ya tell us ya wanted to go away?

Beck No point in actin' the martyr.

Grandma Fraochlán I could as aisy come up next weekend.

The Mai Ah will ye stop – it's pointless. (*She starts to cry.*)

Grandma Fraochlán What's wrong, Mai?

Beck Don't cry, sweetheart.

The Mai (*pushing them off*) I'm all right, I'm all right, I'll be all right in a minute – I'm sorry about this – I didn't mean to spoil your –

> Silence. *Grandma Fraochlán and Beck look at her in dismay.*

(*looking at them*) He gave me this (*birthday card*) and this (*ten-pound note*) and he's gone to Spiddal with her.

Grandma Fraochlán I knew this would happen.

The Mai (*snaps*) Well then you knew more than I did.

Beck Spiddal?

The Mai Yeah, where he used to take me.

Grandma Fraochlán And who is she?

The Mai Everyone knows about it. It's been going on for months apparently. I should have known, I should have known.

Grandma Fraochlán And when did ya find all this out?

The Mai You know, he flew into a rage when I asked him, accused me of hounding him and spying on him and of course he denied it and I believed him – I was suspicious, of course, I am always suspicious of him, though I try not be be – And he was wining me and dining me, showering me with presents, telling me how much he loved me and then he'd be out till all hours, overly attentive to me when he was here. I must be blind – And then I followed him about two weeks ago and sure enough –

Beck And who is she?

The Mai A local woman. I went into her office to talk to her – a cold brazen woman. If I was having an affair with her husband and she came to see me, I think I would die with shame.

Beck Mai, you're too innocent. Half the country's having affairs with married men.

The Mai Well, I could never do it. It's wrong and you can call me a prude if you like, and do you know what she said to me, she said that her relationship with Robert was none of my business. And she asked me to leave her office. I could have her out of this town pronto, if I wanted. Mike Clancy is an old friend, and if I asked him he'd transfer her.

Beck And why don't you?

The Mai He's going to leave me again. I can't bear it a second time. Oh God, please, I can't bear it a second time.

Beck Here, Mai, sit down. Let me get you a drink.

The Mai I know ye've been thinkin' all along that this was going to happen. Well I hope ye're happy now.

Beck Mai, we were hoping that it would all work out for you.

Grandma Fraochlán We were indeed, *a stóir*.

Beck It'll all blow over in a couple of months, you'll see. If he's capable of loving anyone, it's you, Mai. Always has been.

The Mai Love! If there was less talk about love in this house and more demonstration of it we might begin to learn the meaning of the word.

> *Grandma Fraochlán and Beck drift off during Millie's story. The Mai sits at the window, smoking. Waiting for Robert.*

Millie The summer before Robert returned, The Mai found herself in London working as a sweeping girl in an Arab hairdressing salon. The banks would not give her a mortgage for the new house at Owl Lake unless her overdraft was respectable. The Mai figured if she lodged her teaching cheques and worked for the summer she'd be home and dry. We were sent to an old friend of hers, Cassie Molloy, a dressmaker with ten children of her own. What possessed The Mai to land the four of us on that poor woman is another story. What was certain was nothing was going to stop that house being built for Robert. We sat down to dinner in shifts and slept eight to a room while The Mai swept up the curls of Arab royalty. She told me the story of a little princess, already betrothed to some sheik or other, who came into the salon one day and fell for The Mai and insisted it was The Mai and only The Mai who washed and brushed

her hair. The child began to come every day and before
long they were playmates and The Mai's only job was to
entertain the little princess who ran riot in the salon as
long as she was permitted by her docile, shrouded mother
who left magnificent tips. The Mai spoke longingly of
this child, of how they played ring-a-ring-a-rosy, of the
songs she taught her, of a shopping spree they went on
together. A lick of jealousy would curl through me
whenever The Mai mentioned her. I wanted to compete
but I was out of my league and I knew it. But not The
Mai, no, The Mai and the princess were two of a kind,
moving towards one another across deserts and fairytales
and years till they finally meet in a salon under Marble
Arch and waltz around enthralled with one another and
their childish impossible world. Two little princesses on
the cusp of a dream, one five, the other forty.

*It's evening, sound of a car door closing. The Mai
stands at the window. Robert walks past the window,
and stops. He looks at The Mai. The Mai takes off her
knickers, and throws them at him through the window!
They land on his face.*

The Mai (*banging window*) Fuckin' bastard!

*Robert stands there in shock. He passes into the
house. The Mai sits down, kind of smug, pleased with
herself. The Mai listens. We can hear Robert outside
the door. He enters with the cello, the weekend bag
and the knickers. He stands there defiantly a minute:
nervous, guilty, at pains for some peace. The Mai
looks him over, and looks away. He walks across the
room with the knickers, shakes them out, folds them,
and places them on the chair beside her. The Mai
watches their journey.*

That all you can you can think of to do with them?

Robert What you expect me to do, eat them? (*He leaves a bag on the chair beside her.*) I brought you these. (*He goes into the study, and sets up his cello.*)

The Mai Strawberries and *Cosmopolitan* no less.

The Mai looks sarcastically at Robert who is half watching her from the study.

(*reading the magazine*) The zipless fuck and how to achieve it – How to take off seven pounds in seven days – And here's a recipe for peach flan with double cream. I suppose that's to put back on the seven pounds you lost. (*She flings the magazine on the chair.*)

Robert Grandma Fraochlán arrived all right?

The Mai Robert, have you ever seen me reading *Cosmopolitan*? Well, have you? (*She eats some strawberries, a wan figure.*) Did you buy them in Spiddal?

Robert No, why?

The Mai They taste of the salt air.

Robert I bought them in Birr.

The Mai They're lovely, have one? (*She gets up, goes to the study, and proffers a strawberry.*) Go on.

Robert goes to take it. She pulls it away.

Here, let me feed you. Isn't that what lovers do?

Robert Mai, stop it.

The Mai Come on.

Robert moves away from her. The Mai eats the strawberry. She moves around the study, sounds a note on the cello, takes the bow, begins screeching it across the cello to annoy Robert.

Robert Look, will you leave it alone?

The Mai sits down and plays a few phrases expertly.

The Mai Not bad, hah? For someone who hasn't played in over fifteen years. With a bit of practice I'd be as good as you. Now there's a frightening thought – for both of us. How dare you throw ten pounds at me on my fortieth birthday!

Robert What you want me to do, take you to Spiddal and pretend everything is wonderful?

The Mai Just because we're not in the first flush of passion doesn't mean we're pretending. And for your information I don't read *Cosmopolitan*!

Robert Fine.

The Mai Do you know what I did this weekend, Robert, or do you care?

Robert Could you cut out the headmistress tone? You're not addressing Assembly now.

The Mai I collected the children from their schools, I did twelve loads of laundry, I prepared eight meals, I dropped the children back to their schools, and I read Plato and Aristotle on education, because education is my business, and do you know the differences between their philosophies? No, I didn't think you would.

Robert It was I who brought Plato and Aristotle into this house. When I met you, you were reading Mills and Boons!

The Mai You're a fuckin' liar! When you met me I was cellist in the college orchestra! I had a B.A. under my belt and I was halfway through my Masters! You lower me, all the time you lower me. (*She brandishes the cello bow all over the place.*)

Robert Look, will you put that down, you'll break it.

The Mai And so what, you'll replace it, you're good at replacing things. (*She taps the bow along her toes, stops, pulls a string from it, looks at Robert, looks away, resumes playing herself: knees, thighs, stomach. Then she stops to snap a string as it suits her. She plays her breasts and makes notes on her throat with her other hand. Eyes closed, playing herself*) Tell me, Robert – tell me, is it that faraway pussies are greener or is it your mother crowin' on your cock?

Robert You've a filthy tongue and the cut of a tinker.

The Mai This is my house and I'll speak as I fuckin' well like!

Robert It's my house too. I gave you every penny I had for it when I came back here – whatever possessed me. Otherwise we'd have been out on the side of the road. A fact you haven't bothered to mention to any of your relatives! No! You'd rather have them all thinking The Mai has done it single-handedly again in spite of that wayward bastard she married!

The Mai So you want to reduce the conversation to money. Right! Let's talk about money! Add this up! What it costs to feed, clothe, educate four children for five years. Do you know what that cost?

Robert No, I don't.

The Mai Then keep your fuckin' mouth shut about your paltry little contribution. How can you do this to your children! They're haunted! Do you know that! Your children are haunted. And you don't give a fuckin' damn!

Robert I'm not listening to your fuckin' tirade and I refuse to take responsibility for the way you use the kids in our sham of a fuckin' marriage!

He exits slamming the door.
The Mai sits there fuming. After a while she calms
down and begins playing a few phrases until she gets
them right. In full swing she finishes.

Millie Whatever about The Mai and Robert, Sam Brady
had had enough. He'd always treated Robert with a
quiet disdain, but now it was time for action. So one
night he moved the fences in on either side of our house
and we woke to find half the garden gone. He started
throwing the ashes from his fire over our wall, a gesture
considered a curse in that part of the country. He also
figured a dose of Billy the Black was necessary. Billy
the Black was his one obstreperous cow and she could
always be depended on to do the damage. The farmers
around were wary of Billy the Black. If you upset Sam,
the next day you'd find your cornfield torn up by Billy
the Black, and if you dared challenge Sam, well the next
night your beet field would be in ribbons. Billy the Black
was let loose in our garden, or what was left of it, and
tore it to shreds. Sam Brady used to ride Billy like a
horse. A bit of rope through her teeth, and he was off.
If you happened to be walking up the strand at night
and looked left across the churchyard field you would
most probably see Sam galloping across the rise, bare-
backed on Billy the Black, naked except for a pair of
red bloomers it was said he stole from the King of the
Tinkers' Bride. The whole neighbourhood revelled in
nympholeptic glee at the outrageous passion of this mad
bachelor, flying across the night on the flanks of his
wicked cow. They called him the Rodeo Queen and, like
myself, would come out to watch from a safe distance.
Sam's final statement of his disapproval of Robert was
to take his gun and blow the head off the cob feeding
innocently near the bank. It's true what they say: swans
do keen their mates. She circled him for days. The Mai

was transfixed at the window. It's a high haunting sound that sings the once-living out of this world. It's a sound you hope never to hear again and it's a sound you know you will.

It's evening. The Mai comes on and pours a drink. Enter Connie and Beck, who have obviously been drinking.

The Mai (*to Connie*) So you finally came.

Connie The house looks beautiful, Mai, drivin' up the lane and the moon hangin' over it.

The Mai (*looks around*) This house – these days I think it's the kind of house you'd see in the corner of a dream – dark, formless, strangely inviting. It's the kind of house you build to keep out neuroses, stave off nightmares. But they come in anyway with the frost and the draughts and the air bubbles in the radiators. It's the kind of house you build when you've nowhere left to go.

Beck and Connie stand there looking at her.

Sit down for Christ's sake, pour yourselves a drink. (*to Connie*) So you've come to have a look?

Connie Do you want me to go, Mai?

The Mai Of course I don't. Sit down, take it all in. Isn't it strange the fascination families have in the devastation of their nearest and dearest? I've noticed that.

Beck You're in a right mood tonight.

The Mai Maybe they want to pick up a few tips for when their own number is up, or maybe it makes them feel good. They appreciate what they have themselves all the more. But really, Connie, you should have come last summer. Robert was just back, your children could've swam in Owl Lake – (*Whispers passionately.*) It was a Jesus God of a summer!

Connie (*softly*) We were away, Mai.

The Mai You're always away, Connie.

Connie I don't have to explain my life to you, Mai. So you can leave out the big sister act. I'm my own person now and no one tells me what to do.

The Mai I'm sorry, Connie. I'm delighted to see you. I miss you terribly. (*She kisses her.*) How's Derek?

Connie He wanted to come here tonight to see you.

The Mai Then where is he?

Connie Mai, he didn't want to meet Robert.

The Mai He needn't have worried. Be easier get an audience with the Pope. Anyway it's great to see you again – reminds me of – the old days.

Connie Way back before we discovered men. You know I spent my twenties thinkin' I have to get a man, I have to get a man –

The Mai So did I.

Connie Now that I have one, what's the big deal I'd like to know. Sometimes I'd love to be on my own again.

Beck Ara go on outa that. You wouldn't last a day. You've never been without a man as long as I can remember.

The Mai Four engagements before Derek.

Connie And I never slept with any of them. If I could turn the clock back.

Beck Don't be ridiculous. Sex for the sake of it is just sex for the sake of it, like giving someone directions or telling someone the time.

The Mai (*innocently*) Is that what it's like, Beck?

Beck Well I think so, and ye needn't be looking at me now like I'm the Mata Hari.

The Mai Have you slept with a lot of men, Beck?

Beck Put it this way, I've lost count.

Connie I'd like to try it out for myself, just once, go off to a hotel with someone I picked off the street or met in a pub or train, maybe a black man or an Arab – It's just I've never had a room to myself. I'd love a single bed of my own and then to head off to a hotel every now and then. Wouldn't that be just amazing? (*She sits back and laughs.*)

The Mai I think I might like that too.

Beck The pair of ye don't know how lucky ye are.

The Mai Lucky.

Beck OK, Robert's playing puck at the moment but –

The Mai That's putting it mildly.

Connie Is it that bad, Mai?

The Mai I can't see a way out, not any more.

Connie It's very simple, Mai. Just get up and walk, or kick him out. It was you built this house after all! No point in hangin' around to be knocked down again.

The Mai You know the only difference between Robert and us is that Robert does what we dream about doing.

Connie Don't compare me with Robert.

The Mai Robert goes to hotel rooms with this one and that one, like you said you'd like to do, Connie, but he always comes back to me. He always does and has done and always will.

Connie It's not much to be proud of, Mai.

The Mai Think what you like.

Connie You're being very stubborn. You just won't admit to yourself how terrible all this is. Derek thinks it's absolutely dreadful the way he treats you.

The Mai Well I don't like the way Derek treats Robert. All paly-waly for years and suddenly silence.

Connie Well if you want the truth, Derek won't come here because he has nothing to say to Robert, and he feels awkward with you. It's embarrassing, Mai, and I'm sorry, but an awful lot of people no longer speak to Robert. You'd want to hear what they're saying about him in town.

The Mai You think I don't know that! But he's still my husband and I won't have you or anyone else say anything about him. I have the children to think of.

Beck Right, *a stóir*, we won't say another word.

The Mai And you can tell your Mr Perfect, Derek, that he needn't be gettin' up on his high horse. Just because Robert isn't a model husband like himself. Everyone is deranged, Connie. Some manage to hide it better, that's all.

Beck Another one? (*She pours for herself.*)

Connie And what's that supposed to mean?

The Mai Don't be so harsh, Connie. Don't be so harsh and don't be so eager to write off other people's misery with glib observations and glib answers on a subject you know nothing about.

Connie I wasn't being glib, Mai, I'm only tryin' to –

The Mai You don't know what it's like, the humiliation of it. The ground is gone from under me. I'm forty years of age, Connie, I'm on the downward slope.

Connie Indeed'n you are not.

The Mai I am. Let's face facts. Another three, four years, the menopause, and what then?

Connie Life begins at forty, or so they say.

The Mai That's crap from some women's magazine – probably *Cosmopolitan* – to boost the battered egos of haunted middle-aged women who know and feel their lives are falling down around their ears.

Beck C'mon, Mai, lighten up, we're celebratin'. Connie's here.

Connie You'll be all right, *a stóir*.

The Mai For once in ye'er lives, will ye stop this family solidarity shite! You'll be all right *a stóir*! Well I won't be all right! I'll never be all right and neither will ye!

Connie Ara will you stop it. You're drunk!

The Mai I'm not drunk! I'm trapped.

Beck You're tired, sweetheart, and a little drunk. It'll all look better tomorrow.

Connie I mean our lives are far from fairytales but, Christ, we're not dead yet!

The Mai They sure are. Little did I think as I played around the cliffs of Fraochlán that I would ever be like this. I used to dream that a dark-haired prince would come across the waves on the wings of an albatross and he'd take me away to a beautiful land never seen or heard of before and he'd love me as no girl had ever been loved.

Beck My prince had a white horse.

Connie Mine had a chariot with golden bells that could sing my name.

The Mai My God, we were some eejits.

Beck Too much listenin' to Grandma Fraochlán and her wild stories.

The Mai She didn't prepare us at all.

Connie She did her best.

The Mai She filled us with hope – too much hope maybe – in things to come. And her stories made us long for something extraordinary to happen in our lives. I wanted my life to be huge and heroic and pure as in the days of yore. I wanted to march through the world up and up, my prince at my side, and together we'd leave our mark on it.

Connie I suggest you look around for another prince, *a chroí.*

The Mai Don't know any forty-year-old princes.

Beck Try for a king this time. You might have better luck.

The Mai And I started off so well, gained entry everywhere I wanted, did exceedingly well academically, and I was good on the cello – I know I was – The more I think about it, the more I begin to realize that, one by one, I have to let go of all the beautiful things in my life, though I didn't mean to. Does everyone do that or is it just me?

Beck You're a hopeless romantic, Mai.

Connie (*a little jarred, begins singing softly*)
On the wings of the wind o'er the dark rolling deep
Angels are coming to watch o'er thy sleep,

Angels are coming to watch over thee,
So list' to the wind coming over the sea.

Beck (*while Connie is singing*) Remember we used to sing it in bed together?

The Mai Should have stayed in that bed singing.

The Mai and Beck join in with Connie.

All
Hear the wind blow, love,
Hear the wind blow;
Lean your head over
And hear the wind blow.

Robert enters unnoticed. He watches them, stares at The Mai as she begins singing, lost looking, in his overcoat, car keys dangling.

The Mai (*sings*)
Daddy's a-sailing away out on the blue,
Sailing for herring of silvery hue,
Silver the herring and silver the sea,
And soon there'll be silver for baby and me.

All
Hear the wind blow, love,
Hear the wind blow;
Lean your head over
And hear the wind blow.

Millie Joseph, my five-year-old son, has never been to Owl Lake. I thought of having him adopted but would not part with him when the time came, and I'm glad, though I know it's hard for him. Already he is watchful and expects far too little of me, something I must have taught him unknown to myself. He is beginning to get curious about his father and I don't know what to tell him. I tell him all the good things. I say your daddy is an

El Salvadorian drummer who swept me off my feet when I was lost in New York. I tell him his eyes are brown and his hair is black and that he loved to drink Jack Daniels by the neck. I tell him that high on hash or marijuana or god-knows-what we danced on the roof of a tenement building in Brooklyn to one of Robert's cello recordings.

I do not tell him that he is married with two sons to a jaded uptown society girl or that I tricked him into conceiving you because I thought it possible to have something for myself that didn't stink of Owl Lake. I do not tell him that on the day you were born, this jaded society queen sauntered into the hospital, chucked you under the chin, told me I was your daddy's last walk on the wild side, gave me a cheque for five thousand dollars and said, 'You're on your own now, kiddo.' And she was right. I had no business streelin' into her life, however tired it was. I do not tell him that, when you were two, I wrote a sensible letter, enclosing a photograph of you, asking him to acknowledge paternity. And I do not tell him he didn't answer.

The Mai enters in a stunning black ball-gown.

The Mai Will you zip me up, Millie?

Beck (*with a pair of shoes*) These the ones you mean?

The Mai Yeah. (*She does a twirl.*) What do you think?

Beck Beautiful.

Millie You look gorgeous, Mom.

Grandma Fraochlán (*entering*) Oh you're fierce swanky tonight, Mai.

The Mai Are you sure? I want to look my best. We're the guests of honour, you know.

Grandma Fraochlán You'll be the Queen of them all.

The Mai (*examining herself, back and front*) Really, do you think?

Grandma Fraochlán You're stunnin' and ya know ya are.

Beck Relax, Mai, it's only a dress dance.

The Mai (*flustered*) It's not! It's the Lion's Ball, it's a huge affair, the whole county'll be out. I haven't been to the Lion's Ball in over five years. Now, honestly, tell me, am I all right?

Beck Mai, you're a picture.

Millie You are, Mom.

Grandma Fraochlán An apparition if ever I saw one.

Beck Here, that'll start you off (*drink*).

The Mai Pour one for Robert as well. He should be ready by now. And don't say anything about me looking well in front of him. See if he'll notice by himself and, Millie, would you get my cape, it's on the bed.

Millie exits. Robert enters in a dress suit, his car keys dangling.

Robert Right, are you ready?

The Mai (*hands him a drink*) This is poured for you.

Robert Thanks.

He and The Mai drink.

Grandma Fraochlán You're looking very dashing, Robert.

Robert Am I?

He drinks, looks at The Mai. The Mai looks at him. No compliment forthcoming. They finish the drinks.

166

Millie enters with the cape and places it on The Mai's shoulders.

Right, are we off? Goodnight. (*He goes out.*)

The Mai (*kisses Grandma Fraochlán*) Will you be OK?

Grandma Fraochlán Will you?

The Mai I'm going to have a ball!

With mock bravado she turns and smiles at them, and goes out. Beck goes to the stereo and puts on Wagner's 'Liebestod' from Tristan and Isolde, *turns down the lights, pulls an opium pipe out of her shirt, shakes it at Grandma Fraochlán.*

Grandma Fraochlán (*laughs*) A girl after me own heart.

Beck (*lights it up*) Here, you go first.

Grandma Fraochlán takes four or five puffs, holds them in, exhales slowly, smiles. As the conversation goes on and the opium takes effect, it becomes apparent, they're dreamy, slur some words, smile unexpectedly.

Grandma Fraochlán This must be what it's like in Zanzibar.

Beck (*puffing*) What?

Grandma Fraochlán Zanzibar. We'll go in an aeroplane through tha sky an' ax them ta stop at Zanzibar.

Beck Zanzibar, where's that?

Grandma Fraochlán (*one arm out, then the other one*) It's way off that way somewhere. What's it like in an aeroplane, Beck?

Beck Ever sat in a can of beans?

Grandma Fraochlán (*amazed*) Jay, we'll go be the currach so. What d'ya think, Beck? Down the Atlantic Ocean, through the Straits of Gibraltar, on into the Arabian Gulf, the hills of Kilimanjira to the left, down be Mogadisha, a little more to the left or is it the right, anyway there we are in Zanzibar!

She puffs again. Beck lies back, relaxes.

Tha nine-fingered fisherman and meself used to do this tha odd time.

Beck Yeah?

Grandma Fraochlán I often wondered what it'd be like if he was still here, me nine-fingered fisherman, he'd be a hundred and four.

Beck (*laughs*) Would he?

Grandma Fraochlán He would. Isn't the world so strange, Beck?

Beck Always thought it more ordinary than strange.

Grandma Fraochlán People, everyone is strange. I mean we're put here with nothin' and we'll lave with nothin' and why does God in his heaven do that to us?

Beck I've been all over, and everywhere people are the same way. Everything's the same everywhere, they get up and go to work and come home and have their dinner and go to bed and make love or don't make love. And on the weekends they drive to the country if they're from the city and to the city if they're from the country. And some grow weary of that and just stay at home. (*quite spaced*)

Grandma Fraochlán I mean, does God want his children to suffer all the time?

A pause. They both stare ahead, thinking.

(*on her own tangent*) Take my life now, I came into the world without a father – born to an absolute nut. Was that my fault? And she wouldn't let me call her Mother, no, The Duchess, that's what I had to call her, or Duchess for short. And The Duchess told me me father was the Sultan of Spain and that he'd hid The Duchess and meself on Fraochlán because we were too beautiful for the world. But in the summer he was goin' to come in a yacht and take us away to his palace in Spain. And we'd be dressed in silks and pearls and have Blackamoors dancin' attendance on us and everyone on Fraochlán'd be cryin' with jealousy – and I believed her and watched on the cliffs every day for the Sultan of Spain. And at the end of every summer the Sultan would not have arrived and at the end of every summer The Duchess'd say, it must've been next summer he meant.

Beck (*in stitches*) Jesus, what a fruitcake!

Grandma Fraochlán And I don't know which of us believed that story more – her nor me. I was tha only bastard on Fraochlán in living memory and tha stigma must've been terrible for her. I don't know, but I'm not over the dismantlin' of that dream yet. Even still, every summer, I expect somethin' momentous to happen. What's that music anaway?

Beck (*lost in her own thoughts*) What?

Grandma Fraochlán And that's why when Ellen got pregnant, I would not have the scandal. I seen what it done to The Duchess. Oh Ellen – She was heartbroken, Beck, at where she had arrived and no one nor nothin' could console her.

Beck I went to see him.

Grandma Fraochlán Who? What?

Beck My father, passin' through London on my way home.

Grandma Fraochlán Oh that fella! (*Waves her hand dismissively.*)

Beck A pleasant, mild-mannered man was what I met. I had tea with them. He has two teenage daughters. Put on a wonderful spread for me.

Grandma Fraochlán (*wearily*) I'm sure it was all for show.

Beck Can you not leave the man his dignity and his new life, for fuck's sake! Why do you have to trample everything into the dirt! And he wasn't the illiterate boor you'd have us all believe. They went to great efforts to make me feel welcome though I'm sure I was the visit he'd been dreading for years. And do you know what he said to me? 'The last time I saw you, you were peerin' through the bars of the cot.' And I almost answered, 'Why didn't you lift me from that cot and take me away from that house of proud mad women!'

Grandma Fraochlán Did he ask for me?

Beck (*snorts, turns to attack, sees Grandma Fraochlán, a frail, selfish old woman, and relents*) Sure. Sure he did.

Grandma Fraochlán Beck, I was afraid what everyone'd say, afraid they'd blame me and say it was The Duchess' blood that made her wild and immoral.

The Mai stands in the doorway unnoticed.

Beck Ah the past, the past, the past – just forget it.

Grandma Fraochlán But I shouldn't've cared. Ellen could've had The Mai on her own and I could've minded her and she could've gone on and had the very best of lives – a beautiful stillborn baby boy, and Ellen dead beside him – oh the light left my world and I'll not enter heaven without a spell below for what I done to that girl.

The Mai moves into the room. She throws the car keys onto the table. Beck and Grandma Fraochlán jump with fright. Beck goes to hide the pipe.

The Mai Don't bother hidin' it. I've smelt it all over the house. It's an old familiar smell.

Beck We made sure the children were in bed, Mai, before –

The Mai Here, give me a puff and don't worry about the children. They know everything though they pretend not to. They want to protect me. (*She puffs on the pipe.*)

Beck What're you doin' home so early?

Grandma Fraochlán Put it (*the pipe*) away now so Robert doesn't see it.

The Mai Don't mind Robert. You could get used to this. (*Puffs.*)

Grandma Fraochlán Another fight?

The Mai Happy?

Grandma Fraochlán I'm fed up of everyone blamin' me for everythin' around here. Sign meself into a nursin' home if ye're not careful!

The Mai Yeah, another fight.

Beck Poor Cinderella.

She bursts out laughing. The Mai looks at her.

Sorry Mai, it's not me, it's the opium. (*She roars again.*)

Grandma Fraochlán Beck, behavin' yourself. (*Now she bursts out laughing.*) Sorry, Mai. Sit down, what happened?

The Mai What happened? (*Laughs.*) Here, give us another puff of that yoke.

Beck Where's Robert?

The Mai And ye had a great auld heartrendin' reminisce about your darlin' Ellen stranglin' herself in childbirth!

Robert appears in the doorway, sways, looks at them, points a finger vaguely, begins to speak, waves his hand, and makes for the drinks cabinet.

How did you get home? I suppose she ferried you!

Robert Grandma Fraochlán, you'll join me? (*a drink*)

Grandma Fraochlán I won't, Robert. Thank you anaway.

Robert Mai?

He offers decanter. The Mai looks away.

So it's the silent treatment, is it? Well, that's to be expected. *Sláinte.* (*Drinks, toasts himself.*) *Sláinte,* Robert. And did you have a good night, Robert? I've had better, but I'm sure The Mai has told you all about it.

The Mai You're drunk!

Robert Wasn't a crime the last time I checked. What do you think, Grandma Fraochlán, of The Mai and me?

Grandma Fraochlán Ya needn't be usin' me as a decoy. If you've anythin' to say to The Mai, say it to her.

Robert The Mai will not listen, because, you see, The Mai thinks in absolutes. And I am The Mai's absolute husband and when I refuse to behave as The Mai's

absolute husband, The Mai shuts down because the
reality of everyday living is too complicated for The Mai.

The Mai What reality are you speaking about, Robert?

Robert Oh, you are listening.

The Mai What reality?

Robert Love, the reality of love.

The Mai Thought you didn't believe in it.

Robert And neither do I, but I believe in its absence,
I believe in the black hole it leaves after it, like the way –

The Mai He left me in the middle of the floor to dance
with her.

Robert What's the big deal, if you hadn't created such
a fuss! Ah but you love the auld bit of drama and fuss,
don't you, Mai?

The Mai And I was calling you.

Robert (*mimics her*) Robert. Robert. You looked a right
eejit!

The Mai Why wouldn't you give me the car keys?

Robert You got them in the end, so what are you whinin'
about!

The Mai Why wouldn't you give them to me when
I asked you the first time? He needed them to drive her
home! That wagon with her sorry eyes. Even she was
ashamed of you and I'd say it'd take a lot to shame her.
And he's sittin' there with his arm around her! It was me
you were taking out tonight. Me! And I literally begged
him. I said, 'Robert, please don't leave me here on my
own, begging for the car keys,' and everyone was
looking, and do you know what –

Robert Fuck the neighbours! Just look at you, my good wife. You're so fuckin' good, Mai, you even look good when we have a row in public.

The Mai I just wanted the car keys so I could come home, you fucker!

Robert My beautiful wife with her beautiful body and her beautiful face and the goodness shining out of her. What am I supposed to do with all this beauty?

The Mai And that weasel sittin' there, if I'd a knife I'd have put it through her!

Robert You'd do no such thing. You'll calm down as you always do and look me over with that hurt and patient expression that seems to be always on your face these days, at least when I am around, and I'll feel like the bastard I am.

The Mai I want to know what she said about me!

As Robert goes to exit The Mai grabs him.

I said I want to know what she –

Robert Let go of me. Look, she said nothing. I refuse to talk to her about you.

The Mai But she talks about me, doesn't she? Oh yes she does, she talks about me in that arrogant way the loved one talks about the unloved!

Robert She does no such thing!

The Mai She does, she does, she says something like, 'So you no longer love your wife, Robert?' And you say, 'I love my wife but I'm no longer in love with her' or some bullshit like that. Isn't that the way it goes?

Robert No, it's not the way it goes, and I'm not discussing this any further with you!

The Mai You won't discuss me with her and you discuss her with me. What will you discuss?

Robert I've told you a thousand times, my private life is my own business.

The Mai Your private life! I am your private life! You invent these ridiculous compartments! You'll never be a great composer with –

Robert The last thing I need at this hour is a lecture from –

The Mai You'll never be a great composer with such crude and vulgar compartments!

Robert I'm going to bed!

The Mai That's right. Pretend none of this is happening. Go on to bed and dream of that ignorant fucking bitch!

Robert How dare you speak of her like that!

The Mai How dare I? You may be in love with her but don't for one second think that I am, you shit!

Robert Will you for fuck's sake stop cursing. You sound like a fuckin' tinker!

The Mai When you came back here after five years stravagin' up and down the world, you swore to me that you had changed –

Robert I said I would try to change. I promised nothing!

The Mai You told me you loved me. If that's not a promise, what is? You told me you loved me and tonight you left me in the middle of the dance floor in front of everyone –

Robert Oh we're back to the neighbours, are we?

The Mai Leave the neighbours out of this, I'm talking about –

Robert It was you brought them up!

The Mai I'm talking about your treatment of me! Have you no decency left!

Robert The neighbours now are an interesting phenomenon, The Mai –

The Mai That's right, skirt around everything, you fuckin' coward you.

Robert The Mai is fascinated by the neighbours, all her –

The Mai You're a vicious fucking bastard without an ounce of –

Robert All The Mai's efforts go into impressing the neighbours. She even goes so far as to insist she behave exactly like the neighbours on all occasions, but tonight, you see, we had a bit of a tiff and the neighbours hadn't, no, they conducted themselves with their usual dagger decorum, and what has The Mai upset now is –

The Mai You know absolutely nothing. You know fuck all about anything!

Robert What has The Mai upset is not the fact that we had a row in public, but that the neighbours hadn't. If they had, then The Mai could've laughed off all the abuse I showered on her. I don't give a fuck about the neighbours and what upsets me, Mai, is that tonight I discovered I don't give a damn about you any more!

Grandma Fraochlán You've said enough, Robert!

Robert No, you keep out of this, Grandma Fraochlán. With all due respect you're just a visitor here!

The Mai It's you who's the visitor!

Robert C'mon, Mai, you can do better than that!

The Mai wallops him across the face. He grabs her wrist.

Get it through your thick little head that I am not one of your pupils!

Grandma Fraochlán Would ye stop!

The Mai (*shaking her wrist free*) I'll have you know I came first in every exam I ever sat!

Robert Degrees, degrees, you collect them like weapons!

The Mai And what do you have? Just your pissy little job at the college that my family got for you!

Robert I got it myself this time!

The Mai And your pretensions to be a great composer and your mother whingein' in the background, oh, and you've your mistress, all great composers have to have a mistress!

Robert It's like tryin' to reason with a brick wall!

The Mai And I was called up in front of the school board because of you, you bastard!

Robert Poor Mai, the whole town is on your back!

The Mai And I stood up for you. And what about your children? Robert, you cannot treat people the way you are treating me. And that bitch, I went to see her you know and the way she –

Robert I heard all about it!

The Mai And you say you don't talk about me! Of course you do! You fuckin' liar, on top of everything else!

Robert (*turns on Grandma Fraochlán and Beck*) What are ye two doin' here? You can't turn round in this house without findin' one of the Connemara click behind you!

The Mai (*bursting into tears*) And you never collected me from the hospital when Stephen was born. (*She falls to the floor, weeping.*)

Robert Ah now, Mai, come on, come on.

The Mai No, go away from me!

Robert Mai, I tried, the car broke down, for Jesus' sake. What do you want from me, that was fourteen years ago.

The Mai You think I can put up with anything, with the way you look at me these days, the way you despise me and trample over everything I have worked and fought so hard for. You think I can put up with anything, well I can't.

Beck C'mon, Mai, up.

Robert C'mon now. C'mon. (*to Beck*) It's OK. I'll put her to bed.

The Mai No, leave me alone!

> *She gets up herself and exits. Grandma Fraochlán, Beck and Robert look after her. Beck follows.*

Beck Mai.

> *Grandma Fraochlán gets up and exits. Robert, left there, exits.*
> *Millie switches on the Christmas tree lights, and puts on a Christmas record.*
> *The Mai enters with sunglasses on. She pours a drink for herself, sits by the window, apart from the others. Robert enters with a newspaper, sits down, looks at The Mai when she's not looking. She does*

*the same. Silence for a minute. Julie enters with her
handbag, followed by Agnes with hers and Grandma
Fraochlán on her arm, followed by Beck with a tea
tray.*

Julie That was a mighty spread, Mai.

The Mai Beck did it all.

Julie (*to Grandma Fraochlán*) Would you mind not
blowin' that pipe up me nose!

Grandma Fraochlán Sorry, sorry.

Julie Gives me an awful headache.

Agnes And Julie has a very weak chest.

Grandma Fraochlán Will I put it out? That what you're
sayin'!

Julie Ara I'll sit over beside Robert. What're you doin'
readin' the paper on Christmas Day! You're like my
Michael, Lord rest him, he'd read the paper in the dark.

Beck I suppose ye went to the graveyard for Christmas.

Agnes Of course we did, looked in on the whole family,
God rest them all. I love graveyards, so does Julie.

Julie The graves were in an awful state after the winter.
Michael has sunk another foot and his tombstone's
cracked. I'll have to order another one.

Agnes It's the bog, keeps sinkin'.

Julie Such a stupid place to have a graveyard. Maybe my
Christmas present wasn't such a good idea after all,
Agnes.

Agnes Julie bought me a plot beside her own for
Christmas.

Julie Well it's not exactly beside mine. It's the other side of Michael. It was the nearest I could get.

A snort from Robert, behind the newspaper.

Grandma Fraochlán (*half to herself*) Jaysus, poor Michael.

The Mai It's beautiful there though, the way the tide comes in around it.

Grandma Fraochlán When my time comes I'm to be thrun into the wide Atlantic! D'ye all hear that? Twenty mile sou'west of Fraochlán where the nine-fingered fisherman's currach went down! D'ye hear me now!

Julie Ara, would ya stop such morbid talk on Christmas Day.

Robert Well I'll be off. See ye all later. Ye're stopping a few days?

Julie Tonight anyway.

Robert 'Bye everybody.

Beck 'Bye.

Agnes 'Bye Robert.

Julie Where's he off to?

The Mai Oh, visitin' his cronies, I suppose.

Agnes On Christmas Day?

Beck Lots of people go visitin' on Christmas Day.

Julie Not in Connemara they don't, and not on their own. I wouldn't have that, Mai, he should be in playing with the children. That right, Agnes?

Cute wink, returned by Agnes.

The Mai Ah – well –

Agnes You're too soft on him, Mai, isn't that it?

The Mai Yeah, that's it.

Grandma Fraochlán On Christmas Day the nine-fingered fisherman and meself used to go to bed for the afternoon with a bottle a *poitín* and a porter cake and we'd sing all the Christmas carols we knew.

Julie It was some racket!

Grandma Fraochlán A lovely way to spend Christmas Day. Did I ever tell ye as how he came to be called the nine-fingered fisherman?

Julie About ten thousand times.

Agnes Ah, Julie, leave her, she's old.

Julie Well, so am I.

Grandma Fraochlán I won't open me mouth again.

Beck Go on, you tell it every Christmas.

Grandma Fraochlán I will not indeed.

Julie Ara go on outa that, you're dyin' to tell it!

Grandma Fraochlán I am not so.

Beck Ah go on.

Grandma Fraochlán It was my third birth and Tomás was at sea. He didn't want to go out on account of my impendin' delivery but word came the salmon was leppin' on the 'Bofin side. He'd been out a day and a nigh' when he felt there was somethin' wrong of me. And so there was, twenty-two hours gruntin', and not a sign of the child's head. Tomás axed the skipper to turn round and the skipper refused on account of the big haul, anyway the nets was out. So in he jumped and swam for Fraochlán, the skipper follyin' him in the boat, beggin' him to get back on board, fearin' he'd be drowned, every net on Fraochlán in ribbons. Middle of the night it was. I see him arrivin' in the bed chamber drenched and shiverin', his skin a livid purple from the freezin' sea. He examines me and sees I am alive and then he feels for the pulse of the new infant, Donal it was. And then he collapses, doesn't come round for days. He lost the little finger on his left hand and from there on in he was known as the nine-fingered fisherman. He wore that missin' finger like a trophy for me. And up and down the coast the story became known as how he'd lost it. Boats would row up alongside his boat and ax to see his hand and ax to tell how he had come to lose that finger though they'd heard that story a hundred times already because people never tire of great love stories.

Julie If it's true.

Grandma Fraochlán You're determined to leave me with nothin'!

Agnes Ah, of course it's true.

Beck I'd love to have known him.

Grandma Fraochlán Sure ya would.

Julie I hardly remember him though. I was nearly thirteen when –

Grandma Fraochlán I know he was a useless father, Julie, I know, and I was a useless mother. It's the way we were made! There's two types of people in this world from what I can gather, them as puts their children first and them as puts their lover first and for what it's worth, the nine-fingered fisherman and meself belongs ta the latter of these. I would gladly have hurled all seven of ye down the slopes of hell for one night more with the nine-fingered fisherman and may I rot eternally for such unmotherly feelin'.

Beck I hear you're giving a flower arrangin' class, Agnes.

Agnes Ah, it's only a little bit of a class at the Comprehensive.

Grandma Fraochlán Y'always loved the flowers, didn't ya, Agnes?

Agnes I did. I did. Remember we used to go pickin' them up around the cliffs, yourself, myself and Ellen, up by Sruthán na mBláth.

The Mai The river of flowers. I remember Mom talking about it. Once, I said to her, 'Wouldn't you love to be somewhere else, Mom?' 'Yes,' she said. 'Where would you like to be?' 'I'd like to be a child again,' she said, 'up to my knees in Sruthán na mBláth, underneath me the golden sand. I'd like to walk up that river for ever.'

Agnes Ellen was an awful dreamer.

Julie A gangly unbiddable girl with her two feet planted firmly in the clouds.

Agnes She was beautiful and wild, before she met your father.

Julie Wild, don't be talkin'!

The Mai goes out.

Agnes The pair of us were at every dogfight in Connemara lookin' for men and they all fell for Ellen.

Beck I'm sure a few fell for you too.

Agnes Not at all, I was always on the plain side.

Grandma Fraochlán You never were, who told ya that?

Agnes You did.

Grandma Fraochlán I never did, must be thinkin' of somewan else, *a chroí.*

Julie What's up with The Mai?

Beck Ah she's probably tired.

Millie None of The Mai and Robert's children are very strong. We teeter along the fringe of the world with halting gait, reeking of Owl Lake at every turn. I dream of water all the time. I'm floundering off the shore, or bursting towards the surface for air, or wrestling with a black swan trying to drag me under. I have not yet emerged triumphant from those lakes of the night. Sometimes I think I wear Owl Lake like a caul around my chest to protect me from all that is good and hopeful and worth pursuing. And on a confident day when I am considering a first shaky step towards something within my grasp, the caul constricts and I am back at Owl Lake again. Images rush past me from that childhood landscape. There's The Mai talking to the builders about the dimensions of Robert's study and there's Robert playing football with Stephen and Jack, and Orla on her swing. Now Grandma Fraochlán is lighting her pipe as Beck wanders in and pours a drink. There's The Mai again, adding up the bills, a pencil in her mouth, Robert making his cello sing, The Mai at the window, Grandma Fraochlán's oar, Julie and Agnes colluderin' in the corner, The Mai at the window again. The Mai at the window again, and it goes on and on till I succumb and linger among them there in that dead silent world that tore our hearts out for a song.

> *The Mai enters in a nightdress – it is the middle of the night – she goes to the stereo and puts on some cello music, then goes to the window, and stares out.*

Mom?

The Mai Ah Millie, I couldn't sleep. Go on back to bed.

Millie Robert not home yet?

The Mai No.

Millie Why don't you leave him?

The Mai Millie, please.

Millie Or ask him to leave. Or have an affair.

The Mai I already did.

Millie You did not.

The Mai A one-night stand, to be more precise, a one-night stand with a stranger passing through – I shouldn't be telling you all this – I know now why Robert does it, it's the excitement, the newness, it's powerful and it's wonderful, not old and weak like an eighteen-year marriage. You'll be different, won't you, Millie? You won't be like me and Robert – Maybe he still loves me. What do you think, Millie?

Millie Mom, I don't know.

The Mai No, Millie, he does, he loves me in his own high damaged way. Maybe it's just a phase he's going through and in a few years he'll come back to me – What do you think, Millie?

Millie I don't know.

The Mai Millie, I don't think anyone will ever understand, not you, not my family, not even Robert, no one will ever understand how completely and utterly Robert is mine and I am his, no one – People think I've no pride, no dignity, to stay in a situation like this, but I can't think of one reason for going on without him.

Millie Mom, you've never tried.

The Mai I don't want to.

Millie Come on back to bed, you can sleep in beside me.

The Mai You go on, you're tired.

Millie You'll come shortly?

The Mai Yeah.

> *Millie watches The Mai looking out the window. A few seconds later, The Mai turns and drifts from the room. Sounds of geese and swans taking flight, sounds of water. Silence.*
>   *Lights down.*

PORTIA COUGHLAN

Portia Coughlan was commissioned by the National Maternity Hospital, Dublin, and first produced in the Peacock Theatre, Dublin, on 27 March 1996. The play was subsequently produced at the Royal Court Theatre, London, in May 1996. The cast was as follows:

Portia Coughlan Derbhle Crotty
Raphael Coughlan Seán Rocks
Maggie May Doorley Marion O'Dwyer
Senchil Doorley Des Keogh
Damus Halion Don Wycherley
Stacia Doyle Bronagh Gallagher
Fintan Goolan Charlie Bonner
Marianne Scully Stella McCusker
Blaize Scully Pauline Flanagan
Sly Scully Tom Hickey
Gabriel Scully Michael Boylan/Peter Charlesworth Kelly

Director Garry Hynes
Designer Kandis Cook
Lighting Designer Jim Simmons
Music Paddy Cunneen
Stage Director Collette Morris

Characters

Portia Coughlan, thirty
Gabriel Scully, fifteen, Portia's twin, a ghost
Raphael Coughlan, thirty-five, Portia's husband,
has a limp
Marianne Scully, fifty-ish, Portia's mother
Sly Scully, fifty-ish, Portia's father
Maggie May Doorley, fifty-ish, Portia's aunt,
Marianne's sister
Senchil Doorley, fifty-ish, Maggie May's husband
Blaize Scully, eighty, Portia's grandmother
Stacia Doyle, the Cyclops of Coolinarney,
thirty, Portia's friend
Damus Halion, thirty-ish, Portia's lover
Fintan Goolan, thirty-ish,
the barman of the High Chaparral

Time and Place

The present. The play is set in the Belmont Valley in the
Midlands. The stage must incorporate three spaces:
the living room of Portia Coughlan's house; the bank of
the Belmont River; the bar of the High Chaparral

Accent

Midland. I've given a flavour in the text,
but the Midland accent is more rebellious than the
written word permits

Act One

SCENE ONE

Two isolating lights up. One on Portia Coughlan in her living room. She wears a nightdress and a sweatshirt. Dishevelled and barefoot, she stands, staring forward, a drink in her hand; curtains closed. The other light comes up simultaneously on Gabriel Scully, her dead twin. He stands at the bank of the Belmont River, singing. They mirror one another's posture and movements in an odd way; unconsciously. Portia stands there, drinking, lost-looking, listening to Gabriel's voice.

Enter Raphael Coughlan, Portia's husband. He has a limp. He stands there, unnoticed by Portia, watching her, car keys dangling, portable phone. As soon as he speaks Gabriel's voice fades. Lights on Raphael.

Raphael Ah for fuck's sake.

Portia turns to look at him, looks away and takes another drink.

Ten o'clock in the mornin' and you're at it already.

Portia Thought you were at work.

Raphael I were.

Portia Came back to check on me.

Raphael Not especially. (*He holds up brandy bottle, examines level and looks at her.*) And there's dishes in the kitchen as hasn't seen a drop of water this week nor more.

Portia So.

Raphael And the kids, ya didn't drive them to school in that get-up I hope.

Portia Stacia brung them.

Raphael Did they have their breakfast?

Portia A' course they did, what d'ya take me for at all?

Raphael Just askin', Portia.

Portia Well don't, alright! And if you're that worried about them, why don't ya mind them yourself!

Raphael And you'll go out and earn the money.

Portia If ya never made another penny we'd still be rich – Tay?

Raphael Naw.

Portia Busy at the factory?

Raphael Aye.

Portia It's me birthday today.

Raphael That so?

Portia Thirty – half me life's over.

Raphael Me heart goes out to you.

Portia Have one with me – on me birthday (*a drink*).

Raphael At this hour, ya must be out of your mind.

Portia pours another for herself defiantly.

Portia *Sláinte.*

Raphael takes a package from his pocket and throws it to her.

Raphael This is why I came back this mornin'. Happy birthday, Portia.

Portia Thought ya forgot.

Raphael Did ya now?

Portia opens the package – a vulgar diamond bracelet – sort of dismayed at its flashiness; her taste is better.

Portia Diamonds.

Raphael Why not?

Portia Thanks, Raphael – it's lovely. (*Stands there looking at it.*)

Raphael Portia?

Portia What?

Raphael What's wrong of ya?

Portia Nothin'.

Raphael Nothin' – Well I'd better get back. Put that somewhere safe – after settin' me back five grand.

Exit Raphael. Sound of Gabriel's voice begins again. Portia listens a minute, Puts on a CD to drown out voice and turns it up. Gabriel's voice subsides. Exit Portia.

SCENE TWO

Enter Maggie May Doorley, an old prostitute. Black mini-skirt, black tights, white high heels, sexy blouse, loads of costume jewellery, fag in her mouth; she carries a large parcel. Followed by Senchil Doorley, her husband, half the size of her, skinny, fussy, lovely.

Senchil (*following her, half dance, half run*) Let me carry that, pet.

Maggie (*talking through the fag*) S'alright, pet. I have it. Anyways didn't the doctor say as you've to mind your heart. (*Calls.*) Portia!

Senchil Ya sure now, pet?

Maggie Am, pet.

Senchil (*indicating parcel*) Here, put that down, pet.

Maggie S'alright, pet. Portia!

Senchil Don't strain your voice, pet.

Maggie Alright, pet. Portia! Take the cigarette out of me mouth, pet, stingin' the sockets of me eyes.

Senchil (*takes cigarette out of her mouth*) You want another puff before I put it out, pet?

Maggie Aye. (*She takes another puff.*) I wonder is she gone?

Senchil Her car's outside anyways. Sit down, pet, your varicoses, ya shouldn't be wearin' them high heels, pet, don't know how many times I told you that.

Maggie Portia!

Portia (*off*) What?

Senchil She's here, pet.

Maggie Only your auld aunt.

Portia Sit down. I'll be out in a minute.

Maggie Light us a cigarette there, Senchil.

Senchil (*lighting one fussily*) You're smokin' too much, Maggie May, and you didn't get your lungs checked out this five year.

Maggie I will, I will, pet.

Senchil When?

Maggie Soon.

Senchil I'm tired makin' appointments for ya now, Maggie May.

Maggie I know ya are, pet, and sure why wouldn't ya be.

Senchil So long as ya know I'm not to be taken advantage of, Maggie May, now.

Maggie (*not listening to him, smoking away*) I know, pet.

Senchil And you're no use to me dead, Maggie May, and that's the truth of it now.

Maggie Not a sign of me dyin', Senchil, not a sign.

Enter Portia dressed in skirt, sandals and a jumper. The same outfit for Act One and Act Three.

There y'are.

Portia (*kisses Maggie May*) How'ya, Senchil?

Senchil I'm very well thank you, Portia, and yourself? Beautiful day, beautiful, beautiful, a day to set the bull among the heifers, a day to hop the ram in on the ewes.

Maggie (*looking at him*) Aye, if there was e'er a bull or a ram around. Portia, for your birthday. (*Hands her parcel.*)

Portia Ah there was no need, Maggie May.

Maggie A godchild's a godchild. That right, Senchil?

Senchil Is, pet.

Portia What is it?

Senchil Open and see now for yourself.

Portia takes a three-foot white delft horse on its hind legs from wrapping.

Portia (*laughs*) God Almighty, I may jump up on him and ride off on him one of these days.

Maggie Same as I thought meself when I seen him.

Senchil Got him at the garden centre.

Portia I love it, Maggie May. You're fierce good to me.

Maggie Oh Senchil put in for it too.

Senchil Will I make a cup of tay, pet?

Maggie Make one for yourself, pet. I'll have a brandy if Portia offers me one.

Portia Of course ya will.

Senchil (*takes a packet of digestive biscuits out of his pocket, offers them around*) You'll have one, Portia?

Portia I won't, Senchil.

Maggie No thanks, pet.

Senchil Ya don't mind me bringin' my own biscuits, do ya now, Portia?

Maggie And why would she, pet? Sure doesn't Portia know your heart is banjaxed.

Senchil Ya see, same as I was to ate a chocolate biscuit and same as the crumb of the chocolate turned into a clot and same as that very clot went up to me heart. (*Pregnant pause.*) A goner.

Maggie Stick to your digestives, Senchil. That's all I'll say on the matter.

Senchil I will, pet, I will. (*He exits.*)

Maggie Fierce down in yourself, Portia.

Portia (*drinking*) Am I?

Maggie For a birthday girl and all.

Portia Ah.

Maggie Raphael treatin' you alright?

Portia Aye.

Maggie Glad to hear it. And the kids?

Portia Sure they're nearly men, Jason be twelve come December, Peter ten and Quintin's in school already. Had them too young, Maggie May – married at seventeen. Jay, what was I at?

Maggie I know, pet.

Portia And I remember ya tellin' me and all.

Maggie No one ever taken my advice yet barrin' Senchil and look at the state of him – Maybe ya were better off, married to one of the richest men in the county, beautiful house, beautiful clothes, beautiful everythin'.

Portia And I was going to college, had me place and all, but Daddy says no, marry Raphael.

Maggie Auld Sly Scully, never liked him, God forgive me talkin' about your father like that.

Portia Don't care for him aither.

Maggie Turned your mother against me this years now.

Portia Mother – she was always fierce weak.

Maggie She wasn't always, Portia. Me and her had great times together, we'd paint the town regular. Between your father and his auld mother they beat everythin' worth beatin' out of her, that and losin' her son.

Portia Yeah.

Enter Senchil.

Maggie Ya made your tay, pet?

Senchil I did, pet. Ya want me to do the washin' up, Portia?

Portia Whah?

Gabriel's voice has come over and taken her away.

Senchil The washin' up?

Portia Jay, no, Senchil, it's grand, leave it.

Maggie Senchil's mighty at the washin' up.

Senchil I do love it, lookin' out the window at Maggie May's African marigolds and washin' the ware, don't I, pet?

Maggie Ya do.

Portia This lamb of a day and me stuck here for all eternity. I have to get out, Maggie May.

Maggie Come into town with us.

Senchil Aye, do.

Portia I think I'll go walkin', pull the door after yees. (*She exits.*)

Senchil Bye, pet.

Maggie Queer mood.

Senchil Lonely in herself, isn't she now, Maggie May, pet?

Maggie She is.

Senchil I hope now if you was ever to get lonely and fierce basement down in yourself, I hope you'd have the decency to tell me.

Maggie Course I would, pet.

Senchil And I'd have you right as rain before long.

Maggie Ya would, pet. Will we go or will I have another one (*a drink*)?

Senchil Too early, pet.

Maggie Don't start one of your lectures on drinkin', pet; can't abide them.

Senchil I won't, pet. I won't, only it's no good for ya, brandy for breakfast and me after cookin' the full fry for you and d'ya think would ya ate it, not a bit of you! Had to peg it to the cat!

Maggie Pet! Pet! Shut up! Shut up! (*She begins to leave.*)

Senchil (*following her*) Manners, Maggie May! Manners!

SCENE THREE

Enter Damus Halion – swarthy, handsome – by the bank of the Belmont River, he picks a clump of violets, arranges them into a bunch. Enter Portia.

Damus (*kisses her, puts a violet in her hair*) For the birthday girl. (*Gives her flowers, stands back and admires her.*) You'll soon be an auld hag, Portia Coughlan.

Portia Don't seem to deter you none anyways.

Damus What took ya so long?

Portia (*sitting on the bank*) Visitors.

Damus I says to myself, aither she's gone off me again or auld Hopalong's finally found out.

Portia I told you not to call him Hopalong; can't abide it; it's not his fault half his foot got cut off.

Damus Well there's many as says he done it on purpose for the compensation.

Portia All lies and ya know it! Who in their right mind'd cut off their foot for a few quid?

Damus I know plenty as may for half a million, but I find your defence of your husband touchin' and a wee bit sentimental. Coughlan, if ya were mine and ya talked about me the way ya talk about that excuse of a man of yours, I'd chop your head off and ate it for me tay.

Portia Well I'm not yours or anyone else's, Damus Halion.

Damus Are ya not now?

Portia Give us a cigarette.

He lights one for her, she lies back smoking.

Lovely here.

Damus (*kisses her, a long lusty kiss*) Come on up to the boathouse.

Portia In a minute.

Damus I've to be back in an hour.

Portia Then go if you're worried.

Damus One of your bitchy moods again.

Portia I mean for Jaysus' sake, Damus, can't we just sit and talk or do ya not want to talk to me? Why does it always have to be thrashin' and sweatin' in the boathouse?

Damus Missus, it was you gave me the come on and now you want to talk.

Portia To my reckonin', been a long time since I gave you anythin' approachin' a come on.

Damus That a fact? – What keeps ya comin' here so?

Portia I come here because I've always come here and I reckon I'll be comin' here long after I'm gone. I'll lie here when I'm a ghost and smoke ghost cigarettes and watch ye earthlin's goin' about yeer pointless days.

Damus You're cracked as your twin.

Portia And you're as thick as the rest of them. Thought I'd take ya out of the slime but it's still drippin' off of ya.

Damus Wasn't far from slime ya were reared yourself, Portia Coughlan. Your aunt the village bike, your father gettin' auld Tim Lahane drunk and stealin' his land off of him.

Portia Me father bought that land fair and square.

Damus Aye, and auld Tim Lahane scuttered under the table and he signin' it over; never have sold it and him sober.

Portia Ya don't know what you're talkin' about so keep your big thick mouth shut till ya do.

Damus You're more trouble than anythin' else, Portia Coughlan, always were – Once it was me ya were goin' to marry but I wasn't good enough, was I, once you clapped your greedy eyes on Raphael Coughlan – with his big car and his big factory and pound signs lewin' in his eyes.

Portia That's right, get it off of your chest, you'll feel better. Jaysus, you're so fuckin' bitter.

Damus Not exactly a picture of bliss yourself, look at ya.

Portia You're right, I'm not contented and haven't been this long while gone.

Damus Come on to the boathouse, there's still time.

Portia I have to go.

Damus Tomorrow?

Portia If I feel like it. (*She throws flowers into the river.*)

Damus I don't know what it is ya want from me.

Portia (*exiting*) I don't know aither.

Damus Fuck ya! (*Exits.*)

SCENE FOUR

The High Chaparral. Enter Stacia, the Cyclops of Coolinarney, and Portia. They sit at the bar.

Stacia And Quintin was bawlin' his eyes out, had to drag him from the car into the classroom.

Portia (*barely listening*) Fierce difficult, Quintin.

Stacia He's only a child, Portia, ya may go softer on him.

Enter Fintan, the barman, cowboy boots, spurs, medallions.

Fintan Ladies, yees are lookin' extremely beautiful this sultry summer's day.

Stacia It's Portia's birthday.

Portia Now's your excuse to give me a kiss. (*Proffers cheek.*)

Fintan Go 'way outa that with your cheek. Cheeks is for Grannys and auld spinster aunts. I only ever kiss women on the lips nor the legs.

Stacia D'ya hear him? The cheek of ya!

Portia (*offers leg*) Be the leg so, me lips is Raphael's, God help him.

The leg is kissed.

G'way now and leave me leg alone before ya swally it.

Fintan I've swallyed worser.

Stacia A bottle of cider, Fintan, and, Portia, what are ya havin'?

Portia Same as ever.

Fintan Brandy and ginger comin' up.

Stacia Fierce forward, isn't he now? What do ya think of me new eye patch, Portia?

Portia Suits ya.

Stacia Pigskin. Got four of them, one's blue, one's green, one's yellow and one's black for Mass and funerals. Sent away to England for them.

Portia I don't know, Stacia, sometimes I think if I had me eye gouged out, I'd wear ne'er a patch at all.

Stacia Ah no, Portia, it'd frighten the children, as it is they're a bit ashamed of me.

Portia Pity about them.

Enter Fintan with the drinks.

Fintan On the house, ladies, a sort of birthday present, what age are ya anyway?

Stacia Ya know well what age she is, you'd know less and you a class behind her in Miss Sullivan's school. You're only makin' small talk so as ya can ogle her over.

Fintan Do you know what it is, Stacia Doyle, you're gettin' more observant since ya lost the eye.

Stacia All the better to see through you with, Fintan Goolan. Have ya no work to be doin' instead of sniffin' round the skirts of two married women?

Fintan Don't overestimate yourself, Stacia Doyle, when it comes to my attentions and, for your information, I never sniff where there isn't a scent. (*Looks at Portia and exits.*)

Stacia Keep away from him, Portia. Bad news, bad news.

Portia Ah he was only jossin' us. You're too serious, Stacia.

Stacia I'm tellin' ya now, Portia, that fellow'd have ya pillowed and then broadcast it on the mornin' news. Got a cousin of mine up the pole last year, denied it to the hilt. I don't like him one bit.

Portia Cheers anyway. (*Drinks.*)

Stacia Raphael takin' ya out to celebrate tonight?

Portia Celebrate – me and Raphael – can't imagine it.

Stacia He not takin' ya out for dinner or somethin'?

Portia Nah, we're past that kind of lark; leastways I am.

Stacia God, Justin and me goes out regular, yees need time be yeerselves, Portia.

Portia And what do yees talk about, yourself and Justin, when ye're be yeerselves?

Stacia What do ya mean what do we talk about?

Portia I mean is there any differ sittin' opposite him with a candle stuck between ye than there would be if ye were at home facin' one another in armchairs?

Stacia Of course there is.

Portia Explain it to me then, what the differ is.

Stacia Well, Jay, I dunno if I could rightly say what it is.

Portia These days I look at Raphael sittin' opposite me in the armchair. He's always tired, his bad leg up on a stool, addin' up the books from the factory, lost in himself, and I think the pair of us might as well be dead for all the joy we knock out of one another. The kids is asleep, the house creakin' like a coffin, all them wooden doors and floors. Sometimes I can't breathe any more.

Stacia You need to do more things, Portia, get out of that house, get away from that river. Why don't you get him to take you on a holiday? When's the last time you had a holiday?

Portia Haven't never been on one, Stacia.

Stacia Jay, that's right, you've never had a holiday. That's shockin', Portia! Shockin'!

Portia Don't want one, don't think I'd survive a night away from the Belmont Valley.

Stacia Don't be daft, a' course you would, might even enjoy it.

Portia Oh I'm sure I'd live through what other folks calls holidays, but me mind'd be turnin' on the Belmont River. Be wonderin' was it flowin' rough or smooth, was the bank mucky nor dry, was the salmon beginnin' their rowin' for the sea, was the frogs spawnin' the waterlilies, had the heron returned, be wonderin' all of these and a thousand other wonderin's that river washes over me.

Stacia I know, Portia, I know.

Portia (*empties her glass*) Another?

Stacia School's nearly over. Kids'll be waitin'. Just go to the loo.

> *Exit Stacia. Gabriel's voice comes over, faint. Enter Fintan.*

Fintan Ya could keep better company than the Cyclops of Coolinarney.

Portia Don't call her that in front of me and if ya want to screw me, Fintan Goolan, have the decency to ask me like a man instead of fussin' round me like an auld cluckin' hen!

Fintan Fierce sure of yourself, aren't ya?

Portia I seen ya lookin', nigh on every time I come in here.

Fintan Have ya now?

Portia And ya know it, wide boy.

Fintan Well I'm free this evenin'.

Portia I bet ya are – Seven. The Belmont River.

Fintan I'll take ya for dinner.

Portia Can have dinner at home, only want to fuck ya, find out if you're any good, see if there's anythin' behind that cowboy swagger and too honeyed tongue.

> *Exit Portia. Stacia returns to get her bag, overhears Fintan and Portia.*

Stacia Lookin' for somewhere to put it, Goolan? (*Flips up her eye patch.*) Go on, I dare ya! I fuckin' dare ya! (*Exit Stacia.*)

Fintan Jaysus H! (*Exits.*)

SCENE FIVE

Enter Gabriel Scully. He wanders by the Belmont River singing; effect must be ghostly. Portia is in her living room, eyes closed, leaning against the door listening. Hold a while. Doorbell rings. No move from Portia. Again. Still no move. And yet again, impatiently, aggressively, still no move from Portia. Enter Marianne Scully, Portia's mother. She watches Portia leaning against door with eyes closed.

Marianne So you don't even bother answerin' the door any more.

Portia (*still eyes closed, Gabriel's song gets fainter*) Knew by the witchy ring it'd be yourself and you'd be bargin' in before long because ya never learnt, Mother, to allow a person space and quiet.

Marianne One of your bad-tempered moods again. (*Begins tidying up.*) The state of the place! Look at it!

Portia Leave it!

Marianne (*continuing to tidy*) You'd swear you were never taught how to hoover a room or dust a mantel; bloody disgrace, that's what ya are.

She tidies with impotent rage; Portia undoes what she does.

Will you stop it! And where's your children? Playin' round the Belmont River, I suppose. You be lucky they don't fall in and drown themselves one of these days.

Portia You'd like that, wouldn't ya, weepin' at the grave of one of your darlin' grandsons. Be history repeatin' itself, wouldn't it now, be like buryin' Gabriel all over again. I know how your bitter mind works, you think that if one of my sons was drowned that maybe ya could explain away how me twin was lost. Well, Mother, nothin'll ever explain that, nothin'.

Marianne Ah would you stop such nonsense; don't know what you're talkin' about, you're so dark, Portia; always were.

Portia I read subtext, Mother, words dropped be accident, phrases covered over, sentences unfinished, and I know the topography of your mind as well as I know every inch and ditch and drain of Belmont Farm, so don't you bluster in here and put a death wish on my sons just because you couldn't save your own. My sons'll be fine for if I do nothin' else I leave them alone and no mark is better than a black one.

Marianne You've ne'er a right remindin' me of Gabriel in such a bleak and blameful way.

Portia He would've been thirty today as well – sometimes I think only half of me is left, the worst half. Do ya know the only reason I married Raphael? Not because you and Daddy says I should, not because he was rich, I care nothin' for money, naw. The only reason I married Raphael was because of his name, a angel's name, same as Gabriel's, and I thought be osmosis or just pure wishin' that one'd take on the qualities of the other. But Raphael is not Gabriel and never will be – And I dreamt about him again last night, was one of them dreams as is so real you think it's actually happenin'. Gabriel had come to dinner here and after he got up to leave and

I says, 'Gabriel, stay for the weekend,' but Gabriel demurs out of politeness to me and Raphael. And I says, 'Gabriel, it's me, Portia, your twin, don't be polite, there's no need with me' – And then he turns and smiles and I know he's goin' to stay and me heart blows open and stars falls out of me chest as happens in dreams – We were so alike, weren't we, Mother?

Marianne The spit; couldn't tell yees apart in the cradle.

Portia Came out of the womb holdin' hands – When God was handin' out souls he must've got mine and Gabriel's mixed up, aither that or he gave us just the one between us and it went into the Belmont River with him – Oh, Gabriel, ya had no right to discard me so, to float me on the world as if I were a ball of flotsam. Ya had no right. (*Begins to weep uncontrollably.*)

Marianne Stop it! Stop it! Stop it right now! (*Shakes her.*) That's enough of that! If your father hears ya! Control yourself! If ya passed your day like any normal woman there'd be none of this! Stop it! Stop it!

Enter Sly and Blaize.

Blaize Would ya leave me chair alone! You'll destroy me brakes!

Sly Marianne, do somethin' with that one; she has me demented.

Marianne Why didn't ya leave her in the car!

Sly Don't you start, Jaysus!

Marianne Ya alright there, Mrs Scully?

Blaize Am, Mrs Scully.

Sly Happy birthday, Portia.

Blaize Birthday's load of bollix.

Sly Told ya, Mother, not to be cursin'.

Blaize And I told you I spent the first eighty years of me life holdin' me tongue, fuckin' and blindin' into the pillow, and if God sees fit to give me another eighty they'll be spent speakin' me mind foul or fair.

Sly Your mother and me, Portia, set a-thinkin' what'd Portia like for her birthday and we racked our brains, didn't we, Marianne?

Marianne We did.

Sly There be nothin' the girl needs nor wants was the only conclusion we could come to.

Blaize Sly havin' trouble partin' with money again.

Marianne Wasn't from the wind he learnt it.

Blaize Swear to Jaysus if hell were free, you'd go there, sooner than pay a small entry fee to heaven.

Sly Is there anythin' ya want, Portia?

Portia Naw.

Sly See, told ya, nothin' the girl needs nor wants, Marianne.

Portia So yees just brung yeerselves.

Marianne Seen a dress in the boutique yesterday, purple with flecks of gold, told ya we should've got it for her, Sly.

Sly Then we'll get it for the girl, Marianne, OK, we'll get it.

Blaize C'man home.

Sly Not yet, Mother.

Blaize If I had the power of me legs again! Why won't

yees leave me be me own any more? Afraid I'll fall into the fire. Just wanted to lie up against the range listenin' to the Count John McCormack. D'ya think would yees let me?

Portia pours a drink for herself, doing her best to ignore them all.

Marianne At this hour! Sly!

Portia Yees know where the door is if ye can't stand the sight of me – Anyone care to join me?

Sly Tay.

Portia Make yourself at home, Daddy.

Marianne I'll make it seein' as your own daughter haven't the manners to. (*Exits.*)

Sly Seen ya talkin' to young Halion today down be the Belmont River.

Portia Spyin' on me again.

Sly Going about me business mendin' fences on the shallow side. Portia, what're ya up to with him? He's no good, that fella, nor any he came from.

Blaize The Count! Put on the Count!

Sly I'm talkin' to ya, girl!

Portia He knew Gabriel.

Sly Gabriel. Forget Gabriel, that unnatural child that shamed me and your mother so.

Portia Forget Gabriel! He's everywhere, Daddy. Everywhere. There's not a corner of any of your forty fields that don't remind me of Gabriel. His name is in the mouths of the starlin's that swoops over Belmont hill, the cows bellow for him from the barn on frosty winter nights. The very river tells me that once he was here and now he's gone. And you ask me to forget him. When I lie down at the end of another impossible day, I pray for the time – Daddy, ya don't understand nothin'.

Sly Don't talk down to me, you. I've worked long and hard for you to be where ya are today, built Belmont Farm up from twenty acre of bog and scrub to one of the finest farms in the county with them there hands. That don't happen just like that! And do ya think Raphael Coughlan would've looked at you twice if there wasn't land and money goin' with ya? And for you to be hangin' round the likes of Damus Halion. Sure them Halions wouldn't get out of bed in the mornin' to milk the cows. Scrubbers! That's all they are, wouldn't know a heifer from a jackass!

Portia Daddy, I was only talkin' to him.

Sly More than talkin' I seen! I'm tellin' ya now, put a halter on that wayward arse of yours.

Portia I'm sick of you gawkin' at me from behind hedges and ditches and sconces. I'm a grown woman and what I do is none of your concern. (*Begins walking off.*)

Sly Don't you walk away when I'm talkin' to ya! And it's every bit of my concern when it comes to the Scully name. Don't ya know everyone's watchin', been watchin' us this years. Where's your ethics, girl, your morality and your ethics that me and your mother tried to learn you?

Blaize The Count John, where is he!

Enter Marianne with tea as Portia goes to exit.

Marianne And where are you off to and visitors in the house?

Portia Visitors! Jaysus, permanent fixtures be more like. (*Exits.*)

Marianne Sometimes, Sly, I do wonder be that girl stable at all.

Blaize I warned ya and I told ya, Sly, to keep away from the Joyces of Blacklion. Tinkers, the lot of them.

Marianne We were never tinkers and well ya know it!

Blaize Oh, yes, yees were! Came into this area three generations ago with nothin' goin' for yees barrin' flamin' red hair and fat arses. And the County Council buildin' yees houses from our hard-earnt monies. We don't know where ye came from, the histories of yeer blood. I warned ya, Sly! Do ya think you'd listen? There's a devil in that Joyce blood, was in Gabriel, and it's in Portia too. God protect us from that black-eyed gypsy tribe with their black blood and their black souls!

Marianne Are you goin' to stand there and just let her talk to me like that!

Sly Ah, now, Marianne, she doesn't mean it.

Marianne She means every bit of it! And what were you before ya were married? One of the inbred, ingrown, scurvied McGoverns. They say your father was your brother!

Blaize Ya fuckin' tramp, ya!

Sly Ah Jaysus, women, Jaysus.

Blaize All of the McGoverns was bred fair and square which is more than you can say for the Joyces!

Sly Mother, I'm tellin' ya, put a lid on it now!

Blaize Shut up to be fucked, you!

Sly Alright, I'm saying nothin', kill one another for all I care.

Blaize (*trying to get out of the wheelchair*) You, Missus!

Sly That's right, Mother, break that hip, I'm not payin' for another one!

Marianne She comes near me and I'll break it for her.

Blaize I know what's atin' you and I've watched it ate the very heart out of you this fifteen year!

Marianne Ya know nothin!

Blaize Ya killed your son, your beautiful son who had a voice like God himself –

Marianne I never laid a finger on him and well ya know it, just tryin' to upset me, ya vicious evil-minded yoke, ya!

Blaize Ah fingers! Who's talkin' about fingers when the whole world knows ya can kill a body just be lookin' at them if ya look long enough and you look wrong enough. I know your dark auld fuckin' Joyce streak and what it does to a –

Sly Mother, that's enough, warnin' ya now!

Marianne I don't want her next or near me again. You may tend her from here on in. I'll sit in me bedroom if I have to, the way she made me do when first I was a bride, remember that, ya auld witch, sendin' me up to me room when all the work was done, and Portia and Gabriel with me. Six o'clock on summer evenin's, sent to the room, the sun shinin' as if it was midday, because ya couldn't bear to share your kitchen with a Joyce. And you let her and kept your head down, doin' your farm books, dreamin' of acres and what good are they to ya now, you've no one to leave them to, and the twins and

216

me above in the room, too hot to sleep, wonderin' what it was we'd done to be banished from our own kitchen. (*Goes to exit.*)

Sly Marianne?

Marianne Don't call me in that self-pityin' voice, Sly; sickens me, sickens me this long time gone. Take your mother home and mind her, the way you should've minded me and your children, for we need your harsh care no more.(*Exits.*)

Sly Fuckin' happy now, are ya! Why can't ya leave the woman alone?

Blaize Take me home to John McCormack and don't worry about that one, tough as an auld boot, she'll be in the doorway, po-faced, feelin' sorry for sheself before dusk.

And exit the pair.

SCENE SIX

Enter Raphael. Calls.

Raphael Portia.

No answer.
  He begins tidying up the place. Puts on some music. Sets the table for two, lights candles. Opens bottle of wine. Let this go on simultaneously with what's happening by the Belmont River.
  Enter Portia by the river. Smokes. Throws leaves into the river. Dusk. An owl hoots. She sits on her hunkers looking into river. Enter Fintan. Stands there. Watches her a while.

Fintan You're two hours late.

217

Portia (*up from a dream*) What?

Fintan Came at seven like ya says.

Portia Oh, right.

Fintan Couldn't get away I says to meself. Lucky I came back. (*Takes out a naggin of whiskey.*) Whiskey?

Portia Why not?

Fintan (*pours whiskey into two plastic cups*) Cheers.

Portia Aye.

Fintan Fierce close to home – Don't your father's land go by this place?

Portia Aye, and sure I live only up the lane.

Fintan Ya like flyin' in the face of everyone, do ya?

Portia If ya want the honest to Jaysus truth, Fintan, I forgot all about ya. I came down here because I always come down here.

Fintan Forgot all about me! Ya make it very hard for a man, Portia Coughlan.

Portia (*barely listening*) Do I?

Fintan Aye, ya do.

> *Puts a hand on her arm; she looks at the hand, he removes the hand.*

Fierce quiet here.

Portia You can hear the salmon goin' up river if ya listen well enough, strugglin' for the Shannon, on up into the mouth of the sea and from there a slow cruise home to the spawnin' grounds of the Indian Ocean.

Fintan That a fact?

Portia They never made that journey before, just born knowin' the route they'll travel.

Fintan (*not one bit interested*) Fascinatin'. Fascinatin'.

Portia Ever hear tell of how the Belmont River came to be called the Belmont River?

Fintan Heard tell alright. Miss Sullivan used to tell us in school. Fuckin' hated English and all that auld poetic shite she used drum into us – wasn't it about some auld river God be the name of Bel and a mad hoor of a witch as was doin' all sorts of evil round here but they fuckin' put her in her place, by Jaysus they did.

Portia She wasn't a mad hoor of a witch! And she wasn't evil! Just different, is all, and the people round here impaled her on a stake and left her to die. And Bel heard her cries and came down the Belmont Valley and taken her away from here and the river was born. And they say Bel taken more than the girl when he swept through the valley. I don't know enough about that, but I think they do say right for this place must surely be the dungeon of the fallen world.

Fintan The what?

Portia Gabriel used hear the girl when the river was low; said she sounded like a aria from a cave.

Fintan Load of bollix, if ya ask me, them auld stories.

Portia I'm not askin' you.

Fintan There's one story as interests me, Portia Coughlan, the story of you with your knickers off. Now that's a story I'd listen to for a while.

Portia Ya fuckin' turnip head, ya! Just get off me father's land, Fintan Goolan, because you're a fuckin' clodhopper, just like your people before you and like those you'll spawn after you in a wet ditch on a wet night in a drunken stupor!

Fintan You've a lug on ya, Portia Coughlan, that'd turn back a funeral! And you've a tongue on ya that, if I owned ya, I'd mow the big-shot, stuck-up bejaysus out of.

Portia I'm not afraid of ya, so don't waste your time threatenin' me – Think I'll wade home be the river – 'Night. (*Exits.*)

Fintan Fuckin' mickey-dodger! (*Storms off.*)

SCENE SEVEN

Lights on Raphael finishing bottle of wine. Candles have burnt down. He walks around impatiently. Portia appears in doorway, barefoot, carries her sandals, stands there.

Raphael And where were ya till this hour?

Portia (*looks at table*) The candles and the wine. (*Leans against doorway wearily.*)

Raphael Aye – cooked dinner and all for ya – spoilt now.

Portia Dinner – tccch. (*Sighs.*)

Raphael Nigh on midnight, Portia.

Portia Is it?

Raphael Been home since seven, kids atin' rubbish and watchin' videos, no homework done, no lunch, no dinner for them, where were ya?

Portia Ah, Raphael, leave me alone.

Raphael Quintin bawlin' his eyes out all evenin' for ya.

Portia He'll grow out of me eventually. (*Dries her legs with a cushion.*)

Raphael Ah, for Jaysus' sake, Portia, he's only four.

Portia I know what age he is and I want as little as possible to do with him, alright? (*Pours the end of the wine for herself, sits and smokes.*)

Raphael Your own sons.

Portia I never wanted sons nor daughters and I never pretended otherwise to ya; told ya from the start. But ya thought ya could woo me into motherhood. Well, it hasn't worked out, has it? You've your three sons now, so ya better mind them because I can't love them, Raphael. I'm just not able.

Raphael Portia, I know that today of all days you're down and I know why. Now I don't make out to understand the breadth and depth of you and Gabriel. I have heard the bond between twins is ever strange and inexplicable, but surely now it's time to leave it go and try to make your life without him.

Portia (*erupting like a madwoman*) Gabriel! Gabriel! How dare you mention his name! The problem's not Gabriel, I'm over him this years! The problem's you! I fuckin' hate ya! Moochin' up to me with your slick theories on what's wrong of me! Ya haven't a fuckin' clue, ya ignorant auld fuckin' cripple, ya! I can't bear the sight of ya hobblin' around me in your custom-made cowboy boots!

Raphael Stop, Portia! Stop, stop!

Portia And when you touch me at night, sometimes I've just got to sleep, often the first sleep of weeks, and I'm

slidin' into a dream that'll take me away from this livin'
hell and you touch me and lurch me back to Belmont
Valley, and times you're lucky I don't rip ya to pieces or
plunge a breadknife through your lily heart!

Raphael (*going over to her*) Portia, you don't mean any
of this, you're upset, ya can't mean what ya been sayin'.

Portia (*shaking with rage*) Get away from me! You think
I don't? Then hear this and let's be free of all illusions
for evermore. I despise you, Raphael Coughlan, with
your limp and your cheap suits and your slow ways.
I completely and utterly despise you for what you are
in yourself, but more for who you will never be. Now
leave me alone. And light no more candles for me for
fear I blind ya with them. (*Snuffs out candles violently.*)

Raphael Portia, please, don't speak to me like this,
please. Think what you're sayin', this isn't you –

Portia The fool comes back for more. Well, there's more!
You asked me where I was tonight. Well now, I'll tell ya.
I was screwin' the barman from the High Chaparral.
Gettin' angry now, are ya? Good. Beginnin' to hate me?
Better still. I want none of your watery love, Raphael
Coughlan, and while we're on the subject he was useless,
just as I knew he would be, useless, as useless as you.
Go on, cry away, break your heart, Raphael Coughlan,
it'll heal, don't worry, it'll heal, and I'll go guarantor for
you that once's it's healed there'll be nothin' under sun
or moon that'll ever lance its tough hide again.

Lights down.

Act Two

SCENE ONE

By the Belmont River. Evening. A search-light swoops around the river. Raphael, Marianne, Sly, Stacia, Damus, Fintan, Senchil and Maggie May. They stand in silence as a pulley raises Portia out of the river. She is raised into the air and suspended there, dripping water, moss, algae, frogspawn, waterlilies, from the river. Gabriel stands aloof on the other bank, in profile, singing.

Marianne Oh no.

Maggie Sweet sufferin' Jesus.

Senchil Will someone for Christ's sake cover her!

Portia wears only a slip. No one moves, transfixed by the elevated image of the dead Portia. Senchil takes off his jacket, tries to cover her; she's too high, jacket falls, suspends on her foot, hangs there. Hold a couple of beats. Then lower pulley. Raphael moves forward to take her in his arms. Fintan moves to help.

Raphael (*a measured growl*) Keep your paws off of my wife.

Fintan moves back. Sly moves forward, takes rope off pulley. Portia is now free of pulley and in Raphael's arms.

Marianne It's happened again. It's happened again. Oh, Maggie May, what have she gone and done?

Raphael (*a whisper*) Portia. Portia.

Maggie I don't know, pet, I don't know.

Raphael I suppose I may take her up to the house. (*Looks around hopelessly.*) What?

Sly Aye. (*a low sound*)

Raphael moves off followed by all except Damus and Fintan. They light cigarettes, stand there smoking in silence, holding the lighted end of the cigarette in close to the palm. After a while:

Damus Strange bird always – Portia Coughlan.

Fintan Aye.

Damus The twin, too.

Fintan Aye.

Damus Aye.

Fintan Gabriel.

Damus That's right.

Fintan Only fifteen.

Damus Exact same spot he was pulled from, too.

Fintan That a fact?

Damus Looked like a girl.

Fintan Sang like one, too.

Damus Aye – one thing I always found strange about them Scully twins.

Fintan What was that?

Damus You'd ask·them a question and they'd both answer the same answer – at the same time, exact inflexion, exact pause, exact everythin'.

Fintan Forgotten that.

Damus You'd put them in different rooms, still the same answer.

Fintan Aye – remember now.

Damus Remember the school tour?

Fintan Which one?

Damus The one to Bettystown.

Fintan Naw.

Damus Portia and Gabriel sat up in the front of the bus in red shorts and white T-shirts.

Fintan Aye.

Damus Whisperin' to one another as was their wont. We got to Bettystown, still have the photo of the whole class, still can't tell one of them from the other – Anyways, when the time came to get back on the bus Portia and Gabriel was missin'. Mad search went on, ne'er a sign of them, the coastguards called in, helicopters, lifeboats, the works. The pair of them found five mile out to sea in a row boat. They just got in and started rowin'. Poor auld Miss Sullivan in an awful state, 'What were yees at, children, what were yees at at all?' 'We were just goin' away,' says one of them. 'Away! Away where, in the name of God?' says Miss Sullivan. 'Anywhere,' says the other of them, 'just anywhere that's not here.'

Fintan Anywhere that's not here. Jaysus.

Damus Aye.

Fintan Sure auld Hopalong could never manage her.

Damus Lucky to get her, though I wouldn't care for his shoes now.

Fintan What did she ever see in him?

Damus Could have had anyone, Portia Coughlan.

Fintan Aye – she could.

Damus Anyone – anyone.

And exit both in opposite directions.

SCENE TWO

Lights up on Blaize and Stacia manoeuvring Blaize's wheelchair into Portia's living room.

Stacia Are ya alright now?

Blaize Am, Mrs Doyle, thank you.

Stacia I'll leave ya here so and get the ateables ready before they get back from the funeral.

Blaize Put on the Count first.

Stacia Don't know if I should, seein' as the day that's in it.

Blaize Go on, girl. Portia loved the singin'. Go on, it's there lookin' at ya.

Stacia If anyone asks it was you made me, alright?

Voice of McCormack comes over. Blaize listens, enraptured, croons along with him.

Blaize Isn't he magnificent? Born only up the road, but he got away. There was a gramophone and one record in our house when I was a girl. Was the Boston McGovern who brung it home, was a record of the Count, and I listened to that record till it flopped and flapped like a butterfly's wing and me mother used listen to it too – so she used – yes.

Both listen to the Count a minute.

Turn him off now, Stacia, for fear they be accusin' us of disrespect for the dead. They'll be here before long, tomb eyed, stinkin' of the bone orchard. Hate the smell of coffins, don't you, Stacia?

Stacia Haven't smelt enough of them to know, Mrs Scully.

Blaize Very particular smell, cross between honeysuckle and new-mown putrefaction.

Stacia I wish if you'd talk gentler about the dead, Mrs Scully.

Blaize At my age, Stacia, isn't nothin' left to talk gentle about. From here on in it's just bitterness and gums.

Stacia Portia was me friend, Mrs Scully, me only friend, and I realize now I didn't know her at all. Sure, I knew she was unhappy, but who isn't these days, must be a terrible state of mind to do what she done and Maggie May told me about Sly and Marianne but somehow that don't add up to this –

Blaize What did she tell ya about Sly and Marianne?

Stacia Well she told me all about how they were –

Blaize Don't mind that one! Liar! Maggie May Doorley! A rusty tandem, that's all she is! Fit ya better, Stacia Doyle, to mind your own business and not be listenin' to the fabrications of a hoor.

Stacia I'm sorry, Mrs Scully, I didn't mean to upset ya.

Blaize (*calming down*) Not upset, child, not upset at all, just don't pay any attention to that one.

*Enter Raphael, followed by Senchil, Marianne,
Maggie May. All wear black, as do Stacia and Blaize.*

Stacia Sit down, Raphael, and leave the hostesseries to me.

Raphael There's drink and food and all that sort of stuff in the kitchen.

Enter Maggie May from kitchen with tray of drinks. Senchil runs to help her, nearly knocks her down.

Senchil Let me carry that, pet.

Maggie Jay, Senchil, watch where you're goin', near knocked me flat.

Blaize (*to no one in particular*) Buried, is she?

Maggie Aye – God rest her.

Blaize (*to Raphael*) Bereft, be ya? Fuckin' cheek of ya marryin' her in the first place! Who do ya think you are, hah!

Raphael (*calls off*) Sly! Ya may come in here and take charge of your mother.

Blaize None of ours ever had truck with new money before you came skulkin' down the valley with nothin' going for ya except your compensation cheque in your arse pocket!

Raphael I don't need this, Mrs Scully.

Sly Mother, behavin' yourself. I'm sorry, Raphael, she's a bit upset.

Blaize (*to Marianne*) Dry your eyes, girl, been comin' this fifteen year. (*to Sly*) Warned ya and I told you! Would ya listen! (*to Maggie May*) Whiskey! Black Bush, black label!

Maggie Ya know your whiskeys, Granny.

Blaize Mrs Scully to you.

Silence. They all drink awkwardly; some sit, stand, lost in grief, exhaustion, whatever.

Senchil Lovely sermon.

Looks around, glare from Blaize, silence from the others, Maggie May comes to his aid.

Maggie Was, pet, was.

Blaize And what would aither of ye know about sermons, lovely or otherwise. (*to Maggie May*) The sight of you in a church'd blush the host and pale the wine. Fuckin' tinkers, the Joyces, always and ever, with their waxy blood and wanin' souls. Dirty ignorant blood the likes of Belmont never seen before. *Sláinte!* To the Joyces! (*Drinks.*) To Portia in the murky clay of Belmont graveyard where she was headin' from the day she was born, because when you breed animals with humans you can only bring forth poor haunted monsters who've no sense of God or man. Portia and Gabriel. Changelin's. *Sláinte.* (*Finishes her drink, smashes her glass against wall.*) Take me home. The next funeral will be my own.

Sly (*to Marianne*) Be back in a while.

Marianne What are you tellin' me for?

Sly (*erupting*) You blame me for everythin'! For Gabriel and now Portia! I was never hard on the lad! Never! Let him do whatever he wanted when I should've been whippin' him into shape for the farm.

Maggie Ah now take it easy, Sly.

Sly No! Leave me be! I drove that child twice a week every week to Dublin for his singin' lessons, in the hay season, when the cows was calvin', when there was more than enough to be done at home. I drove because you says I should, like a fuckin' slave, seventy mile each way,

and he'd sit in the back of the car, readin' his music
books, hummin' to heeself, wouldn't give me the time of
day not if his life depended on it. God forgive me, but
times I'd look at him through the mirror and the thought
would go through me mind that this is no human child
but some little outcast from hell. And then he'd sing the
long drive home and I knew I was listenin' to somethin'
beautiful and rare though he never sang for me – Christ,
I loved his singin', used stand in the vestry of Belmont
chapel just to listen to his practisin' – those high notes of
God he loved to sing.

Marianne You're great at feelin' long after the need to
feel be gone. This is Portia's funeral! Gabriel died fifteen
year ago. Today is for Portia. Portia is dead. Portia is
dead. And you won't even mourn her.

Blaize Say somethin', Sly, put that upstart in her place
once and for all.

Raphael Will someone get that woman out of me house?

Maggie I will. (*Wheels Blaize out of earshot of the
others.*) One of these days I'm goin' to climb in the
window and burn ya in your bed – and, another thing,
did I ever tell you about the time I gave your husband
a quick one down Mohia Lane?

Blaize (*a hiss*) Liar! I don't believe ya!

Maggie Oh yes, ya do, because you know and I know
what's really goin' on here. You know and I know when
the rot began and how the rot began.

Blaize Don't know what you're talkin' about, hoor ya!

Maggie I did, aye, gave him a job down Mohia Lane,
the dirty auld dog, paid me with your egg money, fifty
quid, and do ya know what he said about you?

Blaize He said nothin'! You're makin' it up.

Maggie He says you were a bitter auld hag and he'd rather hump a bag of rats on a bed of nettles.

Blaize Oh listen to the filth of the hoor with the broken bottle! We were very happy, I'll have you know.

Maggie Happy, were yees, happy? Then how come he beat the lard out of ya every time he looked at ya – How come weeks and weeks would go by and no one would've seen Blaize Scully out and about because her face was in a pulp again? How come he kicked ya down the road once in front of everyone?

Blaize Sly, take me home, Sly.

Senchil (*eating a biscuit out of his pocket*) What were ya sayin' to her, pet?

Stacia (*offering Raphael a sandwich*) Go on, Raphael, ate somethin'.

Raphael The kids.

Stacia They're grand, over in my house, me sister's lookin' after them.

Raphael Quintin?

Stacia He's grand – grand.

> *They eat, drink in silence. Sound of Gabriel's voice comes over. Lights down.*

Act Three

SCENE ONE

Lights up on Portia's living room. It is set as it was at the end of Act One. Portia dozes on couch or at table, wearing the clothes she wore at the end of Act One. It is the morning after her thirtieth birthday. We hear the sound of Gabriel's voice. Portia wakes to this. It grows fainter, she strains to hear it. It stops. Portia – half sitting, half lying – lights a cigarette.

Enter Raphael, fresh suit. He limps across the room to collect his account books, looks at Portia; she meets his look, then turns away. He goes to open curtains.

Portia Leave them.

He does.

Raphael You goin' to get the kids ready for school or ya want me to?

Portia You do – please.

Raphael looks at his watch, stands there.

Raphael Portia.

Portia What?

Raphael I'd be willin' to forget what ya said last night if you'd only take it back.

Portia Do you want dinner this evenin'?

Raphael What?

Portia Dinner.

Raphael Dinner – yeah.

Portia What do ya want?

Raphael For dinner?

Portia Yeah.

Raphael Anythin', I suppose.

Portia Alright.

Raphael Right so. (*He still stands there.*) Ya want to come into the factory for a few hours?

Portia Naw.

Raphael Be good, get ya out of the house – or somethin'.

Portia Can't abide the place, Raphael, ya know.

Raphael Aye – (*Stands there looking at her.*) Well, is there anythin' I can do, Portia? Anythin'?

Portia I'm grand, honest.

Raphael Quintin wants ya to dress him for school.

Portia Will ya just stop! Leave me alone! Told ya I can't! Alright! I'm afraid of them, Raphael! What I may do to them! Don't ya understand! Jaysus! Ya think I don't wish I could be a natural mother, mindin' me children, playin' with them, doin' all the things a mother is supposed to do! When I look at my sons, Raphael, I see knives and accidents and terrible mutilations. Their toys is weapons for me to hurt them with, givin' them a bath is a place where I could drown them. And I have to run from them and lock myself away for fear I cause these terrible things to happen. Quintin is safest when I'm nowhere near him, so teach him to stop whingin' for me for fear I dash his head against a wall or fling him through a window.

Raphael Portia, you're not well.

Portia I'm alright and stop lookin' at me as if I'm goin' to murder ye all in yeer beds, for I won't as long as ye leave me in peace.

Raphael It's not normal the way you're talkin' and thinkin', not normal at all.

Portia Look, if I was goin' to do somethin' dreadful, do ya think I'd be tellin' ya about it? Naw, I'd just go ahead and do it. The fact I'm even talkin' about it means I won't.

Raphael And what sort of logic is that?

Portia Me own, the only logic I know.

Raphael Ya stayin' home all day?

Portia I may.

Raphael Will I ring Stacia to collect the kids from school?

Portia Whatever.

Raphael Portia?

Portia What?

Raphael You've got me scared now. Ya wouldn't do anythin' to them, would ya?

Portia Told ya I wouldn't and I haven't, not a mark on them and I never will – I just want them not to want anythin' from me, that's all.

Raphael Alright so – try and get some sleep – see ya this evenin'.

Portia Yeah.

Exit Raphael.

SCENE TWO

Sound of Gabriel singing. Portia registers this, runs from the living room. Gabriel appears by the bank of the Belmont River. Disappears as Portia arrives, out of breath. Sound of singing fades. She looks around. Silence, except for the flowing river and birdsong. Damus stands there watching her, unobserved.

Portia Can't ya leave me alone or present yourself before me? Is heaven not so lovely after all? Are its streets not paved in alabaster and gold? Do the angels not sit drinkin' coffee and prunin' their wings along the eternal boulevards of paradise? (*close to tears*) Do ya miss me at all?

Damus Talkin' to the dead now, Coughlan?

Portia (*registers him*) And what if I am?

Damus Some do say he still walks.

Portia They do say right – Who told ya anyway?

Damus Still nights he can be heard singin' in his high girly voice. Auld Mahon swears he heard him and he comin' home after a night's poachin' up on O'Connor Morris' belt of the river.

Portia Ah auld Mahon, accordin' to him everyone who ever died walks.

Damus (*puts an arm around her*) Well I'm alive and dyin' for ya, me pretty little ghost fancier, and though I cannot haunt you as ghosts can I can leave me mark on ya well enough.

Kisses her, she neither resists nor complies.

If ya spent less time thinkin' about that silly little brother

235

of yours and more time on how I could please ya, you'd be a happy woman.

Portia (*shrugs him off*) I'm past all pleasures of the body, Damus, long past.

Damus Are ya now?

Portia And if ya really care to know I've always found sex to be a great let-down, all that suckin' and sweatin' and stickin' things into one another makes sense to me no more. Give me a jigsaw or a good opera any day or the Belmont River. I'd liefer sit be the Belmont River for five seconds than have you or any other man beside me in bed.

Damus Strong sentiments from a little cock-teaser who used get her joys and thrills from watchin' men drool as she curved by and who, even as she professes to have found sex to be a great let-down, is leanin' up again' me with a flame creepin' up her throat all the way from the backstairs of her hot little arse.

Portia moves away from him.

Sulkin' now, are we?

Portia I didn't come here to see you, Damus Halion. I came here because this here is me father's land. This be our part of Belmont River. So go on off with yourself and your crude readin' of the world and its inhabitants.

Damus Ah, Portia, come on, don't be gettin' thick over nothin'.

Portia The discos and hotels is full of young ones who'd be only too glad to have ya maulin' them. Leave me be. I won't see you again, so there's no point in comin' here any more.

Damus Portia, I've been comin' here on and off this sixteen year.

Portia I know how long you've been comin'.

Damus Don't that count for anythin'? Once it was me ya wanted and no one else, or have ya forgotten that, have ya?

Portia Ya were never more nor a distraction, Damus Halion.

Damus I don't believe ya.

Portia Believe what ya like, it's the truth.

Damus And who's to say but one of your young lads isn't mine? I've a mind to go and see that cuckold of yours and tell him his sons is not his sons but maybe mine.

Portia Them's all Raphael's, God help them, I made sure of that.

Damus Look, Portia, the last thing I want to do is make your life more difficult than it is. All I want is to be with ya. Why don't ya leave him like ya used to say you'd do?

Portia Used I say I'd leave him?

Damus Aye.

Portia Where did I think I was goin'? Anyway, it makes no differ to me whether I'm with you or Raphael.

Damus I wish to God I'd never laid eyes on ya! I've put up with your messin' for too long now, your runnin' backwards and forwards between me and Raphael and your twin. I'm sick of ya, Coughlan, and don't you come lookin' for me when your mood changes again for I'll not be there for ya. Fuckin' bitch! That's all ya are and ever were! (*Exits.*)

SCENE THREE

Portia sits by the bank of the Belmont River. Maggie May's voice can be heard.

Maggie (*off*) Portia.

Portia Over here.

Maggie (*sees Damus departing*) Halion, right?

Portia Right.

Maggie I'm no one to cast aspersions on extra-marital dalliances but ya could do better than him. Raphael know about this?

Portia Raphael. Only thing Raphael knows be how to make money and then how to save it. Same as Daddy.

Maggie I see. Cigarette?

They light cigarettes. Portia lies back and smokes.

Me and me father used come night-fishin' here.

Portia Used yees?

Maggie Caught a pike here once bigger than a yennin' ewe.

Portia Remember the time –

Maggie What?

Portia Ah nothin' – Just thinkin' aloud is all.

Maggie Go on, tell me.

Portia Just thinkin' about the time the cemetery gates fell on Gabriel.

Maggie Aye. Everyone thought he was a goner.

Portia I think it was a sign – he was never right after that.

Maggie No, he wasn't.

Portia What ya think it meant, Maggie May? Is our lives followin' a minute and careful plan designed on high or are we just flittin' from chance to chance?

Maggie Well, there be some as says it's impossible for a body to be other than they are, but then there's others as would claim ya choose your own life and your own makin' of it. Personally I prefer to believe that everythin' I've done is planned be someone else down to the last detail. I'm a fat auld hoor with bad legs, Portia, and I'd hate to have to lay the blame of everythin' on myself.

Portia When I was a child Mother and Daddy used brandish you as a threat. For years I thought the worst as could ever happen me was to end up like you. Now I wish I could.

Maggie Like me, pet? Sure I've nothin' goin' for me exceptin' Senchil. Did I ever tell ya how I came to meet him?

Portia Naw.

Maggie People has always laughed at him, thinks he's an eegit. Maybe he is. See I was in London, workin' Kings Cross, big angry fuckers with too much money and no respect. Had this rough customer one night, lug on him like a scalded baboon, showed me his fists, done his job, taken me money and shoes so as I couldn't folly him. I'm lyin' there in the doorway of an auld warehouse feelin' a little sorry for meself and along comes Senchil. He's a night watchman. He takes me into his hut, makes me tay, turns out he was brought up not twenty mile from Belmont Valley. We talk all night and in the mornin' he buys me a pair of shoon (*shoes*). T'were the shoon that done it.

Portia Always liked Senchil though he's fierce fernickity.

Maggie Senchil wasn't born, he was knitted on a wet Sunday afternoon. Feel safe when he's around because he's so fuckin' borin' nothin' ever happens.

Portia Suppose he's not there when I go?

Maggie Go where? What're ya talkin' about, pet?

Portia Before I was always sure, was the one thing as kept me goin' – Now I don't know any more, and yet I know that somewhere he lives and that's the place I want to be.

Maggie And where's that, Portia?

Portia There's a wolf tooth growin' in me heart and it's turnin' me from everyone and everythin' I am. I wishin' if the wind or somethin' would carry me from this place without me havin' to do anythin' meself.

Maggie Pet, don't be talkin' like that, give me the shivers.

Portia I knew he was goin' to do it, planned to do it together, and at the last minute I got afraid and he just went on in and I called him back but he didn't hear me on account of the swell and just kept on wadin', and I'm standin' on the bank, right here, shoutin' at him to come back and at the last second he turns thinkin' I'm behind him, his face, Maggie May, the look on his face, and he tries to make the bank but the undertow do have him and a wave washes over him –

Maggie Jay, pet, did ya tell your mother and father about this?

Portia They don't like to talk about Gabriel.

Maggie Do they not?

Portia No one does. Don't know if anyone knows what it's like to be a twin. Everythin's swapped and mixed up and you're aither two people or you're no one. He used call me Gabriel and I used call him Portia. Times we got so confused we couldn't tell who was who and we'd have to wait for someone else to identify us and put us back into ourselves. I could make him cry be just callin' him Portia. We didn't really like one another that much when it came down to it. Oh, how can everyone be alive and not him? If I could just see him, just once, I'd be alright, I know I would.

Maggie But that's not possible, pet.

Pause.

Portia I've to collect the kids from school. (*Begins walking off.*) Ya comin'?

Maggie Aye.

Both exit.

SCENE FOUR

The High Chaparral. Fintan cleans a table. Enter Stacia followed by Portia with a bag of groceries. Fairly dishevelled by now.

Fintan (*cool*) Ladies.

Stacia Bottle of cider, Portia?

Portia Nothin'.

Stacia goes over to jukebox, puts on some Country and Western.

Fintan (*attempting to flirt*) Overdone it on the whiskey last night.

241

Portia I never drink whiskey, Fintan Goolan.

Fintan Ya were drinkin' it last night.

Portia Drinkin' with you don't count – (*Examines him.*) because you're the sort of man as cancels himself out as soon as you appear, the eye fails to register ya – You're the kind of cowboy as gets shot in the first scene of a bad western.

Fintan Do ya know what you need, Portia Coughlan?

Portia What do I need?

Fintan You need the tongue ripped out of ya and the arse flayed off of ya.

Portia Do ya know what we both need?

Fintan Nothin' you've to offer anyway.

Portia Just get Stacia her drink.

Fintan Oh, ya can buy everythin' exceptin' good manners.

Portia A lot you'd know about good manners.

Fintan Bog trash is all you are, Coughlan, trumped-up bog trash!

He storms off. Stacia begins jiving.

Stacia Come on, Portia.

Portia joins her, the pair of them jive expertly, madly. Fintan comes back with drink for Stacia, stands there thick as a bull.

Fintan One ninety! (*price of drink*)

Stacia Leave it on the table.

Portia Brandy and ginger!

Fintan Changed your mind!

Portia Aye.

Enter Maggie May and Senchil.

Maggie Seen your car outside, says I'll join ya for the one.

Senchil Just the one.

A glare from Maggie May.

Maggie Portia, pet, glad to see ya enjoyin' yourself even if it is only two o'clock in the day.

Portia Come and dance with us.

Stacia You too, Senchil.

Senchil puts his hand on his heart for reply. Maggie May takes off her shoes and joins them.

Senchil (*to Fintan*) A pot of tay, tay bag –

Fintan I know, I know! A pot of tay, tay bag on the side, kettle just off the boil and a brandy and ginger for himself! (*indicating Maggie May*)

Senchil Yes, thank ya.

Portia comes over to table to drink, her mood has changed again. She stands there looking off into space, holding drink, cigarette, looks upstage to river. Gabriel is there.

Senchil Alright, pet?

Portia looks at Senchil, knocks back drink, devilish glee, throws glass at Fintan who has been watching her.

Portia Same again! Come on, Senchil.

Takes him by the hand, they dance.

Senchil Just for you, pet.

Maggie May and Stacia sit down, drink, watch Portia and Senchil waltz a while.

Maggie You're very good to her, Stacia.

Stacia Portia always been good to me – When I lost the eye (*touches eye-patch*) no one better – She's not well, Maggie May.

Maggie I know.

Stacia And her kids is in an awful state. I'm not sayin' it as a complaint but they're not minded, exceptin' what Raphael does, and they're very violent and destructive and I don't know how to tell Portia. But she may take charge of them soon – Maybe I'm worryin' too much. Portia herself was a demon of a child but she grew up alright – Didn't she, Maggie May? – Even if she is a bit odd.

Maggie Never knew a gentler child than Portia, like a mouse – Did ya know that Marianne, Portia's mother, was a twin too?

Stacia No, never knew that.

Maggie There's few as does. I'm not even sure Marianne knows. Marianne and Sly is brother and sister. Same father, different mothers, born within a month of one another.

Stacia Jay, how come?

Maggie Me mother told me on her death-bed that Marianne was auld Scully's child, around the same time Blaize was expectin' Sly. She knows. The auld bitch! Always knew. That I'm convinced of.

Stacia And she let them marry?

Maggie Done her best to thwart it, but would never own up as to the why of the thwartin'! Too proud, ya see, and me mother too ashamed. Besides, me father would have killed her if he ever found out – and I mean killed her. Young Gabriel Scully was insane from too much inbreedin' and I'd near swear he walked into the Belmont River be accident. Aither that or his antennae were too high; couldn't take the asphyxiation of that house.

Stacia Portia know all of this?

Maggie No, but her blood do, crossin' me mind these days to tell her if I thought it'd do any good, but I think I'm about thirty year too late – I don't have to tell ya, Stacia, to keep it to yourself.

Stacia Won't even tell Justin, and I tell him everythin'.

Maggie Good girl.

> *Light change on Portia and Senchil dancing, switch from song playing on jukebox to Gabriel taking up the song. Portia rests, eyes closed, on Senchil. Fintan sways from side to side watching them; Maggie May and Stacia sway, drink, smoke, lost in themselves. Senchil takes a biscuit out of his pocket and nibbles on it, with his other hand he pats Portia's head lovingly. Portia looks at him.*

Portia On Judgement Day, Senchil, you'll be atin' your biscuits sittin' opposite of God.

Senchil May even offer him one.

Portia How did ya get to stay so unsoiled, Senchil?

Senchil Unsoiled, that how you'd describe me?

Portia Aye.

Senchil Only an auld eegit, Portia, what the world would call a failure.

Portia Be that so terrible?

Senchil Be – Never met a body yet as didn't want to leave a mark, some sign, however small, that they was on the earth at a point in time. Be some as leaves a good mark, some as leaves a bad one, we shadow people leave ne'er a mark at all.

Portia Would ya say I'm one of the shadow ones?

Senchil No – But even if ya were, you'd still be necessary, a necessary backdrop for the giants who walks this world and mayhap the next.

Stacia Portia, better get a move on, the kids is well out of school.

Fintan (*as Portia and Stacia are exiting, thick*) So high and mighty now yees don't feel it necessary to pay for yeer drinks.

Portia Here.

Fintan I don't have change for fifty pound!

Portia Then keep the change, buy yourself a new medallion.

Exit Portia and Stacia.

Maggie Whoa! I have change! (*Grabs fifty-pound note off him.*) Senchil! A fiver!

Senchil produces a fiver in a flash. Fintan grabs it, storms off. Exit Maggie May and Senchil.

SCENE FIVE

Portia's living room. Gabriel's voice, faint, she strains to hear it, it sounds very high up. She gets up on the table, listens with head upward, sits perched on the table, listening. Enter Marianne. Looks at Portia.

Marianne Portia.

No answer from Portia except an involuntary shudder.

I said, Portia.

Portia (*eyes closed*) Shhh.

Marianne What in the name of God's wrong of ya?

Portia Listen.

Marianne What? (*Looks upward.*) Maggie May rang me up, says ya weren't yourself. When is she, says I? Get down off of that table this minute, young lady!

Portia (*looks at Marianne a while*) I've always wanted to like ya, Mother, but I never could.

Marianne Ah, would you stop such nonsense talk! Now get down. (*gently*) Will I help ya, Portia? (*Offers a hand.*) Is it Gabriel?

Portia Just don't! I don't want to hear you talkin' about him. Ya sully him on me always.

Marianne Gabriel was fierce difficult, obsessed with himself and you.

Portia I said not to talk about him.

Marianne Well I am, and he was obsessed with you! Came out of the womb clutchin' your leg and he's still clutchin' it from wherever he is. Portia, you're goin' to have to cop onto yourself. Your home is a mess, your children is motherless. Raphael has to do it all.

Portia looks at Marianne, a look of complete and utter hatred.

And stop lookin' at me like that! If I didn't know you for me own daughter, I'd swear ya were some evil goblin perched up there glowerin' at me.

Portia leaps, a wildcat leap from the table onto her mother, knocks her down, on top of her.

Me back! Have ya lost the run of yourself!

Portia (*flailing at Marianne who is pinned under her*) You've me suffocated so I can't breathe any more!

Marianne Let me up! Let me up! Portia, please, your mother.

Portia Why couldn't ya have just left us in peace? We weren't doin' nothin'!

Marianne You're not right in the head! Let me up!

Portia Always spyin' on us!

Roars from Marianne.

Interferin' with our games! Out callin' us in your disgustin' hysterical voice! Why couldn't ya have just left us alone? Why?

Marianne Left ye alone to, to yeer unnatural ways and stupid carry-on!

Portia We weren't hurtin' anybody and me and Gabriel locked in that room –

Marianne I was locked in there too –

Portia Aye, sobbin' into the pillow. That sound, that

sound, I think hell be a corridor full of rooms like that one with that sound comin' from every one of them, and then you'd turn on us because we were weaker and smaller than you, but that was nothin' compared with your feeble attempts to love us. We'd sooner have your rage any day! Your hysterical picnics, with your bottle of orange and your crisps –

Marianne That's right, sneer away! I wished to God ye'd never been born!

Portia We wished it too.

Marianne And Gabriel was the one I loved, never you!

Portia A awful pity then ya meant nothin' to him –

Marianne He had all the gifts and you had none!

Portia He hated you! Know what we used to call ya! The stuck pig!

Marianne You were only his shadow, trailin' after him like a slavish pup!

Portia Ya fuckin' liar, ya! You come in here talkin' about Gabriel as if you owned him! He was mine first! And I lost him first! And I was the only one that mattered to him!

Marianne Mattered to him! I seen what he used do to you! How he used start ya chokin' by just lookin' at ya! How he used draw blood from ya when ya tried to defy him!

Portia Mother, he was doin' them things to himself for he thought I was him!

Marianne I know he did. But you're not him, Portia, ya have to forget him, ya can't go on like this.

Portia Why did ya have to sever us?

Marianne Wasn't me as severed yees and well you know it.

Portia Ya fuckin' bitch! Get out! Get out! Get out!

Attacks her again, Marianne resists her.

Marianne Stop it! Stop it! That's enough of that!

Portia It wasn't me as severed us! Was you and Daddy! Was ye stopped hees singin' lessons!

Marianne Me and your father would've stopped lots of things if we could've –

Portia Didn't you know the only fuckin' thing he could do was sing!

Marianne Gabriel stopped singin', Portia, when you stopped talkin' to him, when ya refused to go anywhere with him, when ya refused to ate at the table with him, when ya ran from every room he walked into, when you started runnin' round with Stacia and Damus Halion. That's when Gabriel stopped singin'. Oh, Portia, you done away with him as if he were no more than an ear of corn at the threshin' and me and your father could do nothin' only look on.

Enter Sly unobserved, with package.

Portia Mother, stop – I can't bear it – Mother, the night he died, the night after our fifteenth birthday, I walked down to the river with him and he whispered to me before he went in. 'Portia,' he says, 'I'm goin' now but I'll come back and I'll keep comin' back until I have you.'

Marianne You were with him, Portia?

Sly (*whisper*) With him.

Marianne And ya didn't stop him?

Portia Stop him! One of us was goin', were killin' each other, and ye just left us to fight it to the death. Well, we fought it to the death and I won. Mother, I can hear him comin' towards me, can hear him callin' me –

Sly Ya were with him, Portia, how could ya, and ya let him go.

Marianne Sly, leave it.

Sly And ya let us search high and low for him, hopin' against hope we'd find him alive, puttin' off draggin' the river, and you knew where he was the whole fuckin' time. Me only son and you let him go like a swallow at the close of summer.

Portia I didn't plan for not to go with him – just happened.

Sly Ya cunt! Ya dark fuckin' cunt! I watched how you played with him, how ya teased him, I watched yeer perverted activities, I seen yees, dancin' in yeer pelts, disgustin', and the whole world asleep barrin' ye and the river – I'll sort you out once and for all, ya little hoor, ya, ya rip, ya fuckin' bitch ya!

Portia I'm not your wife nor your mother so don't you come in here takin' your rage out on me, ya fuckin' coward ya!

Marianne Sly! Go home! Now! Your own daughter!

Portia I didn't kill your precious Gabriel! We all did.

Sly You're not my daughter any more.

Portia I'm just tryin' to tell ya how it was, he's closin' in on me, I hear his footfall crossin' the worlds.

Sly What ya want me to do, girl? I deal with animals, not ghosts. What ya want me to do? Marianne, say somethin' to her – (*Goes to exit, picks up package.*) And there's the dress ya told me to collect from town for her birthday. (*Goes to exit, stops to look at Portia.*)

Marianne Go on, Sly, go on.

Exit Sly. Silence. Marianne opens package, takes out a beautiful dress, holds it against Portia.

Do ya like it?

Portia (*a whisper*) Mother.

Marianne It'll be beautiful on ya – wanted to have it for yesterday – for your thirtieth birthday.

Exit Marianne. Portia puts on dress.

SCENE SIX

Portia sets the table, lights candles, opens wine, pours a glass, drinks, sits, puts on diamond bracelet. Enter Raphael, phone, car keys, factory books, looks at table with pleasure.

Raphael Kids in bed?

Portia Just gone.

Raphael Got held up in the factory.

Portia Did ya? (*Pours him a glass of wine.*)

Raphael Thanks – Feelin' better?

Portia Feel just fine.

Raphael Glad to hear it.

Portia I'll bring in the dinner if you're ready.

Raphael Belt away.

Portia brings in the dinner, serves it up. They dig in, eat like peasants, horse it down, heads close to the plate, no conversation, finished.

Portia There's more.

Raphael Grand for the minute.

Raphael lights a cigar, Portia a cigarette.

I went to see the barman of the High Chaparral – Goolan, that his name?

Portia Fintan Goolan, aye.

Raphael Swears he never laid a finger on ya.

Portia Aye.

Raphael Is it true? It is, isn't it? Portia, why would ya lie about somethin' like that?

Portia Mayhap to hide a bigger one.

Raphael What do ya mean?

Portia Can't we just leave it, Raphael? Look, I cooked your dinner, I poured your wine, I bathed Quintin, read him a story and all. Can't we knock a bit of pleasure out of one another for once?

Raphael Pleasure? The pair of us, the mind boggles. Anyway, long realized ya want very little to do with me.

Portia May have wanted more to do with ya if ya weren't always so calm and unneedy, Raphael – Never learnt how to deal with that – And I never told anyone this before – ya see, me and Gabriel made love all the time down be the Belmont River among the swale, from the age of five – That's as far back as I can remember anyways – But I think we were doin' it before we were

253

born. Times I close me eyes and I feel a rush of water around me and above we hear the thumpin' of me mother's heart, and we're a-twined, his foot on my head, mine on his foetal arm, and we don't know which of us is the other and we don't want to, and the water swells around our ears, and all the world is Portia and Gabriel packed for ever in a tight hot womb, where there's no breathin', no thinkin', no seein', only darkness and heart drums and touch – And when I was fifteen I slept with Damus Halion – should've known better, he meant nothin' to me – and Gabriel seen and Gabriel seen and never spoke to me after.

Raphael It's me you're married to, Portia, not Gabriel, and it's me you been fuckin' round on, not Gabriel. Damus Halion. Jaysus! Portia, you're so much better than him! Why do ya lower yourself and me with him.

Portia Told ya he meant nothin' to me, Raphael, nothin'.

Raphael Ah, I don't care about Damus Halion any more, thought I did, he's only a fuckin' eegit of a gobshite fucker. Gabriel's the one. I've waited thirteen year for you to talk about me the way you've just talked about him. I'm weary of it all. (*Goes to exit.*)

Portia Raphael, don't leave me here be me own.

Raphael Don't know what way I'm supposed to behave with ya any more. Ya think ya can do what ya like with me. Once ya could. When I first seen you walkin' by the river, I prayed to God to let me have ya, I showered ya with everythin' I thought a woman could want, and what do ya do? You've savaged me to the scut and now ya want love talk – well, I've none for ya, I'm goin' to bed.

Portia Raphael.

Raphael What?

Portia I seen you long before you ever seen me, seen ya fishin' one Sunday afternoon and the stillness and sureness that came off of you was a balm to me, and when I asked who ya were and they said that's Raphael Coughlan, I thought, how can anyone with a name like that be so real, and I says to meself, if Raphael Coughlan notices me I will have a chance to enter the world and stay in it, which has always been the battle for me. And you say you want me to talk about ya the way I talk about Gabriel – I cannot, Raphael, I cannot. And though everyone and everythin' tells me I have to forget him, I cannot, Raphael, I cannot.

Exit Raphael. Sound of Gabriel's voice, triumphant.

BY THE BOG OF CATS . . .

By the Bog of Cats . . . was first produced at the Abbey Theatre, Dublin, as part of the Dublin Theatre Festival, on 7 October 1998, with the following cast:

Hester Swane Olwen Fouéré
Josie Kilbride Siobhan Cullen/Kerry O'Sullivan
Carthage Kilbride Conor MacDermottroe
Monica Murray Pat Leavy
Mrs Kilbride Pauline Flanagan
Xavier Cassidy Tom Hickey
Caroline Cassidy Fionnuala Murphy
Catwoman Joan O'Hara
Ghost Fancier Pat Kinevane
Ghost of Joseph Swane Ronan Leahy
Young Dunne/Waiter Conan Sweeny
Father Willow Eamon Kelly
Waiters Gavin Cleland, Kieran Grimes

Director Patrick Mason
Designer Monica Frawley
Lighting Nick Chelton
Stage Director Finola Eustace
ASM Stephen Dempsey

Characters

Hester Swane, forty
Carthage Kilbride, thirty
Josie Kilbride, seven, Hester and Carthage's daughter
Mrs Kilbride, sixties, Carthage's mother
Monica Murray, sixties, a neighbour
Catwoman, fifties, lives on the bog
Xavier Cassidy, sixties, a big farmer
Caroline Cassidy, twenty, his daughter
The Ghost Fancier, a handsome creature in a dress suit
The Ghost of Joseph Swane, eighteen
Young Dunne, a waiter
Father Willow, eighty
Two Other Waiters
Voice of Josie Swane

Time and Place

The present.

Act One takes place in the yard of Hester Swane's
house and by the caravan on the Bog of Cats.
Act Two takes place in Xavier Cassidy's house.
Act Three opens in Hester's yard and then
reverts to the caravan on the Bog of Cats

Accent

Midland. I've given a slight flavour in the text,
but the real Midland accent is a lot flatter and rougher
and more guttural than the written word allows

Songs of Josie Swane*

BY THE BOG OF CATS . . .

By the Bog of Cats I finally learned false from true,
Learned too late that it was you and only you
Left me sore, a heart brimful of rue
By the Bog of Cats in the darkling dew.

By the Bog of Cats I dreamed a dream of wooing.
I heard your clear voice to me a-calling
That I must go though it be my undoing.
By the Bog of Cats I'll stay no more a-rueing.

To the Bog of Cats I one day will return,
In mortal form or in ghostly form,
And I will find you there and there with you sojourn,
Forever by the Bog of Cats, my darling one.

THE BLACK SWAN

I know where a black swan sleeps
On the bank of grey water,
Hidden in a nest of leaves
So none can disturb her.

I have lain outside her lair,
My hand upon her wing,
And I have whispered to her
And of my sorrows sung.

I wish I was a black swan
And could fly away from here,
But I am Josie Swane,
Without wings, without care.

* *to be recorded and used during the play*

Act One

SCENE ONE

*Dawn. On the Bog of Cats. A bleak white landscape of
ice and snow. Music, a lone violin. Hester Swane trails
the corpse of a black swan after her, leaving a trail of
blood in the snow. The Ghost Fancier stands there
watching her.*

Hester Who are you? Haven't seen you around here
before.

Ghost Fancier I'm a ghost fancier.

Hester A ghost fancier. Never heard tell of the like.

Ghost Fancier You never seen ghosts?

Hester Not exactly, felt what I thought were things from
some other world betimes, but nothin' I could grab on to
and say, 'That is a ghost.'

Ghost Fancier Well, where there's ghosts there's ghost
fanciers.

Hester That so? So what do you do, Mr Ghost Fancier?
Eye up ghosts? Have love affairs with them?

Ghost Fancier Dependin' on the ghost. I've trailed you a
while. What're you doin' draggin' the corpse of a swan
behind ya like it was your shadow?

Hester This is auld Black Wing. I've known her the
longest time. We used play together when I was a young
wan. Wance I had to lave the Bog of Cats and when
I returned years later this swan here came swoopin' over

the bog to welcome me home, came right up to me and kissed me hand. Found her frozen in a bog hole last night, had to rip her from the ice, left half her underbelly.

Ghost Fancier No one ever tell ya it's dangerous to interfere with swans, especially black wans?

Hester Only an auld superstition to keep people afraid. I only want to bury her. I can't be struck down for that, can I?

Ghost Fancier You live in that caravan over there?

Hester Used to; live up the lane now. In a house, though I've never felt at home in it. But you, Mr Ghost Fancier, what ghost are you ghoulin' for around here?

Ghost Fancier I'm ghoulin' for a woman be the name of Hester Swane.

Hester I'm Hester Swane.

Ghost Fancier You couldn't be, you're alive.

Hester I certainly am and aim to stay that way.

Ghost Fancier (*looks around, confused*) Is it sunrise or sunset?

Hester Why do ya want to know?

Ghost Fancier Just tell me.

Hester It's that hour when it could be aither dawn or dusk, the light bein' so similar. But it's dawn, see there's the sun comin' up.

Ghost Fancier Then I'm too previous. I mistook this hour for dusk. A thousand apologies.

Goes to exit, Hester stops him.

Hester What do ya mean you're too previous? Who are ya? Really?

Ghost Fancier I'm sorry for intrudin' upon you like this. It's not usually my style. (*Lifts his hat, walks off.*)

Hester (*shouts after him*) Come back! – I can't die – I have a daughter.

   Monica enters.

Monica What's wrong of ya, Hester? What are ya shoutin' at?

Hester Don't ya see him?

Monica Who?

Hester Him!

Monica I don't see anywan.

Hester Over there. (*Points.*)

Monica There's no wan, but ya know this auld bog, always shiftin' and changin' and coddin' the eye. What's that you've there? Oh, Black Wing, what happened to her?

Hester Auld age, I'll wager, found her frozed last night.

Monica (*touches the swan's wing*) Well, she'd good innin's, way past the life span of swans. Ya look half frozed yourself, walkin' all night again, were ya? Ya'll cetch your death in this weather. Five below the forecast said and worser promised.

Hester Swear the age of ice have returned. Wouldn't ya almost wish if it had, do away with us all like the dinosaurs.

Monica I would not indeed – are you lavin' or what, Hester?

Hester Don't keep axin' me that.

Monica Ya know you're welcome in my little shack.

Hester I'm goin' nowhere. This here is my house and my garden and my stretch of the bog and no wan's runnin' me out of here.

Monica I came up to see if ya wanted me to take Josie down for her breakfast.

Hester She's still asleep.

Monica The child, Hester, ya have to pull yourself together for her, you're goin' to have to stop this broodin', put your life back together again.

Hester Wasn't me as pulled it asunder.

Monica And you're goin' to have to lave this house, isn't yours any more. Down in Daly's doin' me shoppin' and Caroline Cassidy there talkin' about how she was goin' to mow this place to the ground and build a new house from scratch.

Hester Caroline Cassidy. I'll sourt her out. It's not her is the problem anyway, she's just wan of the smaller details.

Monica Well, you've left it late for dealin' with her for she has her heart set on everythin' that's yours.

Hester If he thinks he can go on treatin' me the way he's been treatin' me, he's another thing comin'. I'm not to be flung aside at his biddin'. He'd be nothin' today if it wasn't for me.

Monica Sure the whole parish knows that.

Hester Well, if they do, why're yees all just standin' back and gawkin'. Thinks yees all Hester Swane with her tinker blood is gettin' no more than she deserves. Thinks yees all she's too many notions, built her life up from a caravan on the side of the bog. Thinks yees all she's taken a step above herself in gettin' Carthage Kilbride into her bed. Thinks yees all yees knew it'd never last. Well, yees are thinkin' wrong. Carthage Kilbride is mine for always or until I say he is no longer mine. I'm the one who chooses and discards, not him, and certainly not any of yees. And I'm not runnin' with me tail between me legs just because certain people wants me out of their way.

Monica You're angry now and not thinkin' straight.

Hester If he'd only come back, we'd be alright, if I could just have him for a few days on me own with no wan stickin' their nose in.

Monica Hester, he's gone from ya and he's not comin' back.

Hester Ah you think ya know everythin' about me and Carthage. Well, ya don't. There's things about me and Carthage no wan knows except the two of us. And I'm not talkin' about love. Love is for fools and children. Our bond is harder, like two rocks we are, grindin' off of wan another and maybe all the closer for that.

Monica That's all in your own head, the man cares nothin' for ya, else why would he go on the way he does.

Hester My life doesn't hang together without him.

Monica You're talkin' riddles now.

Hester Carthage knows what I'm talkin' about – I suppose I may bury auld Black Wing before Josie wakes and sees her. (*Begins walking off.*)

Monica I'll come up to see ya in a while, bring yees up some lunch, help ya pack.

Hester There'll be no packin' done around here.

And exit both in opposite directions.

SCENE TWO

The sound of a child's voice comes from the house. She enters after a while, Josie Kilbride, seven, barefoot, pyjamas, kicking the snow, singing.

Josie
By the Bog of Cats I dreamed a dream of wooing.
I heard your clear voice to me a-calling
That I must go though it be my undoing.
By the Bog of Cats I'll stay no more a-rueing –

Mam – Mam – (*Continues playing in the snow, singing.*)

To the Bog of Cats I one day will return,
In mortal form or in ghostly form,
And I will find you there and there with you sojourn,
Forever by the Bog of Cats, my darling one.

Mrs Kilbride has entered, togged up against the biting cold, a shawl over her face.

Mrs Kilbride Well, good mornin', ya little wagon of a girl child.

Josie Mornin' yourself, y'auld wagon of a Granny witch.

Mrs Kilbride I tould ya not to call me Granny.

Josie Grandmother – Did ya see me Mam, did ya?

Mrs Kilbride Aye, seen her whooshin' by on her broom half an hour back.

Josie Did yees crash?

Mrs Kilbride Get in, ya pup, and put on some clothes before Jack Frost ates your toes for breakfast. Get in till I dress ya.

Josie I know how to dress meself.

Mrs Kilbride Then dress yourself and stop braggin' about it. Get in. Get in.

And exit the pair to the house.

SCENE THREE

Enter Hester by the caravan. She digs a grave for the swan. Enter the Catwoman, a woman in her late fifties, stained a streaky brown from the bog, a coat of cat fur that reaches to the ground, studded with cats' eyes and cats' paws. She is blind and carries a stick.

Catwoman What're ya doin' there?

Hester None of your business now, Catwoman.

Catwoman You're buryin' auld Black Wing, aren't ya?

Hester How d'ya know?

Catwoman I know everythin' that happens on this bog. I'm the Keeper of the Bog of Cats in case ya forgotten. I own this bog.

Hester Ya own nothin', Catwoman, except your little house of turf and your hundred-odd mousetraps and anythin' ya can rob and I'm missin' a garden chair so ya better bring it back.

Catwoman I only took it because ya won't be needin' it any more.

Hester Won't I? If ya don't bring it back I'll have to go down meself and maybe knock your little turf house down.

Catwoman You just dare.

Hester I'll bring down diesel, burn ya out.

Catwoman Alright! Alright! I'll bring back your garden chair, fierce uncomfortable anyway, not wan of the cats'd sleep on it. Here, give her to me a minute, auld Black Wing.

Hester does.

She came to my door last night and tapped on it as she often did, only last night she wouldn't come in. I bent down and she puts her wing on me cheek and I knew this was farewell. Then I heard her tired auld wingbeat, shaky and off kilter and then the thud of her fallin' out of the sky onto the ice. She must've died on the wing or soon after. (*Kisses the black swan.*) Goodbye, auld thing, and safe journey. Here, put her in the ground.

Hester does and begins shovelling in clay. Catwoman stands there leaning on her stick, produces a mouse from her pocket.

A saucer of milk there, Hester Swane.

Hester I've no milk here today. You may go up to the house for your saucer of milk and, I told ya, I don't want ya pawin' mice around me, dirty auld yokes, full of diseases.

Catwoman And you aren't, you clean as the snow, Hester Swane?

Hester Did I say I was?

Catwoman I knew your mother, I helped her bring ya into the world, knew ya when ya were chained like a rabied pup to this auld caravan, so don't you look down on me for handlin' a mouse or two.

Hester If ya could just see yourself and the mouse fur growin' out of your teeth. Disgustin'.

Catwoman I need mice the way you need whiskey.

Hester Ah, go on and lave me alone, Catwoman, I'm in no mood for ya today.

Catwoman Bet ya aren't. I had a dream about ya last night.

Hester Spare me your visions and dreams, enough of me own to deal with.

Catwoman Dreamt ya were a black train motorin' through the Bog of Cats and, oh, the scorch off of this train and it blastin' by and all the bog was dark in your wake, and I had to run from the burn. Hester Swane, you'll bring this place down by evenin'.

Hester I know.

Catwoman Do ya now? Then why don't ya lave? If ya lave this place you'll be alright. That's what I came by to tell ya.

Hester Ah, how can I lave the Bog of Cats, everythin' I'm connected to is here. I'd rather die.

Catwoman Then die ya will.

Hester There's sympathy for ya! That's just what I need to hear.

Catwoman Ya want sugar-plum platitudes, go talk to Monica Murray or anyone else around here. You're my match in witchery, Hester, same as your mother was, it may even be ya surpass us both and the way ya go on as if God only gave ya a little frog of a brain instead of the gift of seein' things as they are, not as they should be, but exactly as they are. Ya know what I think?

Hester What?

Catwoman I been thinkin' a while now that there's some fierce wrong ya done that's caught up with ya.

Hester What fierce wrong?

Catwoman Don't you by-talk me, I'm the Catwoman. I know things. Now I can't say I know the exact wrong ya done but I'd put a bet on it's somethin' serious judgin' by the way ya go on.

Hester And what way do I go on?

Catwoman What was it ya done, Hester?

Hester I done nothin' – Or if I did I never meant to.

Catwoman There's a fine answer.

Hester Everywan has done wrong at wan time or another.

Catwoman Aye, but not everywan knows the price of wrong. You do and it's the best thing about ya and there's not much in ya I'd praise. No, most manage to stay a step or two ahead of the pigsty truth of themselves, not you though.

Hester Ah, would ya give over. Ya lap up people's fears, you've too much time on your own, concoctin' stories about others. Go way and kill a few mice for your dinner, only lave me alone – Or tell me about me mother, for what I remember doesn't add up.

Catwoman What ya want to know about big Josie Swane?

Hester Everythin'.

Catwoman Well, what ya remember?

Hester Only small things – Like her pausin'.

Catwoman She was a great wan for the pausin'.

Hester 'G'wan to bed, you,' she'd say, 'I'll just be here pausin'.' And I'd watch her from the window. (*Indicates window of caravan.*) Times she'd smoke a cigar which she had her own particular way of doin'. She'd hould it stretched away from her and, instead of takin' the cigar to her mouth, she'd bring her mouth to the cigar. And her all the time pausin'. What was she waitin' for, Catwoman?

Catwoman Ya'd often hear her voice comin' over the bog at night. She was the greatest song stitcher ever to have passed through this place and we've had plenty pass through but none like Josie Swane. But somewhere along the way she lost the weave of the song and in so doin' became small and bitter and mean. By the time she ran off and left ya I couldn't abide her.

Hester There's a longin' in me for her that won't quell the whole time.

Catwoman I wouldn't long for Josie Swane if I was you. Sure the night ya were born she took ya over to the black swan's lair, auld Black Wing ya've just buried there, and laid ya in the nest alongside her. And when I axed her why she'd do a thing like that with snow and ice everywhere, ya know what she says, 'Swane means swan.' 'That may be so,' says I, 'but the child'll die of pneumonia.' 'That child,' says Josie Swane, 'will live as long as this black swan, not a day more, not a day less.' And each night for three nights she left ya in the black swan's lair and each night I snuck ya out of the lair and took ya home with me and brung ya back to the lair before she'd come lookin' for ya in the mornin'. That's when I started to turn again' her.

Hester You're makin' it up to get rid of me like everywan else round here. Xavier Cassidy put ya up to this.

Catwoman Xavier Cassidy put me up to nothin'. I'm only tellin' ya so ya know what sourt of a woman your mother was. Ya were lucky she left ya. Just forget about her and lave this place now or ya never will.

Hester Doesn't seem to make much difference whether I stay or lave with a curse like that on me head.

Catwoman There's ways round curses. Curses only have the power ya allow them. I'm tellin' ya, Hester, ya have to go. When have I ever been proved wrong? Tould ya ya'd have just the wan daughter, tould ya the day and hour she'd be born, didn't I now?

Hester Ya did alright.

Catwoman Tould ya Carthage Kilbride was no good for ya, never grew his backbone, would ya listen? Tould Monica Murray to stop her only son drivin' to the city that night. Would she listen? Where's her son? In his grave, that's where he is. Begged her till she ran me off with a kittle of bilin' water. Mayhap she wanted him dead. I'll say nothin'. Gave auld Xavier Cassidy herbs to cure his wife. What did he do? Pegged them down the tilet and took Olive Cassidy to see some swanky medicine man in a private hospital. They cured her alright, cured her so well she came back cured as a side of ham in an oak coffin with golden handles. Maybe he wanted her dead too. There's many gets into brown studies over buryin' their loved wans. That a fact, Hester Swane. I'll be off now and don't say the Catwoman never tould ya. Lave this place now or ya never will.

Hester I'm stoppin' here.

Catwoman Sure I know that too. Seen it writ in a bog hole.

Hester Is there anythin' them blind eyes doesn't see writ in a bog hole?

Catwoman Sneer away. Ya know what the Catwoman says is true, but sneer away and we'll see will that sneer be on your puss at dusk. Remember the Catwoman then for I don't think I'll have the stomach for this place tonight.

And exit the Catwoman and exit Hester.

SCENE FOUR

Josie and Mrs Kilbride enter and sit at the garden table as the Catwoman and Hester exit. Josie is dressed: wellingtons, trousers, jumper on inside out. They're playing snap. Mrs Kilbride plays ruthlessly, loves to win. Josie looks on in dismay.

Mrs Kilbride Snap – snap! Snap! (*stacking the cards*) How many games is that I'm after winnin' ya?

Josie Five.

Mrs Kilbride And how many did you win?

Josie Ya know right well I won ne'er a game.

Mrs Kilbride And do ya know why ya won ne'er a game, Josie? Because you're thick, that's the why.

Josie I always win when I play me Mam.

Mrs Kilbride That's only because your Mam is thicker than you. Thick and stubborn and dangerous wrong-headed and backwards to top it all. Are you goin' to start cryin' now, ya little pussy babby, don't you dare cry,

277

ya need to toughen up, child, what age are ya now? – I says what age are ya?

Josie Seven.

Mrs Kilbride Seven auld years. When I was seven I was cookin' dinners for a houseful of men, I was thinnin' turnips twelve hour a day, I was birthin' calves, sowin' corn, stookin' hay, ladin' a bull be his nose, and you can't even win a game of snap. Sit up straight or ya'll grow up a hunchback. Would ya like that, would ya, to grow up a hunchback? Ya'd be like an auld camel and everyone'd say, as ya loped by, 'There goes Josie Kilbride the hunchback,' would ya like that, would ya? Answer me.

Josie Ya know right well I wouldn't, Granny.

Mrs Kilbride What did I tell ya about callin' me Grandmother.

Josie (*defiantly*) Granny.

Mrs Kilbride (*leans over the table viciously*) Grandmother! Say it!

Josie (*giving in*) Grandmother.

Mrs Kilbride And you're lucky I even let ya call me that. Ya want another game?

Josie Only if ya don't cheat.

Mrs Kilbride When did I cheat?

Josie I seen ya, loads of times.

Mrs Kilbride A bad loser's all you are, Josie, and there's nothin' meaner than a bad loser. I never cheat. Never. D'ya hear me, do ya? Look me in the eye when I'm talkin' to ya, ya little bastard. D'ya want another game?

278

Josie No thanks, Grandmother.

Mrs Kilbride And why don't ya? Because ya know I'll win, isn't that it? Ya little coward ya, I'll break your spirit yet and then glue ya back the way I want ya. I bet ya can't even spell your name.

Josie And I bet ya I can.

Mrs Kilbride G'wan then, spell it.

Josie (*spells*) J-o-s-i-e K-i-l-b-r-i-d-e.

Mrs Kilbride Wrong! Wrong! Wrong!

Josie Well, that's the way Teacher taught me.

Mrs Kilbride Are you back-answerin' me?

Josie No, Grandmother.

Mrs Kilbride Ya got some of it right. Ya got the 'Josie' part right, but ya got the 'Kilbride' part wrong, because you're not a Kilbride. You're a Swane. Can ya spell Swane? Of course ya can't. You're Hester Swane's little bastard. You're not a Kilbride and never will be.

Josie I'm tellin' Daddy what ya said.

Mrs Kilbride Tell him! Ya won't be tellin' him anythin' I haven't tould him meself. He's an eegit, your Daddy. I warned him about that wan, Hester Swane, that she'd get her claws in, and she did, the tinker. That's what yees are, tinkers. And your poor Daddy, all he's had to put up with. Well, at least that's all changin' now. Why don't yees head off in that auld caravan, back to wherever yees came from, and give your poor Daddy back to me where he rightfully belongs. And you've your jumper on backwards.

Josie It's not backwards, it's inside out.

Mrs Kilbride Don't you cheek me – and tell me this, Josie Swane, how much has your Mam in the bank?

Josie I don't know.

Mrs Kilbride I'll tell ya how much, a great big goose egg. Useless, that's what she is, livin' off of handouts from my son that she flitters away on whiskey and cigars, the Jezebel witch. (*smugly*) Guess how much I've saved, Josie, g'wan, guess, guess.

Josie I wish if me Mam'd came soon.

Mrs Kilbride Ah g'wan, child, guess.

Josie Ten pound.

Mrs Kilbride (*hysterical*) Ten pound! A' ya mad, child? A' ya mad! Ten pound! (*Whispers avariciously.*) Three thousand pound. All mine. I saved it. I didn't frig it away on crame buns and blouses. No. I saved it. A thousand for me funeral, a thousand for the Little Sisters of the Poor and a thousand for your Daddy. I'm lavin' you nothin' because your mother would get hould of it. And d'ya think would I get any thanks for savin' all that money? Oh no, none, none in the world. Would it ever occur to anywan to say, 'Well done, Mrs Kilbride, well done, Elsie,' not wance did your Daddy ever say, 'Well done, Mother,' no, too busy fornicatin' with Hester Swane, too busy bringin' little bastards like yourself into the world.

Josie Can I go and play now?

Mrs Kilbride Here, I brung ya sweets, g'wan ate them, ate them all, there's a great child, ya need some sugar, some sweetie pie sweetness in your life. C'mere and give your auld Grandmother a kiss.

Josie does.

Sure it's not your fault ya were born a little girl bastard.
D'ya want another game of snap? I'll let ya win.

Josie No.

Mrs Kilbride Don't you worry, child, we'll get ya off of
her yet. Me and your daddy has plans. We'll batter ya
into the semblance of legitimacy yet, soon as we get ya
off –

Enter Carthage.

Carthage I don't know how many times I tould ya to
lave the child alone. You've her poisoned with your bile
and rage.

Mrs Kilbride I'm sayin' nothin' that isn't true. Can't
I play a game of snap with me own granddaughter?

Carthage Ya know I don't want ya around here at the
minute. G'wan home, Mother. G'wan!

Mrs Kilbride And do what? Talk to the range? Growl at
God?

Carthage Do whatever ya like, only lave Josie alone, pick
on somewan your own size. (*He turns Josie's jumper the
right way around.*) You'll have to learn to dress yourself.

Mrs Kilbride Ah now, Carthage, don't be annoyed with
me. I only came up to say goodbye to her, found her in
her pyjamas out here playin' in the snow. Why isn't her
mother mindin' her?

Carthage Don't start in on that again.

Mrs Kilbride I never left you on your own.

Carthage Ya should have.

Mrs Kilbride And ya never called in to see the new dress I got for today and ya promised ya would.

Carthage glares at her.

Alright, I'm goin', I'm goin'. Just don't think now ya've got Caroline Cassidy ya can do away with me, the same as you're doin' away with Hester Swane. I'm your mother and I won't be goin' away. Ever. (*Exits.*)

Carthage Where's your Mam?

Josie Isn't she always on the bog? Can I go to your weddin'?

Carthage What does your mother say?

Josie She says there'll be no weddin' and to stop annoyin' her.

Carthage Does she now?

Josie Will you ax her for me?

Carthage We'll see, Josie, we'll see.

Josie I'll wear me Communion dress. Remember me Communion, Daddy?

Carthage I do.

Josie Wasn't it just a brilliant day?

Carthage It was, sweetheart, it was. Come on, we go check the calves.

And exit the pair.

SCENE FIVE

Enter Caroline Cassidy in her wedding dress and veil. Twenty, fragile-looking and nervous. She goes to the window of Hester's house and knocks.

Caroline Hester – are ya there?

Hester comes up behind her.

Hester Haven't you the gall comin' here, Caroline Cassidy.

Caroline (*jumps with fright*) Oh! (*Recovers.*) Can come here whenever I want, this is my house now, sure ya signed it over and all.

Hester Bits of paper, writin', means nothin', can as aisy be unsigned.

Caroline You're meant to be gone this weeks, it's just not fair.

Hester Lots of things isn't fair, Daddy's little ice-pop.

Caroline We're goin' ahead with the weddin', me and Carthage, ya think ya'll disrupt everythin', Hester Swane. I'm not afraid of ya.

Hester Ya should be. I'm afraid of meself – What is it ya want from me, Caroline? What have I ever done on you that ya feel the need to take everythin' from me?

Caroline I'm takin' nothin' ya haven't lost already and lost this long while gone.

Hester You're takin' me husband, you're takin' me house, ya even want me daughter. Over my dead body.

Caroline He was never your husband, he only took pity on ya, took ya out of that auld caravan on the bog, gave ya a home, built ya up from the ground.

Hester Them the sweet nothin's he's been tellin' ya? Let's get wan thing straight, it was me built Carthage Kilbride up from nothin', him a labourer's son you wouldn't give the time of day to and you trottin' by in your first bra, on your half-bred mare, your nose nudgin' the sun.
It was me who tould him he could do better. It was my money that bought his first fine acres. It was in my bed he slowly turned from a slavish pup to a man and no frigid little Daddy's girl is goin' to take him from me. Now get off of my property before I cut that dress to ribbons.

Caroline I'll have to get Daddy. He'll run ya off with a shotgun if he has to.

Hester Not everyone is as afraid of your Daddy as you are, Caroline.

Caroline Look, I'll give ya more money if ya'll only go. Here's me bank book, there's nearly nineteen thousand pounds in it, me inheritance from me mother. Daddy gave it to me this mornin'. Ya can have it, only please go. It's me weddin' day. It's meant to be happy. It's meant to be the best day of me life.

She stands there, close to tears. Hester goes over to her, touches her veil.

Hester What ya want me to do, Caroline? Admire your dress? Wish ya well? Hah? I used babysit you. Remember that?

Caroline That was a long time ago.

Hester Not that long at all. After your mother died, several nights ya came down and slept with me. Ya were glad of the auld caravan then, when your Daddy'd be off at the races or the mart or the pub, remember that, do ya? A pasty little thing, and I'd be awake half the night listenin' to your girly gibberish and grievances. Listen to me now, Caroline, there's two Hester Swanes, one that is decent and very fond of ya despite your callow treatment of me. And the other Hester, well, she could slide a knife down your face, carve ya up and not bat an eyelid. (*Grabs her hair suddenly and viciously.*)

Caroline Ow! Lave go!

Hester Listen to me now, Caroline. Carthage Kilbride is mine and only mine. He's been mine since he was sixteen. You think you can take him from me? Wrong. All wrong. (*Lets go of her.*) Now get out of me sight.

Caroline Ya'll be sorry for this, Hester Swane.

Hester We all will.

And exit Caroline, running.

SCENE SIX

Hester lights a cigar, sits at her garden table. Enter Josie with an old shawl around her head and a pair of high heels. She is pretending to be her Granny.

Josie Well good mornin', Tinker Swane.

Hester (*mock surprise*) Oh, good mornin', Mrs Kilbride, what a lovely surprise, and how are ya today?

Josie I've been savin' all night.

Hester Have ya now, Mrs Kilbride.

Josie Tell me, ya Jezebel witch, how much have ya in the bank today?

Hester Oh, I've three great big goose eggs, Mrs Kilbride. How much have ya in the bank yourself?

Josie Seventeen million pound. Seventeen million pound. I saved it. I didn't frig it away on love stories and silk stockin's. I cut back on sugar and I cut back on flour. I drank biled socks instead of tay and in wan night I saved seventeen million pound.

Hester Ya drank biled socks, Mrs Kilbride?

Josie I did and I had turf stew for me dinner and for dessert I had snail tart and a big mug of wee-wee.

Hester Sounds delicious, Mrs Kilbride.

Josie Ya wouldn't get better in Buckin'am Palace.

Hester Josie, don't ever say any of that in front of your Granny, sure ya won't?

Josie I'm not a total eegit, Mam.

Hester Did ya have your breakfast?

Josie I had a sugar sammige.

Hester Ya better not have.

Josie Granny made me disgustin' porridge.

Hester Did she? Did ya wash your teeth?

Josie Why do I always have to wash me teeth? Every day. It's so borin'. What do I need teeth for anyway?

Hester Ya need them for snarlin' at people when smilin' doesn't work any more. G'wan in and wash them now.

Enter Carthage in his wedding suit. Hester looks at him, looks away.

Josie Did ya count the cattle, Daddy?

Carthage I did.

Josie Were they all there?

286

Carthage They were, Josie.

Josie Daddy says I can go to his weddin'.

Carthage I said maybe, Josie.

Hester G'wan round the back and play, Josie.

Josie Can I go, Mam, can I? Say yeah, g'wan, say yeah.

Hester We'll see, g'wan, Josie, g'wan, good girl.

And exit Josie. They both watch her. Silence.

Carthage I'd like to know what ya think you're playin' at.

Hester Take a better man than you to cancel me out, Carthage Kilbride.

Carthage Ya haven't even started packin'.

Hester Them your weddin' clothes?

Carthage They're not me farm clothes, are they?

Hester Ya've a cheek comin' here in them.

Carthage Well, you, missus, are meant to be gone.

Hester And ya've a nerve tellin' Josie she can go to your weddin'.

Carthage She's mine as well as yours.

Hester Have ya slept with her yet?

Carthage That's none of your business.

Hester Every bit of me business. Ya think ya can wipe out fourteen years just like that. Well she's welcome to ya and any satisfaction she can squeeze out of ya.

Carthage Never heard ya complainin' when I was in your bed.

Hester Ya done the job, I suppose, in a kindergarten sourt of way.

Carthage Kindergarten, that what ya call it?

Hester You were nothin' before I put me stamp on ya and ya'll be nothin' again I'm finished with ya.

Carthage Are you threatenin' me, Hetty? Because, if ya are, ya better know who you're dealin' with, not the sixteen-year-auld fool snaggin' hares along the Bog of Cats who fell into your clutches.

Hester It was you wooed me, Carthage Kilbride, not the other way round as ya'd like everywan to think. In the beginnin' I wanted nothin' to do with ya, should've trusted me first instinct, but ya kept comin' back. You cut your teeth on me, Carthage Kilbride, gnawed and sucked till all that's left is an auld bone ya think to fling on the dunghill, now you've no more use for me. If you think I'm goin' to let you walk over me like that, ya don't know me at all.

Carthage That at least is true. I've watched ya now for the best part of fourteen years and I can't say for sure I know the first thing about ya. Who are ya and what sourt of stuff are ya made of?

Hester The same as you and I can't abide to lose ya. Don't lave me. Don't – is it I've gotten old and you just hittin' thirty?

Carthage Ya know right well it isn't that.

Hester And I haven't had a drink since the night ya left.

Carthage I know.

Hester I only ever drank anyway to forget about –

Carthage I don't want to talk about that. Lave it.

Hester And still ya took the money and bought the land, the Kilbrides who never owned anythin' till I came along, tinker and all. Tell me what to do, Carthage, and I'll do it, anythin' for you to come back.

Carthage Just stop, will ya –

Hester Anythin', Carthage, anythin', and I'll do it if it's in me power.

Carthage It's not in your power – Look, I'm up to me neck in another life that can't include ya any more.

Hester You're sellin' me and Josie down the river for a few lumpy auld acres and notions of respectability and I never thought ya would. You're better than all of them. Why must ya always look for the good opinion from them that'll never give it. Ya'll only ever be Xavier Cassidy's work horse. He won't treat ya right. He wouldn't know how.

Carthage He's treatin' me fine, signin' his farm over to me this evenin'.

Hester Ya know what they're sayin' about ya? That you're a jumped-up land-hungry mongrel but that Xavier Cassidy is greedier and craftier and he'll spancel ya back to the scrubber ya are.

Carthage And ya know what they're sayin' about you? That it's time ya moved onto another haltin' site.

Hester I was born on the Bog of Cats and on the Bog of Cats I'll end me days. I've as much right to this place as any of yees, more, for it holds me to it in ways it has never held yees. And as for me tinker blood, I'm proud of it. It gives me an edge over all of yees around here, allows me see yees for the inbred, underbred, bog-brained shower yees are. I'm warnin' ya now, Carthage, you go through with this sham weddin' and you'll never see Josie again.

Carthage If I have to mow ya down or have ya declared an unfit mother to see Josie I will, so for your own sake don't cause any trouble in that department. Look, Hetty, I want Josie to do well in the world, she'll get her share of everythin' I own and will own. I want her to have a chance in life, a chance you never had and so can never understand –

Hester Don't tell me what I can and can't understand!

Carthage Well understand this. Ya'll not separate me and Josie or I'll have her taken off of ya. I only have to mention your drinkin' or your night roamin' or the way ya sleep in that dirty auld caravan and lave Josie alone in the house.

Hester I always take Josie to the caravan when I sleep there.

Carthage Ya didn't take her last night.

Hester I wasn't in the caravan last night. I was walkin' the bog, but I checked on her three, four times.

Carthage Just don't cross me with Josie because I don't want to have to take her off of ya, I know she's attached to ya, and I'm not a monster. Just don't cross me over her or I'll come down on ya like a bull from heaven.

Hester So I'm meant to lie back and let Caroline Cassidy have her way in the rearin' of my child. I'm meant to lave her around Xavier Cassidy – sure he's capable of anythin'. If it's the last thing I do I'll find a way to keep her from ya.

Carthage I want you out of here before dusk! And I've put it to ya now about Josie. Think it over when ya've calmed down. And here. (*producing envelope*) There's your blood money. It's all there down to the last penny.

Hester No! I don't want it!

Carthage (*throws it in the snow*) Neither do I. I never should've took it in the first place. I owe ya nothin' now, Hester Swane. Nothin'. Ya've no hold over me now. (*Goes to exit.*)

Hester Carthage – ya can't just walk away like this.

Carthage I can and I am – Ya know what amazes me, Hetty?

Hester What?

Carthage That I stayed with ya so long – I want peace, just peace – Remember, before dusk.

And exit Carthage. Hester looks after him. Josie comes running on.

Josie What's wrong of ya, Mam?

Hester Ah go 'way, would ya, and lave me alone.

Josie Can I go down to Daly's and buy sweets?

Hester No, ya can't. Go on off and play, you're far too demandin'.

Josie Yeah well, just because you're in a bad humour it's not my fault. I'm fed up playin' on me own.

Hester You'll get a clatter if you're not careful. I played on me own when I was your age, I never bothered me mother, you're spoilt rotten, that's what ya are. (*in a gentler tone*) G'wan and play with your dolls, give them a bath, cut their hair.

Josie Ya said I wasn't to cut their hair.

Hester Well now I'm sayin' ya can, alright.

Josie But it won't grow back.

Hester So! There's worse things in this world than your dolls' hair not growin' back, believe me, Josie Swane.

Josie Me name is Josie Kilbride.

Hester That's what I said.

Josie Ya didn't, ya said Josie Swane. I'm not a Swane. I'm a Kilbride.

Hester I suppose you're ashamed of me too.

Enter Xavier Cassidy and Caroline, both in their wedding clothes.

Josie Caroline, your dress, is that your weddin' dress? It's beautiful.

Caroline Hello Josie.

Josie runs over to Caroline to touch her dress. Hester storms after her, picks her up roughly, carries her to corner of the house. Puts her down.

Hester Now stay around the back.

And exit Josie.

Xavier Was hopin' I wouldn't find ya still here, Swane.

Hester So ya came back with your Daddy, ya know nothin', Caroline, nothin'. (*Sits at her garden table, produces a naggin of whiskey from her pocket, drinks.*)

Xavier Thought ya'd given up the drink.

Hester I had. Me first in months, but why should I try and explain meself to you?

Xavier Might interest Carthage to know you lashin' into a naggin of whiskey at this hour.

Hester Carthage. If it wasn't for you, me and Carthage'd be fine. Should've eradicated ya, Cassidy, when I could've.

God's punishin' me now because I didn't take steps
that were right and proper concernin' you. Aye. God's
punishin' me but I won't take his blows lyin' down.

Caroline What are ya talking about, Hester?

Hester What am I talkin' about? I'm talkin' about you,
ya little fool, and I'm talkin' about James.

Caroline Me brother James?

Xavier You keep a civil tongue, Swane, over things ya
know nothin' about.

Hester Oh, but I do know things, and that's why ya
want me out of here. It's only your land and money and
people's fear of ya that has ya walkin' free. G'wan home
and do whatever it is ya do with your daughter, but keep
your sleazy eyes off of me and Josie. This is my property
and I've a right to sit in me own yard without bein' ogled
by the likes of you.

Xavier There's softer things on the eye, Swane, if it's
oglin' I was after. This is no longer your property and
well ya know it, ya signed it over six months ago, for a
fine hefty sum, have the papers here.

Hester I wasn't thinkin' right then, was bein' coerced
and bullied from all sides, but I have regained me pride
and it tells me I'm stayin'. Ya'll get your money back.
(*Picks up envelope Carthage has thrown in the snow.*)
Here's some of it.

Xavier I'm not takin' it. A deal's a deal.

Hester Take it! Take it! (*Stuffs it into his breast pocket.*)
And it might interest ya to know, Caroline, that Carthage
was just here in his weddin' clothes and he didn't look
like no radiant groom and he axed me to take him back,
but I said –

Xavier I'd say he did alright –

Hester He did! He did! Or as much as, but I said I couldn't be played with any more, that I was made for things he has lost the power to offer. And I was. I was made for somethin' different than these butchery lives yees all lead here on the Bog of Cats. Me mother taught me that.

Xavier Your mother. Your mother taught ya nothin', Swane, except maybe how to use a knife. Let me tell ya a thing or two about your mother, big Josie Swane. I used see her outside her auld caravan on the bog and the fields covered over in stars and her half covered in an excuse for a dress and her croonin' towards Orion in a language I never heard before or since. We'd peace when she left.

Hester And what were you doin' watchin' her? Catwoman tould me ya were in a constant swoon over me mother, sniffin' round the caravan, lavin' little presents and Christmas dinners and money and drink, sure I remember the gatch of ya meself and ya scrapin' at the door.

Xavier Very presumptuous of ya, Swane, to think I'd have any interest in your mother beyond Christian compassion.

Hester Christian compassion! That what it's called these days!

Xavier Aye, Christian compassion, a thing that was never bet into you. Ya say ya remember lots of things, then maybe ya remember that that food and money I used lave was left so ya wouldn't starve. Times I'd walk by that caravan and there'd be ne'er a sign of this mother of yours. She'd go off for days with anywan who'd buy her a drink. She'd be off in the bars of Pullagh and Mucklagh gettin' into fights. Wance she bit the nose off a woman

294

who dared to look at her man, bit the nose clean off
her face. And you, you'd be chained to the door of the
caravan with maybe a dirty nappy on ya if ya were
lucky. Often times –

Hester Lies! All lies!

Xavier Often times I brung ya home and gave ya over to
me mother to put some clothes on ya and feed ya. More
times than I can remember it'd be from our house your
mother would collect ya, the brazen walk of her, and
not a thank you or a flicker of guilt in her eye and her
reekin' of drink. Times she wouldn't even bother to
collect ya and meself or me mother would have to bring
ya down to her and she'd hardly notice that we'd come
and gone or that you'd returned.

Hester Ya expect me to believe anythin' that comes from
your siled lips, Xavier Cassidy.

Xavier And wan other thing, Swane, for you to cast
aspersions on me just because I'm an auld widower,
that's cheap and low. Not everywan sees the world
through your troubled eyes. There's such a thing as a
father lovin' his daughter as a father should, no more,
no less, somethin' you have never known, and I will –

Hester I had a father too! Ya'd swear I was dropped
from the sky the way ya go on. Jack Swane of Bergit's
Island, I never knew him – but I had a father. I'm as
settled as any of yees –

Xavier Well, he wasn't much of a father, never claimin'
ya when your mother ran off.

Hester He claimed me in the end –

Xavier Look, Swane, I don't care about your family or
where ya came from. I care only about me own and all
I've left is Caroline and if I have to plough through you

to have the best for her, then that's what I'll do. I don't want to unless I have to. So do it the aisy way for all of us. Lave this place today. (*Takes envelope from breast pocket, puts it into her hand.*) This is yours. Come on, Caroline.

Caroline Ya heard what Daddy says. Ya don't know his temper, Hester.

Hester And you don't know mine.

And exit Xavier followed by Caroline. Hester sits at her garden table, has a drink, looks up at the cold winter sky.

(*a whisper*) Dear God on high, what have ya in store for me at all?

Enter Josie in her Communion dress, veil, buckled shoes, handbag, the works.

(*Looks at her a minute.*) What are ya doin' in your Communion dress?

Josie For Daddy's weddin'. I'm grown out of all me other dresses.

Hester I don't think ya are.

Josie I am. I can go, can't I, Mam?

Hester Ya have her eyes.

Josie Whose eyes – whose eyes, Mam?

Hester Josie Swane's, me mother.

Josie Granny said me real name is Josie Swane.

Hester Don't mind your Granny.

Josie Did ya like her, Josie Swane?

Hester – More than anythin' in this cold white world.

Josie More than me and Daddy?

Hester I'm talkin' about when I was your age. Ya
weren't born then, Josie – Ya know the last time I seen
me mother I was wearin' me Communion dress too, down
by the caravan, a beautiful summer's night and the bog
like a furnace. I wouldn't go to bed though she kept tellin'
me to. I don't know why I wouldn't, I always done what
she tould me. I think now – maybe I knew. And she says,
'I'm goin' walkin' the bog, you're to stay here, Hetty.'
And I says, 'No,' I'd go along with her, and made to
folly her. And she says, 'No, Hetty, you wait here, I'll be
back in a while.' And again I made to folly her and again
she stopped me. And I watched her walk away from me
across the Bog of Cats. And across the Bog of Cats I'll
watch her return.

Lights down.

Act Two

Interior of Xavier Cassidy's house. A long table covered in a white tablecloth, laid for the wedding feast. Music off, a band setting up. The Catwoman sits at centre table lapping wine from a saucer. A waiter, a lanky, gawky young fellow, hovers with a bottle of wine waiting to refill the saucer.

Waiter You're sure now ya wouldn't like a glass, Catwoman?

Catwoman No, no, I love the saucer, young man. What's your name? Do I know ya?

Waiter I'm a Dunne.

Catwoman Wan of the long Dunnes or wan of the scutty fat-legged Dunnes?

Waiter Wan of the long Dunnes. Ya want a refill, Catwoman?

Catwoman I will. Are ya still in school? Your voice sounds as if it's just breakin'.

Waiter I am.

Catwoman And what're ya goin' to be when ya grow up, young Long Dunne?

Waiter I want to be an astronaut but me father wants me to work on the bog like him and like me grandfather. The Dunnes has always worked on the bog.

Catwoman Oh go for the astronaut, young man.

Waiter I will so, Catwoman. Have ya enough wine?

Catwoman Plenty for now.

Exit young Dunne crossed by the ghost of Joseph Swane, entering; bloodstained shirt and trousers, a throat wound. He walks across the stage. Catwoman cocks her ear, starts sniffing.

Joseph Hello. Hello.

Catwoman Ah Christ, not another ghost.

Joseph Who's there?

Catwoman Go 'way and lave me alone. I'm on me day off.

Joseph Who are ya? I can't see ya.

Catwoman I can't see you aither. I'm the Catwoman but I tould ya I'm not talkin' to ghosts today, yees have me heart scalded, hardly got a wink's sleep last night.

Joseph Please, I haven't spoken to anywan since the night I died.

Catwoman Haven't ya? Who are ya anyway?

Joseph I'm Joseph Swane of Bergit's Island. Is this Bergit's Island?

Catwoman This is the Bog of Cats.

Joseph The Bog of Cats. Me mother had a song about this place.

Catwoman Josie Swane was your mother?

Joseph Ya know her?

Catwoman Oh aye, I knew her. Then Hester must be your sister?

Joseph Hester, ya know Hester too?

Catwoman She lives only down the lane. I never knew Hester had a brother.

Joseph I doubt she'd be tellin' people about me.

Catwoman I don't mean to be short with ya, Joseph Swane, but Saturday is me day off. I haven't a minute to meself with yees, so tell me what is it ya want and then be on your way.

Joseph I want to be alive again. I want to stop walkin'. I want to rest, ate a steak, meet a girl, I want to fish for wild salmon and sow pike on Bergit's Lake again.

Catwoman You'll never do them things again, Joseph Swane.

Joseph Don't say that to me, Catwoman, I'm just turned eighteen.

Catwoman Eighteen. That's young to die alright. But it could be worse. I've a two-year-old ghost who comes to visit, all she wants to do is play Peep. Still eighteen's young enough. How come ya went so young? An accident, was it? Or by your own hand?

Waiter (*going by*) Ya talkin' to me, Catwoman?

Catwoman No, Long Dunne, just a ghost, a poor lost ghost.

Waiter Oh. (*Exits.*)

Joseph Are ya still there, Catwoman?

Catwoman I am but there's nothin' I can do for ya, you're not comin' back?

Joseph Is there no way?

Catwoman None, none in this world anyway, and the sooner ya realize that the better for ya. Now be on your way, settle in to your new world, knock the best out of it ya can.

Joseph It's fierce hard to knock the best out of nothin', fierce hard to enjoy darkness the whole time, can't I just stay here with ya, talk to ya a while?

Catwoman Ya could I suppose, only I'm at a weddin' and they might think I'm not the full shillin' if I have to be talkin' to you all day. Look, I'll take ya down to Hester Swane's house, ya can talk to her.

Joseph Can she hear ghosts?

Catwoman (*getting up*) Oh aye, though she lets on she can't.

Joseph Alright so, I suppose I may as well since I'm here.

Catwoman C'mon, folly me voice till I lead ya there.

Joseph (*following her*) Keep talkin' so I don't take a wrong turnin'.

Catwoman I will and hurry up now, I don't want to miss the weddin'. Ya still there?

Joseph I am.

> *And they're off by now. Enter Caroline and Carthage as they exit.*

Caroline This is the tablecloth me mother had for her weddin' and it's the same silver too. I'd really like for her to have been here today – Aye, I would.

Carthage A soft-boned lady, your mother. I used see her in town shoppin' with you be the hand, ya wanted to bow when she walked by. She had class, and you have too, Caroline, like no wan else around here.

Caroline I can't stop thinkin' about Hester.

Carthage (*kisses her*) Hester'll be fine, tough as an auld boot. Ya shouldn't concern yourself with her on your weddin' day. I've provided well for her, she isn't goin' to ever have to work a day in her life. Josie's the wan I worry about. The little sweetheart all done up in her Communion dress. Hetty should've got her a proper dress.

Caroline But Hester didn't want her here, Carthage.

Carthage Ya know what I wish?

Caroline What?

Carthage That she'd just give Josie to me and be done with it.

Caroline You're still very tangled up with Hester, aren't ya?

Carthage I'm not wan bit tangled with her, if she'd just do what she's supposed to do which is fierce simple, clear out of the Bog of Cats for wance and for all.

Caroline And I suppose ya'll talk about me as callously wan day too.

Carthage Of course I won't, why would I?

Caroline It's all fierce messy, Carthage. I'd hoped ya'd have sourted it out by today. It laves me in a fierce awkward position. You're far more attached to her than ya'd led me to believe.

Carthage Attached to her? I'm not attached to her, I stopped lovin' her years ago!

Caroline I'm not jealous as to whether ya love her or don't love her, I think maybe I'd prefer if ya still did.

Carthage Then what's botherin' ya?

Caroline You and Hester has a whole history together, stretchin' back years that connects yees and that seems more important and real than anythin' we have. And I wonder have we done the wrong thing.

Carthage Ya should've said all this before ya took your vows at the altar.

Caroline I've been tryin' to say it to ya for weeks.

Carthage So what do we do now?

Caroline Get through today, I suppose, pretend it's the best day of our lives. I don't know about you but I've had better days than today, far better.

Carthage Caroline, what's wrong of ya?

Caroline Nothin', only I feel like I'm walkin' on somewan's grave.

Enter Mrs Kilbride in what looks extremely like a wedding dress, white, a white hat, with a bit of a veil trailing off it, white shoes, tights, bag, etc.

Mrs Kilbride (*flushed, excited, neurotic*) Oh the love birds! The love birds! There yees are, off hidin'. Carthage, I want a photo of yees. Would you take it, Caroline?

Carthage She means she wants wan of herself.

Mrs Kilbride Shush now, Carthage, and stand up straight.

They pose like a bride and groom, Carthage glaring at Mrs Kilbride.

That's it. Wan more, smile, Carthage, smile, I hate a glowery demeanour in a photograph. That's great, Caroline, did ya get me shoes in?

Caroline I don't think I –

Mrs Kilbride Doesn't matter, doesn't matter, thank ya, what a glorious day, what a glorious white winter's day, nothin' must spoil today for me, nothin'. (*Begins photographing her shoes, first one, then the other.*)

Carthage What in the name of God are ya at now?

Mrs Kilbride I just want to get a photo of me shoes while they're new and clean. I've never had such a beautiful pair of shoes, look at the diamonds sparklin' on them. I saved like a Shylock for them, seen them in O'Brien's six months ago and I knew instantly them were to be me weddin' shoes. And I put by every week for them. Guess how much they were, Carthage, g'wan guess, Caroline, guess, guess.

Caroline I don't know, Mrs Kilbride.

Mrs Kilbride Elsie! Elsie! Call me Elsie, ah g'wan guess.

Caroline Fifty pound.

Mrs Kilbride (*angrily*) Fifty pound! Are ya mad! Are ya out of your tiny mind!

Carthage Tell us how much they were, Mother, before we die of the suspense.

Mrs Kilbride (*smug, can hardly believe it herself*) A hundred and fifty pound. The Quane herself wouldn't pay more.

Monica and Xavier have entered, Monica has Josie by the hand.

Monica – And Father Willow seems to have lost the run of himself entirely.

Xavier They should put him down, he's eighty if he's a day.

Monica The state of him with his hat on all durin' the Mass and the vestments inside out and his pyjamas peepin' out from under his trousers.

Xavier Did you hear he's started keepin' a gun in the tabernacle?

Monica I did, aye.

Xavier For all them robbers, is it?

Monica No, apparently it's for any of us that's late for Mass. Ya know what I was thinkin' and I lookin' at Caroline up there on the altar, I was thinkin' about my young fella Brian and I decided not to think about him today at all.

Xavier Then don't, Monica. Don't.

Monica Don't you never think about your own young fella?

Xavier Never, I never think about him. Never. Children! If they were calves we'd have them fattened and sould in three weeks. I never think of James. Never.

Monica Or Olive aither?

Xavier Ah, Olive had no fight in her, wailed like a ewe in a storm after the young lad and then lay down with her face to the wall. Ya know what she died of, Monica? Spite. Spite again' me. Well, she's the wan who's dead. I've the last laugh on her.

Monica Strange what these weddin's drag up.

Xavier Aye, they cost a fortune. (*Takes two glasses of champagne from a passing waiter.*) Here, Monica, and cheers. (*to Josie*) Child, a pound for your handbag.

Mrs Kilbride What d'ya say, Josie?

Xavier Lave her. Two things in this world get ya nowhere, sayin' sorry and sayin' thanks – that right, Josie?

Josie That's right, Mr Cassidy.

Mrs Kilbride (*taking Josie a little aside*) Here give me that pound till I mind it for ya.

Josie First give me back me Communion money.

Mrs Kilbride What Communion money?

Carthage Aye and ya can give me back mine while you're at it.

> *The Catwoman and Father Willow have entered, linking arms, both with their sticks. Father Willow has his snuff on hand, pyjamas showing from under his shirt and trousers, hat on, adores the Catwoman.*

Father Willow I'm tellin' ya now, Catwoman, ya'll have to cut back on the mice, they'll be the death of ya.

Catwoman And you'll have to cut back on the snuff.

Father Willow Try snails instead, far better for ya, the French ate them with garlic and tons of butter and Burgundy wine. I tried them wance meself and I in Avalon. Delicious.

Catwoman We should go on a holiday, you and me, Father Willow.

Father Willow Ah, ya say that every winter and come the summer I can't budge ya.

Catwoman I'll go away with ya next summer and that's a promise.

Father Willow Well, where do ya want to go and I'll book the tickets in the mornin'?

Catwoman Anywhere at all away from this auld bog, somewhere with a big hot sun.

Father Willow Burgundy's your man then.

Monica God help Burgundy is all I say.

Catwoman Anywhere it's not rainin' because it's goin' to rain here all next summer, seen it writ in the sky.

Mrs Kilbride Writ in the sky, me eye, sure she's blind as a bat. Xavier, what did ya have to invite the Catwoman for? Brings down the tone of the whole weddin'.

Monica Hasn't she as much right to walk God's earth as you, partake of its pleasures too.

Mrs Kilbride No, she hasn't! Not till she washes herself. The turf-smoke stink of her. Look at her moochin' up to Father Willow and her never inside the door of the church and me at seven Mass every mornin' watchin' that auld fool dribblin' into the chalice. And would he call to see me? Never. Spends all his time with the Catwoman in her dirty little hovel. I'd write to the Archbishop if I thought he was capable of anythin'. Why did ya have to invite her?

Xavier Ya know as well as me it's bad luck not to invite the Catwoman.

Father Willow shoots Mrs Kilbride in the back of the head with an imaginary pistol as he walks by or as she walks by.

Mrs Kilbride I'd love to hose her down, fling her in onto the milkin' parlour floor, turn the water on full blast and hose her down to her kidneys.

Carthage (*with his arm around Caroline*) Well, Catwoman, what do ya predict for us?

Catwoman I predict nothin'.

Carthage Ah g'wan now, ya must have a blessin' or a vision or somethin'.

Caroline Lave it, Carthage. You're welcome, Catwoman and Father Willow.

Father Willow Thank you, Hester, thank you.

Carthage You mean, Caroline, Father Willow, this is Caroline.

Father Willow Whatever.

Carthage Come on now, Catwoman, and give Caroline and me wan of your blessin's.

Catwoman Seein' as ya insist. Separate tombstones. I'm sorry but I tould ya not to ax me.

Josie Granny, will ya take a photo of just me and Daddy for to put in me scrapbook?

Mrs Kilbride Don't be so rude, you, to Caroline. (*Hisses.*) And I tould ya to call me Grandmother!

Josie (*whispers boldly from the safety of her father's side*) Granny, Granny, Granny.

Caroline She's alright. Here, I'll take the photo of you and Carthage for your scrapbook. (*Does.*)

Mrs Kilbride She's ruined, that's what she is, turnin' up in her Communion dress, makin' a holy show of us all.

Carthage It's you that's the holy show in that stupid dress.

Mrs Kilbride What! I am not! There's gratitude for ya. Ya make an effort to look your best. (*close to tears*) I cut

back on everythin' to buy this dress. How was
I supposed to know the bride'd be wearin' white as well.

Carthage Don't start whingin' now in front of everywan,
sit down will ya, ya look fine, ya look great – Alright,
I'm sorry. Ya look stunnin'!

Mrs Kilbride (*beginning to smile*) I don't, do I?

Carthage Christ! *Yes!*

*They've all made their way to the table by now and
are seated. Xavier tinkles his glass for silence.*

Xavier Thank you. Now before we dig in I'd like to
welcome yees all here on wan of the happiest days of me
life. Yees have all long known that Caroline has been my
greatest joy and reason for livin'. Her mother, if she was
here today, would've been proud too at how she has
grown into a lovely and graceful woman. I can take no
credit for that, though I've taken the greatest pride these
long years in watchin' her change from a motherless
child to a gawky girl, to this apparition I see before
me eyes today. We auld fathers would like to keep our
daughters be our sides for ever and enjoy their care and
gentleness but it seems the world does have a different
plan entirely. We must rear them up for another man's
benefit. Well if this is so, I can't think of a better man
than Carthage Kilbride to take over the care of me only
child. (*Raises his glass.*) I wish yees well and happiness
and infants rompin' on the hearth.

All Hear! Hear!

Xavier Father Willow, would ya do us the –

Mrs Kilbride (*standing up*) I'd like to say a few words
too –

Xavier Go ahead, Mrs Kilbride.

Mrs Kilbride As the proud mother of the groom –

Carthage Mother, would ya whisht up –

Mrs Kilbride (*posh public speaking voice*) As the proud mother of the groom, I feel the need to answer Xavier's fine speech with a few words of me own. Never was a mother more blessed than me in havin' Carthage for a son. As a child he was uncommon good, never cried, never disobeyed, never raised his voice wance to me, never went about with a grumpy puss on him. Indeed he went to the greatest pains always to see that me spirits was good, that me heart was uplifted. When his father died he used come into the bed to sleep beside me for fear I would be lonely. Often I woke from a deep slumber and his two arms would be around me, a small leg thrown over me in sleep –

Catwoman The craythur –

Mrs Kilbride He was also always aware of my abidin' love for Our Lord, unlike some here (*Glares at the Catwoman.*) and on wan occasion, me birthday it was, I looked out the back window and there he was up on the slope behind our house and what was he doin'? He was buildin' Calvary for me. He'd hammered three wooden crosses and was erectin' them on the slope Calvary-style. Wan for him, wan for me and wan for Our Lord. And we draped ourselves around them like the two thieves in the holy book, remember, Carthage?

Carthage I do not, would ya ever sit down.

Mrs Kilbride Of course ya do, the three crosses ya made up on the slope and remember the wind was howlin' and the pair of us yellin' 'Calvary! Calvary!' to wan another. Of course ya remember. I'm only tellin' yees this story as wan of the countless examples of Carthage's kind nature and I only want to say that Caroline is very welcome into the Kilbride household. And that if Carthage will be as good a son to Caroline as he's been a husband to me then she'll have no complaints. (*Raises her glass.*) Cheers.

All Hear! Hear!

Xavier And now, Father Willow, ya'll say grace for us?

Father Willow It'd be an honour, Jack, thank you –

Mrs Kilbride Who's Jack?

Father Willow gets up. All stand and bless themselves for the grace.

Father Willow In the name of the Father and of the Son and of the Holy Ghost, it may or may not surprise yees all if I tould yees I was almost a groom meself wance. Her name was Elizabeth Kennedy, no that was me mother's name, her name was – it'll come to me, anyway it wasn't to be, in the end we fell out over a duck egg on a walkin' holiday by the Shannon, what was her name at all? Helen? No.

Mrs Kilbride Would ya say the grace, Father Willow, and be –

Father Willow The grace, yes, how does it go again?

Mrs Kilbride Bless us, oh Lord, and these thy gifts which of –

Father Willow Rowena. That was it. Rowena Phelan. I should never have ate that duck egg – no – (*Stands there lost in thought.*)

Enter Hester in her wedding dress, veil, shoes, the works.

Mrs Kilbride Ya piebald knacker ya.

Xavier What's your business here, Swane, besides puttin' a curse on me daughter's weddin'?

Mrs Kilbride The brazen nerve of her turnin' up in that garb.

Hester The kettle callin' the pot white. Remember this dress, Carthage? He bought it for me –

Caroline Daddy, would ya do somethin'.

Hester Oh must be near nine year ago. We'd got to the stage where we should've parted and I said it to ya and ya convinced me otherwise and axed me to marry ya. Came home wan evenin' with this dress in a box and somehow it got put away. Ya only ever wanted me there until ya were strong enough to lave me.

Carthage Get outa here right now!

Hester You thought ya could come swaggerin' to me this mornin' in your weddin' clothes, well, here I am in mine. This is my weddin' day be rights and not wan of yees can deny it. And yees all just sit there glarin' as if I'm the guilty wan. (*Takes Carthage's glass of wine, drinks from it.*)

Mrs Kilbride Run her off, Xavier! Run her off or I will. (*Gets up.*)

Carthage (*pulls her back*) Would you keep out of this!

Mrs Kilbride And let her walk all over us?

Monica Hester, go home, g'wan.

Mrs Kilbride (*getting up again*) I've had the measure of you this long time, the lazy shiftless blood in ya, that savage tinker eye ya turn on people to frighten them –

Carthage Would ya shut up! Ya haven't shut up all

day! We're not havin' a brawl here.

Mrs Kilbride There's a nice way to talk to your mother on your weddin' day, I'm not afraid of ya, Hester Swane, you're just a sad lost little woman –

Hester I still stole your son from ya, didn't I, Elsie? Your sissy boy that I tried to make a man of.

Mrs Kilbride Ya took advantage of him, ya had to take advantage of a young boy for your perverted pleasures for no grown man would stomach ya.

Hester And weren't they great, Carthage, all them nights in the caravan I 'took advantage' of ya and you bangin' on the window and us stuffin' pillows in our mouths so ya wouldn't hear us laughin' –

Mrs Kilbride You're absolutely disgustin', that's what ya are!

Hester Have you ever been discarded, Elsie Kilbride? – the way I've been discarded. Do ya know what that feels like? To be flung on the ashpit and you still alive!

Xavier No wan's flingin' ya anywhere! We done everythin' proper by you –

Hester Proper! Yees have taken everythin' from me. I've done nothin' again' any of yees. I'm just bein' who I am, Carthage, I'm axin' ya the wance more, come away with me now, with me and –

Mrs Kilbride Come away with her, she says –

Hester Yes! Come away with me and Josie and stop all this –

Xavier Come away with ya! Are ya mad! He's married to Caroline now –

Carthage Go home, Hester, and pack your things.

Monica C'mon, Hester, I'll take ya home.

Hester I have no home any more for he's decided to take it from me.

Monica Then come and live with me, I've no wan –

Hester No, I want to stay in me own house. Just let me stay in the house, Carthage. I won't bother anywan if yees'd just lave me alone. I was born on the Bog of Cats, same as all of yees, though ya'd never think it the way yees shun me. I know every barrow and rivulet and bog hole of its nine square mile. I know where the best bog rosemary grows and the sweetest wild bog rue. I could lead yees around the Bog of Cats in me sleep.

Carthage There's a house bought and furnished for ya in town as ya agreed to –

Hester I've never lived in a town. I won't know anywan there –

Monica Ah, let her stay in the house, the Bog of Cats is all she knows –

Mrs Kilbride And since when do we need you stickin' your snout in, Monica Murray?

Monica Since you and your son have forgotten all dacency, Elsie Kilbride. Ya've always been too hard on her. Ya never gave her a chance –

Mrs Kilbride A waste of time givin' chances to a tinker. All tinkers understands is the open road and where the next bottle of whiskey is comin' from.

Monica Well, you should know and your own grandfather wan!

Mrs Kilbride My grandfather was a wanderin' tinsmith –

Monica And what's that but a tinker with notions!

Hester Carthage, ya could aisy afford another house for yourself and Caroline if ya wanted –

Carthage No! We're stickn' by what we agreed on –

Hester The truth is you want to eradicate me, make out I never existed –

Carthage If I wanted to eradicate ya, I could've, long ago. And I could've taken Josie off of ya. Facts are, I been more than generous with ya.

Hester You're plentiful with the guilt money alright, showerin' buckets of it on me. (*Flings envelope he had given her in Act One at him.*) There's your auld blood money back. Ya think you're gettin' away that aisy! Money won't take that guilt away, Carthage, we'll go to our grave with it!

Carthage I've not an ounce of guilt where you're concerned and whatever leftover feelin' I had for ya as the mother of me child is gone after this display of hatred towards me. Just go away, I can't bear the sight of ya!

Hester I can't lave the Bog of Cats –

Mrs Kilbride We'll burn ya out if we have to –

Hester Ya see –

Mrs Kilbride Won't we, Xavier –

Xavier Ya can lave me out of any low-boy tactics. You're lavin' this place today, Swane, aren't ya?

Hester I can't lave – Ya see me mother said she'd come back here. Father Willow, tell them what they're doin' is wrong. They'll listen to you.

Father Willow They've never listened to me, sure they

even lie in the Confession box. Ya know what I do?
I wear ear-plugs.

Hester (*close to tears*) I can't go till me mother comes.
I'd hoped she'd have come before now and it wouldn't
come to this. Don't make me lave or somethin' terrible'll
happen. Don't.

Xavier We've had enough of your ravin', Swane, so take
yourself elsewhere and let us try to recoup as best we
can these marred celebrations.

Josie I'll go with ya, Mam, and ya look gorgeous in that
dress.

Carthage Stay where ya are, Josie.

Josie No, I want to go with me Mam.

Carthage (*stopping her*) Ya don't know what ya want.
And reconsiderin', I think it'd be better all round if Josie
stays with me till ya've moved. I'll bring her back to ya
then.

Hester I've swallyed all me pride over you. You're lavin'
me no choice but a vicious war against ya. (*Takes a bottle
of wine from the table.*) Josie, I'll be back to collect ya
later. And you just try keepin' her from me! (*Exits.*)

Act Three

*Dusk. Hester, in her wedding dress, charred and muddied.
Behind her, the house and sheds ablaze. Joseph Swane
stands in the flames watching her.*

Hester Well, Carthage, ya think them were only idle
threats I made? Ya think I can be flung in a bog hole like
a bag of newborn pups? Let's see how ya like this – Ya
hear that sound? Them's your cattle howlin'. Ya smell
that smell? That's your forty calves roastin'. I tied them
all in and flung diesel on them. And the house, I burnt
the bed and the whole place went up in flames. I'd burn
down the world if I'd enough diesel – Will somewan not
come and save me from meself before I go and do worse.

   Joseph starts to sing.

Joseph
  By the Bog of Cats I finally learned false from true,
  Learned too late that it was you and only you
  Left me sore, a heart brimful of rue
  By the Bog of Cats in the darkling dew.

Hester Who's there? Who dares sing that song? That's
my song that me mother made up for me. Who's there?

Joseph I think ya know me, Hester.

Hester It's not Joseph Swane, is it?

Joseph It is alright.

Hester I thought I done away with you. Where are ya?
I can't see ya. Keep off! Keep away! I'm warnin' ya.

Joseph I'm not here to harm ya.

Hester Ya should be. If you'd done to me what I done to you I'd want your guts on a platter. Well come on! I'm ready for ya! Where are ya?

Joseph I don't know, somewhere near ya. I can't see you aither.

Hester Well, what do ya want, Joseph Swane, if you're not here to harm me? Is it an apology you're after? Well, I've none for ya. I'd slit your throat again if ya stood here in front of me in flesh and bone.

Joseph Would ya? What're ya so angry about? I've been listenin' to ya screamin' your head off this while.

Hester You've a nerve singin' that song. That song is mine! She made it for me and only me. Can't yees lave me with anythin'!

Joseph I didn't know it was yours. She used sing it to me all the time.

Hester You're lyin'! Faithless! All of yees! Faithless! If she showed up now I'd spit in her face, I'd box the jaws off of her, I'd go after her with a knife. (*heartbroken wail*) Where is she? She said she'd return. I've waited so long. I've waited so long – Have you come across her where you are?

Joseph Death's a big country, Hester. She could be anywhere in it.

Hester No, she's alive. I can smell her. She's comin' towards me. I know it. Why doesn't she come and be done with it! If ya see her tell her I won't be hard on her, will ya?

Joseph Aye, if I see her.

Hester Tell her there's just a couple of things I need to ax her, will ya?

Joseph I will.

Hester I just want to know why, that's all.

Joseph What are ya on about, Hester?

Hester Was it somethin' I done on her? I was seven, same as me daughter Josie, seven, and there isn't anythin' in this wide world Josie could do that'd make me walk away from her.

Joseph Ya have a daughter?

Hester Aye, they're tryin' to take her from me. Just let them try!

Joseph Who's tryin'?

Hester If it wasn't for you, me and Carthage'd still be together!

Joseph So it's my fault ya killed me, that what you're sayin'?

Hester He took your money after we killed ya –

Joseph To my memory Carthage did nothin' only look on. I think he was as shocked as I was when ya came at me with the fishin' knife –

Hester He took your money! He helped me throw ya overboard! And now he wants to put it all on me.

Joseph Ya came at me from behind, didn't ya? Wan minute I'm rowin' and the next I'm a ghost.

Hester If ya hadn't been such an arrogant git I may have left ya alone but ya just wouldn't shut up talkin' about her as if she wasn't my mother at all. The big smug neck of ya! It was axin' to be cut. And she even called ya after her. And calls me Hester. What sourt of a name is

Hester? Hester's after no wan. And she saves her own name for you – Didn't she ever tell ya about me?

Joseph She never mentioned ya.

Hester She must've. It's a long time ago. Think, will ya. Didn't she ever say anythin' about me?

Joseph Only what she tould me father. She never spoke to me about ya.

Hester Listen to ya! You're still goin' on as if she was yours and you only an auld ghost! You're still talkin' as if I never existed.

Joseph I don't know what you're on about, Hester, but if it's any consolation to ya, she left me too and our father. Josie Swane hung around for no wan.

Hester What was she like, Joseph? Every day I forget more and more till I'm startin' to think I made her up out of the air. If it wasn't for this auld caravan I'd swear I only dreamt her. What was she like?

Joseph Well, she was big for starters . . . and gentle.

Hester Gentle! She was a rancorous hulk with a vicious whiskey temper.

Joseph You'd have liked the old man, Hester. All he wanted to do was go fishin'.

Hester Well, it wasn't me that shunned him.

Joseph It wasn't his fault, Hester, she told him you were dead, that ya died at birth, it wasn't his fault. Ya would've liked the old man, but she told him ya died, that ya were born with your heart all wrong.

Hester Nothin' wrong of me heart till she set about banjaxin' it. The lyin' tongue of her. And he just believed her.

Joseph Didn't he send me lookin' for ya in the end, see was there any trace of ya, told me to split the money with ya if I found ya. Hester, I was goin' to split the money with ya. I had it there in the boat. I was goin' to split it with ya when we reached the shore, ya didn't have to cut me throat for it.

Hester Ya think I slit your throat for the few auld pound me father left me?

Joseph Then why?

Hester Should've been with her for always and would have only for you.

Joseph If ya knew what it was like here ya'd never have done what ya done.

Hester Oh I think I know, Joseph, for a long time now I been thinkin' I'm already a ghost.

Joseph I'll be off, Hester, I just wanted to say hello.

Hester Where are ya goin'?

Joseph Stravagin' the shadows. (*And he's gone.*)

Hester Joseph?

Hester sits on the steps of the caravan, drinks some wine from the bottle she took from the wedding, lights a cigar. Monica shouts offstage.

Monica Hester! Hester! Your house! It's on fire! Hester! (*Runs on.*) Come quick, I'll get the others!

Hester Don't bother.

Monica But your house – Ya set it yourself?

Hester I did.

Monica Christ almighty woman, are ya gone mad?

Hester Ya want a drink?

Monica A drink, she says! I better go and get Carthage, the livestock, the calves –

Hester Would ya calm down, Monica, only an auld house, it should never have been built in the first place. Let the bog have it back. Never liked that house anyway.

Monica That's what the tinkers do, isn't it, burn everythin' after them?

Hester Aye.

Monica They'll skin ya alive, Hester, I'm tellin' ya, they'll kill ya.

Hester And you with them.

Monica I stood up for ya as best I could, I've to live round here, Hester. I had to pay me respects to the Cassidys. Sure Xavier and meself used walk to school together.

Hester Wan of these days you'll die of niceness, Monica Murray.

Monica A quality you've never had any time for.

Hester No, I'm just wan big lump of maneness and bad thoughts. Sit down, have a drink with me, I'll get ya a glass. (*Goes into the caravan, gets one.*) Sit down before ya fall.

Monica (*sitting on steps, tipsily*) We'll go off in this yoke, you and me.

Hester Will we?

Monica Flee off from this place, flee off to Eden.

Hester Eden – I left Eden, Monica, at the age of seven. It was on account of a look be this caravan at dusk.

Monica And who was it gave ya this look, your mother, was it? Josie Swane?

Hester Oh aye, Monica, she was the wan alright who looked at me so askance and strangely – Who'd believe an auld look could do away with ya? I never would've 'cept it happened to me.

Monica She was a harsh auld yoke, Hester, came and went like the moon. Ya'd wake wan mornin' and look out over the bog and ya'd see a fire and know she had returned. And I'd bring her down a sup of milk or a few eggs and she'd be here sittin' on the step just like you are, with her big head of black hair and eyes glamin' like a cat and long arms and a powerful neck all knotted that she'd stretch like a swan in a yawn and me with ne'er a neck at all. But I was never comfortable with her, riddled by her, though, and I wasn't the only wan. There was lots spent evenin's tryin' to figure Josie Swane, somethin' cold and dead about her except when she sang and then I declare ya'd fall in love with her.

Hester Would ya now?

Monica There was a time round here when no celebration was complete without Josie Swane. She'd be invited everywhere to sing, funerals, weddin's, christenin's, birthdays of the bigger farmers, the harvest. And she'd make up songs for each occasion. And it wasn't so much they wanted her there, more they were afraid not to have her.

Hester I used go with her on some of them singin' sprees before she ran off. And she'd make up the song as we walked to wherever we were goin'. Sometimes she'd sing somethin' completely different than the song she'd been makin' on the road. Them were her 'Blast from God' songs as opposed to her 'Workaday' songs, or so she

called them. And they never axed us to stay, these people,
to sit down and ate with them, just lapped up her songs,
gave her a bag of food and a half a crown and walked us
off the premises, for fear we'd steal somethin', I suppose.
I don't think it bothered her, it did me – and still rankles
after all these years. But not Josie Swane, she'd be off to
the shop to buy cigars and beer and sweets for me.

Monica Is there another sup of wine there?

Hester (*pours for her*) I'm all the time wonderin'
whatever happened to her.

Monica You're still waitin' on her, aren't ya?

Hester It's still like she only walked away yesterday.

Monica Hester, I know what it's like to wait for
somewan who's never walkin' through the door again.
But this waitin' is only a fancy of yours. Now I don't
make out to know anythin' about the workin's of this
world but I know this much, it don't yield aisy to mortal
wishes. And maybe that's the way it has to be. You up
on forty, Hester, and still dreamin' of storybook endin's,
still whingin' for your Mam.

Hester I made a promise, Monica, a promise to meself
a long while back. All them years I was in the Industrial
School I swore to meself that wan day I'm comin' back
to the Bog of Cats to wait for her there and I'm never
lavin' again.

Monica Well, I don't know how ya'll swing to stay
now, your house in ashes, ya after appearin' in that
dress. They're sayin' it's a black art thing ya picked up
somewhere.

Hester A black art thing. (*Laughs.*) If I knew any black
art things, by Christ, I'd use them now. The only way I'm
lavin' this place is in a box and if it comes to that I'm not

lavin' alone. I'll take yees all with me. And, yes, there's things about me yees never understood and makes yees afraid and yees are right for other things goes through my veins besides blood that I've fought so hard to keep wraps on.

Monica And what things are they?

Hester I don't understand them meself.

Monica Stop this wild talk then, I don't like it.

Hester Carthage still at the weddin'?

Monica And where else would he be?

Hester And what sourt of mood is he in?

Monica I wasn't mindin'. Don't waste your time over a man like him, faithless as an acorn on a high wind – wine all gone?

Hester Aye.

Monica I'll go up to the feast and bring us back a bottle unless you've any objections.

Hester I'll drink the enemy's wine. Not the wine's fault it fell into the paws of cut-throats and gargiyles.

Monica Be back in a while, so.

Hester And check see Josie's alright, will ya?

Monica She's dancin' her little heart out.

Exit Monica. Hester looks around, up at the winter sky of stars, shivers.

Hester Well, it's dusk now and long after and where are ya, Mr Ghost Fancier. I'm here waitin' for ya, though I've been tould to flee. Maybe you're not comin' after all, maybe I only imagined ya.

Enter Josie running, excited.

Josie Mam! – Mam! I'm goin' on the honeymoon with Daddy and Caroline.

Hester You're goin' no such where.

Josie Ah, Mam, they're goin' drivin' to the sea. I never seen the sea.

Hester It's just wan big bog hole, Josie, and blue, that's all, nothin' remarkable about it.

Josie Well, Daddy says I'm goin'.

Hester Don't mind your Daddy.

Josie No, I want to go with them. It's only for five days, Mam.

Hester There's a couple of things you should know about your precious Daddy, you should know how he has treated me!

Josie I'm not listenin' to ya givin' out about him. (*Covers her ears with her hands.*)

Hester That's right, stand up for him and see how far it'll get ya. He swore to me that after you'd be born he'd marry me and now he plans to take ya off of me. I suppose ya'd like that too.

Josie (*still with ears covered*) I said I'm not listenin'!

Hester (*pulls Josie's hands from her ears*) You'll listen to me, Josie Swane, and you listen well. Another that had your name walked away from me. Your perfect Daddy walked away from me. And you'll walk from me too. All me life people have walked away without a word of explanation. Well, I want to tell ya somethin', Josie, if you lave me ya'll die.

Josie I will not.

Hester Ya will! Ya will! It's a sourt of curse was put on ya be the Catwoman and the black swan. Remember the black swan?

Josie (*frightened*) Aye.

Hester So ya have to stay with me, d'ya see, and if your Daddy or anywan else axes ya who ya'd prefer to live with, ya have to say me.

Josie Mam, I would've said you anyway.

Hester Would ya? – Oh, I'm sorry, Josie, I'm sorry, sweetheart. It's not true what I said about a curse bein' put on ya, it's not true at all. If I'm let go tonight I swear I'll make it up to ya for them awful things I'm after sayin'.

Josie It's alright, Mam, I know ya didn't mean it – Can I go back to the weddin'? The dancin's not over yet.

Hester Dance with me.

Begins waltzing with Josie. Music.

Come on, we'll have our own weddin'.

Picks her up, they swirl and twirl to the music of the song 'By the Bog of Cats . . .'. They sing it together.

Ya beautiful, beautiful child, I could ate ya.

Josie I could ate ya too – Can I go back to the weddin' for a while?

Hester Ya can do anythin' ya want 'cept lave me. (*Puts her down.*) G'wan then, for half an hour.

Josie I brung ya a big lump of weddin' cake in me handbag. Here. Why wasn't it your weddin', Mam?

Hester It sourt of was. G'wan and enjoy yourself.

And exit Josie running. Hester looks after her eating the wedding cake. Xavier Cassidy comes up behind her from the shadows, demonic, red-faced, drink taken, carries a gun.

Xavier Ya enjoyin' that, are ya, Swane, me daughter's weddin' cake?

Hester Oh it's yourself, Xavier, with your auld gun. I was wonderin' when I'd see ya in your true colours. Must've been an awful strain on ya behavin' so well all day.

Xavier Ya burnt the bloody house to the ground.

Hester Did ya really think I was goin' to have your daughter livin' there?

Xavier Ya won't best me, Swane, ya know that. I ran your mother out of here and I'll run you too like a frightened hare.

Hester It's got nothin' to do with ya, Cassidy, it's between me and Carthage.

Xavier Got everythin' to do with me and ya after makin' a mockery of me and me daughter in front of the whole parish.

Hester No more than yees deserve for wheedlin' and cajolin' Carthage away from me with your promises of land and money.

Xavier He was aisy wheedled.

Hester He was always a feckless fool.

Xavier Aye, in all respects bar wan. He loves the land and like me he'd rather die than part with it wance he gets his greedy hands on it. With him Cassidy's farm'll be safe, the name'll be gone, but never the farm. And who's to say but maybe your little bastard and her offspring won't be farmin' my land in years to come.

Hester Josie'll have nothin' to do with anythin' that's yours. I'll see to that. And if ya'd looked after your own son better ya wouldn't be covetin' Josie nor any that belongs to me.

Xavier Don't you talk about my young fella.

Hester Wasn't it me that found him, strychnined to the eyeballs, howlin' 'long the bog and his dog in his arms?

Xavier My son died in a tragic accident of no wan's makin'. That's what the inquest said. My conscience is clear.

Hester Is it now? You're not a farmer for nothin', somethin' about that young lad bothered ya, he wasn't tough enough for ya probably, so ya strychnined his dog, knowin' full well the child'd be goin' lookin' for him. And ya know what strychnine does, a tayspoonful is all it takes, and ya'd the dog showered in it. Burnt his hands clean away. Ya knew what ya were at, Cassidy, and ya know I know. I can tell the darkness in you, ya know how? Because it mirrors me own.

Xavier Fabrications! Fabrications of a mind unhinged! If ya could just hear the mad talk of yourself, Swane, and the cut of ya. You're mad as your mother and she was a lunatic.

Hester Nothin' lunatic about her 'cept she couldn't breathe the same air as yees all here by the Bog of Cats.

Xavier We often breathed the same air, me and Josie Swane, she was a loose wan, loose and lazy and aisy, a five-shillin' hoor, like you.

Hester If you're tryin' to destroy some high idea I have of her you're wastin' your time. I've spent long hours of all the long years thinkin' about her. I've lived through every mood there is to live concernin' her. Sure there was

329

a time I hated her and wished the worst for her, but I've taught meself to rise above all that is cruel and unworthy in me thinkin' about her. So don't you think your five shillin' hoor stories will ever change me opinion of her. I have memories your cheap talk can never alter.

Xavier And what memories are they, Swane? I'd like to know if they exist at all.

Hester Oh they exist alright and ya'd like to rob them from me along with everythin' else. But ya won't because I'm stronger than ya and ya'll take nothin' from me I don't choose to give ya.

Xavier (*puts gun to her throat*) Won't I now? Think ya'll outwit me with your tinker ways and –

Hester Let go of me!

Xavier (*a tighter grip*) Now let's see the leftovers of Carthage Kilbride.

Uses gun to look down her dress.

Hester I'm warnin' ya, let go!

A struggle, a few blows, he wins this bout.

Xavier Now are ya stronger than me? I could do what I wanted with ya right here and now and no wan would believe ya. Now what I'd really like to know is when are ya plannin' on lavin'?

Hester What're ya goin' to do, Cassidy? Blow me head off?

Xavier Ya see, I married me daughter today! Now I don't care for the whiny little rip that much, but she's all I've got, and I don't want Carthage changin' his mind after a while. So when are ya lavin', Swane? When?

Hester Ya think I'm afraid of you and your auld gun.

(*Puts her mouth over the barrel.*) G'wan shoot! Blow me away! Save me the bother meself. (*Goes for the trigger.*) Ya want me to do it for ya?

Another struggle, this time Xavier trying to get away from her.

Xavier You're a dangerous witch, Swane.

Hester (*laughs at him*) You're sweatin'. Always knew ya were yella to the bone. Don't worry, I'll be lavin' this place tonight, though not the way you or anywan else expects. Ya call me a witch, Cassidy? This is nothin', you just wait and see the real –

Enter Carthage running, enraged, shakes her violently.

Carthage The cattle! The calves! Ya burnt them all, they're roarin' in the flames! The house in ashes! A' ya gone mad altogether? The calves! A' ya gone mad?

Hester (*shakes him off*) No, I only meant what I said. I warned ya, Carthage, ya drove me to it.

Xavier A hundred year ago we'd strap ya to a stake and roast ya till your guts exploded.

Carthage That's it! I'm takin' Josie off of ya! I don't care if I've to drag ya through the courts. I'll have ya put away! I'll tell all about your brother! I don't care!

Hester Tell them! And tell them your own part in it too while you're at it! Don't you threaten me with Josie! This pervert has just been gropin' me with his gun and you want Josie round him –

Xavier The filthy lies of her –

Hester Bringin' a child on a honeymoon, what are ya at, Carthage? Well, I won't let ya use Josie to fill in the silences between yourself and Caroline Cassidy –

Xavier She's beyond reasonin' with, if she was mine I'd cut that tinker tongue from her mouth, I'd brand her lips, I'd –

Carthage (*exploding at Xavier*) Would you just go back to the weddin' and lave us alone, stop interferin'. If ya'd only let me handle it all the way I wanted to, but, no, ya had to push and bring the weddin' forward to avoid your taxes, just lave us alone, will ya!

Xavier I will and gladly. You're a fiasco, Kilbride, like all the Kilbrides before ya, ya can't control a mere woman, ya'll control nothin', I'm havin' serious doubts about signin' over me farm –

Carthage Keep your bloody farm, Cassidy. I have me own. I'm not your scrubber boy. There's other things besides land.

Xavier There's nothin' besides land, boy, nothin'! And a real farmer would never think otherwise.

Carthage Just go back to the weddin', I'll follow ya in a while and we can try hammerin' out our differences.

Xavier Can we? (*Exits.*)

Hester All's not well in paradise.

Carthage All'd be fine if I could do away with you.

Hester If ya just let me stay I'll cause no more trouble. I'll move into the caravan with Josie. In time ya may be glad to have me around. I've been your greatest friend around here, Carthage, doesn't that count for nothin' now?

Carthage I'm not havin' me daughter livin' in a caravan!

Hester There was a time you loved this caravan.

Carthage Will ya just stop tryin' to drag up them years! It won't work!

Hester Ya promised me things! Ya built that house for me. Ya wanted me to see how normal people lived. And I went along with ya again' me better judgement. All I ever wanted was to be by the Bog of Cats. A modest want when compared with the wants of others. Just let me stay here in the caravan.

Carthage And have the whole neighbourhood makin' a laughin' stock of me?

Hester That's not why ya won't let me stay. You're ashamed of your part in me brother's death, aren't ya?

Carthage I had no part in it!

Hester You're afraid I'll tell everywan what ya done. I won't. I wouldn't ever, Carthage.

Carthage I done nothin' except watch!

Hester Ya helped me tie a stone around his waist!

Carthage He was dead by then!

Hester He wasn't! His pulse was still goin'!

Carthage You're only sayin' that now to torture me! Why did ya do it, Hetty? We were doin' fine till then.

Hester How does anywan know why they done anythin'? Somethin' evil moved in on me blood – and the fishin' knife was there in the bottom of the boat – and Bergit's Lake was wide – and I looked across the lake to me father's house and it went through me like a spear that she had a whole other life there – How could she have and I a part of her?

Carthage Ya never said any of this before – I always thought ya killed your brother for the money.

Hester I met his ghost tonight, ya know –

Carthage His ghost?

Hester Aye, a gentle ghost and so lost, and he spoke so softly to me, I didn't deserve such softness –

Carthage Ah, would you stop this talk!

Hester You rose in the world on his ashes! And that's what haunts ya. You look at me and all you see is Joseph Swane slidin' into Bergit's Lake again. You think doin' away with me will do away with that. It won't, Carthage. It won't. You'll remember me, Carthage, when the dust settles, when ya grow tired scourin' acres and bank balances. Ya'll remember me when ya walk them big, empty, childless rooms in Cassidy's house. Ya think now ya won't, but ya will.

Carthage Ya always had a high opinion of yourself. Aye, I'll remember ya from time to time. I'll remember ya sittin' at the kitchen table drinkin' till all hours and I'll remember the sound of the back door closin' as ya escaped for another night roamin' the bog.

Hester The drinkin' came after, long after you put it into your mind to lave me. If I had somewan to talk to I mightn't have drunk so hard, somewan to roam the bog with me, somewan to take away a tiny piece of this guilt I carry with me, but ya never would.

Carthage Seems I done nothin' right. Did I not?

Hester You want to glane lessons for your new bride. No, Carthage, ya done nothin' right, your bull-headed pride and economy and painful advancement never moved me. What I wanted was somewan to look me in the eye and know I was understood and not judged. You thought I had no right to ax for that. Maybe I hadn't, but the way ya used judge me – didn't it ever occur to ya, that however harshly ya judged me, I

334

judged meself harsher. Couldn't ya ever see that.

Carthage I'm takin' Josie, Hester. I'm takin' her off of ya. It's plain as day to everywan 'cept yourself ya can't look after her. If you're wise ya'll lave it at that and not have us muckin' through the courts. I'll let ya see her from time to time.

Hester Take her then, take her, ya've taken everythin' else. In me stupidity I thought ya'd lave me Josie. I should've known ya always meant to take her too.

Enter Caroline with a bottle of wine.

Caroline (*to Carthage*) Oh, this is where ya are.

Carthage She's after burnin' all the livestock, the house, the sheds in ruins. I'm away up there now to see what can be salvaged. G'wan back home, I'll be there in a while. (*Exits.*)

Caroline Monica said ya wanted wine, I opened it for ya.

Hester Take more than wine to free me from this place. Take some kind of dark sprung miracle. (*Takes the wine.*)

Carthage (*coming back*) Caroline, come on, come on, I don't want ya around her.

Hester G'wan back to your weddin' like Carthage says.

Caroline goes to exit, stops.

Caroline I just wanted to say –

Hester What? Ya just wanted to say what?

Caroline Nothin' – Only I'll be very good to Josie whenever she stays with us.

Hester Ya better be!

Caroline I won't let her out of me sight – I'll go everywhere with her – protect her from things. That's all. (*Goes to exit.*)

Hester Didn't ya enjoy your big weddin' day, Caroline?

Caroline No, I didn't – Everywan too loud and frantic – and when ya turned up in that weddin' dress, knew it should've been you – and Daddy drinkin' too much and shoutin', and Carthage gone away in himself, just watchin' it all like it had nothin' to do with him, and everywan laughin' behind me back and pityin' me – When me mother was alive, I used go into the sick room to talk to her and she used take me into the bed beside her and she'd describe for me me weddin' day. Of how she'd be there with a big hat on her and so proud. And the weddin' was goin' to be in this big ballroom with a fountain of mermaids in the middle, instead of Daddy's idea of havin' the do at home to save money – None of it was how it was meant to be, none of it.

Hester Nothin' ever is, Caroline. Nothin'. I've been a long time wishin' over me mother too. For too long now I've imagined her comin' towards me across the Bog of Cats and she would find me here standin' strong. She would see me life was complete, that I had Carthage and Josie and me own house. I so much wanted her to see that I had flourished without her and maybe then I could forgive her – Caroline, he's takin' Josie from me.

Caroline He's not, he wouldn't do that, Hester.

Hester He's just been here tellin' me.

Caroline I won't let him, I'll talk to him, I'll stand up for ya on that account.

Hester Ya never stood up for nothin' yet, I doubt ya'll stand up for me. Anyway, they won't listen to ya. You're only a little china bit of a girl. I could break ya aisy as a tay cup or a wine glass. But I won't. Ya know why? Because I knew ya when ya were Josie's age, a scrawky little thing that hung on the scraps of my affection. Anyway, no need to break ya, you were broke a long while back.

Caroline There's somethin' wrong of me, isn't there? (*Stands there, lost-looking.*)

Hester G'wan back to your weddin' and lave me be.

Caroline I promise ya I'll do everythin' I can about Josie.

Hester (*softly*) G'wan. G'wan.

Exit Caroline. Hester stands there alone, takes a drink, goes into the caravan, comes out with a knife. She tests it for sharpness, teases it across her throat, shivers.

Come on, ya done it aisy enough to another, now it's your own turn.

Bares her throat, ready to do it. Enter Josie running, stops, sees Hester with the knife poised.

Josie Mam – What's that ya've got there?

Hester (*stops*) Just an auld fishin' knife, Josie, I've had this years.

Josie And what are ya doin' with it?

Hester Nothin', Josie, nothin'.

Josie I came to say goodbye, we'll be goin' soon. (*Kisses Hester.*)

Hester Goodbye, sweetheart – Josie, ya won't see me again now.

Josie I will so. I'm only goin' on a honeymoon.

Hester No, Josie, ya won't see me again because I'm goin' away too.

Josie Where?

Hester Somewhere ya can never return from.

Josie And where's that?

Hester Never mind. I only wanted to tell ya goodbye, that's all.

Josie Well, can I go with ya?

Hester No ya can't.

Josie Ah, Mam, I want to be where you'll be.

Hester Well, ya can't, because wance ya go there ya can never come back.

Josie I wouldn't want to if you're not here, Mam.

Hester You're just bein' contrary now. Don't ya want to be with your Daddy and grow up big and lovely and full of advantages I have not the power to give ya?

Josie Mam, I'd be watchin' for ya all the time 'long the Bog of Cats. I'd be hopin' and waitin' and prayin' for ya to return.

Hester Don't be sayin' them things to me now.

Josie Just take me with ya, Mam. (*Puts her arms around Hester.*)

Hester (*pushing her away*) No, ya don't understand. Go away, get away from me, g'wan now, run away from me quickly now.

Josie (*struggling to stay in contact with Hester*) No, Mam, stop! I'm goin' with ya!

338

Hester Would ya let go!

Josie (*frantic*) No, Mam. Please!

Hester Alright, alright! Shhh! (*Picks her up.*) It's alright, I'll take ya with me, I won't have ya as I was, waitin' a lifetime for somewan to return, because they don't, Josie, they don't. It's alright. Close your eyes.

Josie closes her eyes.

Are they closed tight?

Josie Yeah.

Hester cuts Josie's throat in one savage movement.

(*softly*) Mam – Mam – (*And Josie dies in Hester's arms.*)

Hester (*whispers*) It's because ya wanted to come, Josie.

Begins to wail, a terrible animal wail. Enter the Catwoman.

Catwoman Hester, what is it? What is it?

Hester Oh, Catwoman, I knew somethin' terrible'd happen, I never thought it'd be this. (*Continues this terrible sound, barely recognizable as something human.*)

Catwoman What have ya done, Hester? Have ya harmed yourself?

Hester No, not meself and yes meself.

Catwoman (*comes over, feels around Hester, feels Josie*) Not Josie, Hester? Not Josie? Lord on high, Hester, not the child. I thought yourself, maybe, or Carthage, but never the child. (*Runs to the edge of the stage shouting.*) Help, somewan, help! Hester Swane's after butcherin' the child! Help!

Hester walks around demented with Josie. Enter Carthage, running.

Carthage What is it, Catwoman? Hester? What's wrong with Josie? There's blood all over her.

Hester (*brandishing knife*) Lave off, you. Lave off. I warned ya and I tould ya, would ya listen, what've I done, what've I done?

Enter Monica.

Carthage Give her to me!

Monica Sweet Jesus, Hester –

Carthage Give her to me! You've killed her, she's killed her.

Hester Yees all thought I was just goin' to walk away and lave her at yeer mercy. I almost did. But she's mine and I wouldn't have her waste her life dreamin' about me and yees thwartin' her with black stories against me.

Carthage You're a savage!

Enter the Ghost Fancier. Hester sees him, the others don't. He picks up the fishing knife.

Hester You're late, ya came too late.

Carthage What's she sayin'? What? Give her to me, come on now. (*Takes Josie off Hester.*)

Hester Ya won't forget me now, Carthage, and when all of this is over or half remembered and you think you've almost forgotten me again, take a walk along the Bog of Cats and wait for a purlin' wind through your hair or a soft breath be your ear or a rustle behind ya. That'll be me and Josie ghostin' ya. (*She walks towards the Ghost Fancier.*) Take me away, take me away from here.

Ghost Fancier Alright, my lovely.

They go into a death dance with the fishing knife, which ends plunged into Hester's heart. She falls to the ground. Exit Ghost Fancier with knife.

Hester (*whispers as she dies*) Mam – Mam –

Monica goes over to her after a while.

Monica Hester – She's gone – Hester – She's cut her heart out – it's lyin' there on top of her chest like some dark feathered bird.

Music. Lights.